Y0-AGI-828

Clinical Management of Sexual Disorders

Clinical Management of Sexual Disorders

EDITED BY

Jon K. Meyer, M.D.
Director, Sexual Behaviors Consultation Unit
The Johns Hopkins Medical Institutions
Baltimore, Maryland

with 19 contributors

The Williams & Wilkins Company
Baltimore

428 E. Preston Street
Baltimore, Md. 21202, U.S.A.

Made in the United States of America

Library of Congress Cataloging in Publication Data
Main entry under title:
Clinical management of sexual disorders.
Includes index.
1. Sexual disorders. I. Meyer, Jon K., 1938- [DNLM: 1. Sex disorders—Therapy. WM610 C641] RC556.C57 616.6 75-19064
ISBN 0-683-05969-6

Composed and printed at the
Waverly Press, Inc.
Mt. Royal and Guilford Aves.
Baltimore, Md. 21202, U.S.A.

TO ELEANOR AND DAVID,
who have been so consistently supportive and encouraging.

Acknowledgements

This volume would not have been possible without the untiring efforts of Miss Donna Reter, and the continuing inspiration of the staff of the Sexual Behaviors Consultation Unit, the Johns Hopkins Medical Institutions.

Foreword

This volume grew out of experience across the country in more direct, or directive, intervention in the treatment of sexual disabilities.

A reawakening of interest in sexual problems, in and of themselves, has been noticeable among the public and in medicine, psychology, and the social, experimental, and applied sciences. Sadly, among certain groups and individuals, this surge of interest has led, at worst, to faddishness, hyperbole, and invective or, at best, to questionable claims of efficacy for one particular treatment, unsubstantiated cure rates, and unethical conduct. Such exploitation of recent concern is in marked contrast *to the responsible clinician* or investigator who wishes *to make reasonable and proper use of new techniques and recent information.*

This volume represents an attempt to combine between two covers the best of recent thought, minus unsubstantiated claims, regarding the approach to patients with sexual disorders, the diagnosis and classification of these disorders, the determination of significant variables in sexual conditions, and the application of selected treatment techniques.

The philosophy of this volume is that *the treatment of sexual disorders is analogous to the treatment of any other major spectrum of disorders in medical practice: i.e.*, there is no one treatment modality sufficient to cover all possible dysfunctional conditions; rather, the complete practitioner must have a broad range of treatment modalities at his fingertips so that the most appropriate technique may be selected according to the patient's particular symptoms, life style, interpersonal relationships, financial resources, and emotional health. *Although the empha-*

sis in Clinical Management of Sexual Disorders is on direct manipulation and directive techniques, the full range of appropriate modalities for treatment of sexual disorders is considered to extend from formal psychoanalysis through behavior modification and desensitization, to surgical intervention.

This volume attempts to represent an evolutionary step and not a revolutionary one. Considerable past experience in medicine, psychiatry, surgery, and psychology is applicable to sexual disorders, so that it is not appropriate to throw the baby of prior observation and understanding out with the bath water of unnecessary past hesitance to inquire more frankly and explicitly about aspects of an individual's sexual life.

Clinical Management of Sexual Disorders is *addressed to the clinician of whatever specialty*, since individuals with sexual disorders are no respectors of jurisdictional lines among disciplines. The book will supplement the skills of *the clinician and practitioner who is faced daily with problems of sexual dysfunction.* Additionally, the authors have provided adequate documentation so that the more serious student may pursue any particular area in the original sources. This volume may also be used as a reference handbook, selected chapters being useful to broaden the capabilities of those individuals whose clinical experience and training already has encompassed one or more of the specific interventions. It is hoped over-all that it will make a contribution to the better care of those individuals suffering from a sexual disability.

Jon K. Meyer, M.D.
Baltimore

List of Contributors

Oliver J. W. Bjorksten, M.D.
Assistant Professor of Psychiatry
Medical University of South Carolina
Charleston, South Carolina

Carol Sue Carter, Ph.D.
Assistant Professor
Departments of Ecology, Ethology, and Evolution and Psychology
School of Basic Medical Sciences, University of Illinois
Urbana-Champaign, Illinois

John M. Davis, M.D.
Director of Research, Illinois State Psychiatric Institute
Associate Professor of Psychiatry
University of Chicago, Pritzer School of Medicine
Chicago, Illinois

Leonard R. Derogatis, Ph.D.
Assistant Professor of Medical Psychology
The Johns Hopkins University, School of Medicine
Director of Research, Sexual Behaviors Consultation Unit
The Johns Hopkins Medical Institutions
Baltimore, Maryland

Ernest R. Griffith, M.D.
Professor and Acting Director
Department of Rehabilitation Medicine
Medical College of Virginia
Virginia Commonwealth University
Richmond, Virginia

Donald R. Laub, M.D.
Associate Professor of Surgery
Chief, Division of Plastic and Reconstructive Surgery
Stanford University Medical School
Stanford, California

Arnold A. Lazarus, Ph.D.
Professor of Psychology
Graduate School of Applied and Professional Psychology
Rutgers—The State University
Piscataway, New Jersey

Mary Jane Lucas, R.N.
Instructor in Psychiatry
The Johns Hopkins University, School of Medicine
Assistant Director, Sexual Behaviors Consultation Unit
The Johns Hopkins Medical Institutions
Baltimore, Maryland

Jon K. Meyer, M.D.
Assistant Professor of Psychiatry and Surgery
The Johns Hopkins University, School of Medicine
Director, Sexual Behaviors Consultation Unit
The Johns Hopkins Medical Institutions
Baltimore, Maryland

Joel M. Noe, M.D.
Instructor of Plastic and Reconstructive Surgery
Harvard Medical School
Beth Israel Hospital
Boston, Massachusetts

John F. O'Connor, M.D.
Director, Behavioral Sciences Unit
International Institute for the Study of Human Reproduction
College of Physicians and Surgeons of Columbia University
New York, New York

Raymond C. Rosen, Ph.D.
Assistant Professor of Psychiatry
Director of Sexual Counselling Service
College of Medicine and Dentistry of New Jersey
Rutgers Medical School
Piscataway, New Jersey

James J. Ryan, M.D.
Assistant Professor of Plastic Surgery
The Johns Hopkins University, School of Medicine
Baltimore, Maryland

Chester W. Schmidt, Jr., M.D.
Associate Professor of Psychiatry
The Johns Hopkins University, School of Medicine
Chief, Department of Psychiatry, Baltimore City Hospitals
Associate Director, Sexual Behaviors Consultation Unit
The Johns Hopkins Medical Institutions
Baltimore, Maryland

Werner P. Schulz
Consulting Engineer
Department of Surgery, Stanford University Medical School
Stanford, California

Roberta B. Trieschmann, Ph.D.
Associate Professor of Physical Medicine and Rehabilitation
Associate Professor of Psychology
Director of Psychological Services
Department of Physical Medicine and Rehabilitation
University of Cincinnati, School of Medicine
Cincinnati, Ohio

Roy M. Whitman, M.D.
Professor of Psychiatry, Department of Psychiatry
University of Cincinnati, College of Medicine
Cincinnati, Ohio

Leon Zussman, M.D.
Director, Human Sexuality Center
Long Island Jewish, Hillside Medical Center
New Hyde Park, New York

Shirley Zussman, Ed.D.
Assistant Director, Human Sexuality Center
Long Island Jewish, Hillside Medical Center
New Hyde Park, New York

Contents

ONE

Sexual Problems in Office Practice: Guidelines for Identification and Management

JON K. MEYER, M.D.

Since all acute illnesses and chronic diseases exact their toll upon sexual performance, sexual problems are to be found routinely among the patients in physicians' and surgeons' offices. In addition, individuals whose difficulties are on a functional basis will first seek medical consultation, believing or hoping that they are suffering from organic impairment. Some patients in the consultation room will come directly to their sexual complaint, a larger number will speak of related physical or interpersonal complaints leading indirectly to the sexual problem, and others will attempt to deny or disguise it altogether. A careful history of the presenting complaint, together with questions about satisfaction with the marriage, will often elicit the sexual disturbance.

For the physician who is either presented with or uncovers a sexual disability, there are certain basic issues to be addressed:

1. What are the physiological and emotional correlates of sexual experience?
2. What are the known etiologies of sexual dysfunction?
3. What are the skills and attitudes required to deal with sexual problems?
4. What is the best way to approach assessment of the sexual disability?
5. What are the common disorders?
6. What is the differential diagnosis between organic and functional sexual disorders?
7. What techniques are useful within the time constraints of office practice?
8. What specialized techniques are available?

9. What are the indications for referral?
The remainder of this paper will attempt to sketch out some of the answers to these questions.

PHYSIOLOGICAL AND EMOTIONAL CORRELATES OF SEXUAL EXPERIENCE

Variations in sex drive and arousal speed occur. The perjorative terms "oversexed" and "undersexed," on the other hand, are comparative labels best used only in referring to a specific partnership. To stretch a point, one woman's hopelessly inadequate partner may be another's sexual athlete, depending upon needs and arousal patterns. If sexual interest between husband and wife is consistently and markedly discrepant, the one with greater need may withdraw in order to avoid frustration.

Hormones are often invoked to explain sexual variations, but, except in clear deficiency states, a cause and effect relationship is seldom clear. A general observation regarding the role of hormones is as follows: "The . . . job of the sex hormones is to set [and maintain] the stage properties . . . so that the drama of eroticism can be enacted" (Money, 1961). Hormones *per se* do not determine the type, direction, or—within limits—the frequency of activity. For example, the evidence indicates that homosexuality versus heterosexuality is not dependent upon hormonal irregularity. Sexual activity after orchiectomy or ovariectomy is also not absolutely correlated with diminished hormonal output.

Masters and Johnson are better known for treatment of sexual disabilities, but their landmark contribution has been their observations on the physiology of sexual response (Masters and Johnson, 1966). They have divided the orgasmic response of both males and females into four phases: excitement, plateau, orgasm, and resolution. The excitement phase in the male is indicated by erection, in the female by vaginal lubrication. Plateau phase arousal in the male is indicated by additional penile tumescence, apposition of the testes to the perineum due to contraction of the cremasterics, and the appearance at the meatus of Cowper's gland secretions. The *sine qua non* of female plateau levels is further vascular engorgement and color change (from pink to deep red) in the labia minora. It should be emphasized that all four stages involve a total body response. Certain aspects are omitted for the sake of space (see Masters and Johnson, 1966). Male and female experiences of orgasm are outlined separately below. This description is taken largely from Masters and Johnson (1966) but has been confirmed and modified slightly by work within the Sexual Behaviors Consultation Unit. Variations in the male pattern are related more to duration and less to intensity of response. The female pattern varies both in intensity and in duration of response.

The basic physiological responses to sexual stimulation are widespread vasocongestion and generalized increase in muscle tension, both voluntary and involuntary. The excitement phase derives from appropriate somatic or psychic stimulation. This stimulation establishes sufficient increments of sexual tension to extend the cycle leading to and through the plateau phase. Subjective appreciation of orgasm is based on psychological integration of physiological events.

The male subjective experience of orgasm is important, since the quality of male orgasm varies more than is generally assumed. For example, the premature ejaculator often has poor subjective experience of orgasm until sufficient control is achieved to allow stimulus buildup. The following are the usual stages of male orgasmic experience:

Stage 1

The first stage is that of ejaculatory inevitability—the feeling of fullness along with a feeling of "activity" deep to the symphysis—which indicates that ejaculation is forthcoming and can no longer be voluntarily controlled.

Stage 2

This stage may be divided into two phases: (a) the contraction of the urethra *per se*, and (b) an appreciation of the semen bulk and its movement along the urethra.

Stage 3

This is the stage of release and relaxation, often with semivoluntary vocalization. This is followed by a desire for closeness and then a wish to rest or sleep. In good relationships, a component of this stage may be afterplay (as distinct from foreplay).

After ejaculation in the male there is a refractory period of varying lengths (according to age, state of satiation, and physical condition) during which further erection and ejaculation is inhibited.

The following are the stages of female orgasmic experience:

Stage 1

Orgasm has its onset with a suspension, or momentary cessation, in arousal, followed almost immediately by an intense sensual awareness oriented toward the clitoris but radiating upward into the pelvis. This clitoral-pelvic awareness has been described as occurring concomitantly with a sense of bearing down or expelling.

Stage 2

A sensation of spreading warmth moving outward from the pelvic area suffusing the body.

Stage 3

Consists of a feeling of involuntary contraction focused in the vagina or lower pelvis—often described as "pelvic throbbing."

Stage 4

Release and relaxation associated oftentimes with spontaneous vocalization, a desire for closeness, and in good relationships, a desire for afterplay or "cuddling."

After orgasm in the female there is no obligatory refractory phase, and serial orgasms may be experienced if effective stimulation continues.

Patient descriptions do not match textbook accounts since an analytic mind is not often turned toward the experience of orgasm. In general, for orgasm to have occurred in females, there must be a feeling of warmth, pelvic contraction, and release; for males, a sense of ejaculatory inevitability, followed by expulsive contractions, and a sense of release.

ETIOLOGY OF SEXUAL DYSFUNCTIONS

Although there is considerable clinical overlap between organic and psychological sexual dysfunction, the two processes may be conveniently separated in reviewing etiology. Since the organic etiologies seen in practice vary according to the particular specialty, no attempt will be made to deal comprehensively with the many possible disorders. The emphasis will be on factors in psychological development which contribute to functional etiologies.

It is well to keep in mind that primarily organic disorders may have significant functional overlay which will not necessarily remit with effective treatment of the pathological condition. By the same token, treatment of an "obvious" functional disorder may come to a standstill unless the complicating organic condition is diagnosed and remedied.

Organic

Organic etiologies may occur on an embryological basis, *e.g.*, the intersex conditions, vaginal atresia, epispadias, and bladder exstrophy, etc. (Jones and Park, 1974; Engel, 1974; Jones, 1974). They may occur secondary to trauma (Horton, 1973), or secondary to medical illness, acute or chronic (Kaplan, 1974). They may also occur related to ingestion of drugs—socially and for medical indications (see Chapter 9). Endocrine deficit or excess states are often invoked to account for sexual disability. In general, certain organic conditions are commonly seen in different specialty practices and are familiar to those specialists. Urologists commonly see postprostatectomy and postorchiectomy conditions; internists, diabetic impotence; and surgeons, anatomical deficit cases.

Functional

Genetic inheritance, maturation of the fetus, and hormonal conditioning *in utero* are viewed as establishing the physical wherewithal and the operating range of the emotional thermostat as substrates for psychological sexual development. Such basic parts of sexuality as being able to relate trustingly to another human, the fantasy involved in foreplay, and erotic competition for a loved person are developmental milestones of childhood. Frustrating, overindulging, or skewed, idiosyncratic responses on the part of parents and sibs have the capacity for building in conflicting, inappropriate behaviors and emotional responses in subsequent situations of intimacy or relatedness, including sexual intimacy.

Infants must first have the experience of relating trustingly with the adults in their environment, accepting reasonable nurturance and physical contact from them. In the newborn, human contact and emotional feedback are essential to the development of basic trust so important in later relationships.

At 1 year and earlier, with crawling and then walking, the platform of basic trust is utilized to establish some separation and individuation. These basic early experiences will allow a mature person to relate trustingly without melding or losing a sense of identity. From the earliest stages, masturbation among infants and toddlers, as well as cuddling with various shades of eroticism, are to be expected. Parents should be nonpunitive of such behavior, while establishing limits which are comfortable for them. Overstimulation may clearly be as detrimental to the child as prohibition. Nothing can replace parental sensitivity to the developmental stages of the child in terms of setting reasonable limits. It should go almost without saying that parental eroticized play and lovemaking *are* overstimulating to the child and should be conducted in privacy. The same may be said for parental nudity.

Gender identity—sense of maleness or femaleness—is in the process of consolidation from ages 1½ to 6. Occasional "girlish" behavior in young boys, or tomboyish behavior in girls, is no cause for alarm. However, consistent opposite sex patterns in dress, toys, friends, and interests, particularly with often voiced wishes to be of the opposite sex, are a different matter and require consultation. A solidly fixed gender identity is a precursor for adequate sexual identification and the established role as a sexual partner.

A critical developmental period for the child is the phase of the "family triangle" or oedipal period. In the simplified situation, this consists of eroticized attachment to the opposite sex parent with anger and rebelliousness directed toward the other. Little boys will speak of marrying their mothers and getting rid of their fathers in one way or another. This situation may be handled by pointing out its reality: namely, that the child is too young to marry anyone and that when he is of sufficient age, mother will be too old; besides, mother is already married and loves the husband she has. Furthermore, little boys need their fathers, for how else are they going to learn to be men. Successful resolution of the triangular conflict of eroticized possessiveness and rebellion with parents will make the individual less susceptible to repeating a triangular situation through compulsive pursuits of someone else's partner in unrelenting and unrewarding extramarital conquests with their subsequent guilt.

The sexualized relationships of the "family triangle" generally submerge about age 5 or 6, with the beginning of school. In those situations in which sexualized attachments openly continue through ages 6 to 10, the child is probably being overstimulated by parents or sibs. Children experience too much sexual excitement as frustrating, disorganizing, or enraging.

With the gradual onset of androgen and estrogen production, at about ages 10 to 12, sexual latency comes to an end. Menarche or nocturnal emissions and secondary sexual characteristics are the hallmarks of this change.

Masturbation and frank sex become part of the adolescent spectrum of behavior. Masturbation often presents conflicts, which are largely unspoken, however, and seldom brought into the consultation room. Sexual activity is usually brought into consultation as either a troublesome problem representing a three-way conflict between peer pressures, personal moral code, and family morality, or as a direct request for birth control measures.

Masculinity and femininity are in the process of consolidation in adolescence, and sexual identity is in some flux even in the normal situation. Occasional homosexual experimentation is not abnormal, but repeated or preferential homosexuality must be taken seriously and will not necessarily be outgrown.

Mature sexuality requires the normal maturation in physical apparatus, freedom from disease, and progression through the stages of psychological development without too much residual conflict. Mature sexuality is built on a capacity for intimate assertiveness and receptivity and the recognition of the sexual partner as a real person (with actual personal needs, desires, and responses) rather than a substitute for childhood figures. What has gone before developmentally serves as the prototype for what comes later. Maturity in the sexual sphere assumes that early experiences with intimacy have been satisfactory, that foreplay fantasies are not burdened with leftover anger or fear, that gender is secure, that conflicts growing out of the family triangle have mellowed, and that peers have provided sufficient opportunity for sexual experimentation. Mature sexuality can best be captured as the realization, put into practice, that satisfaction, as against simple discharge, requires the mutual cooperation and involvement of two real people. (For a more detailed discussion of sexual development, see Meyer, 1975.)

Functional sexual disorders may clearly grow out of disharmonious relationships between partners, real-life events such as economic crisis, and lack of experience or education. In a majority of instances, however, the factors that render the relationship, the real-life events, or the paucity of experience pathological are rooted in developmental arrests or conflicts in the psychological history of the individual (Meyer *et al.*, 1975).

SKILLS AND ATTITUDES IN DEALING WITH SEXUAL DISORDERS

A physician who elects to deal with sexual problems in his practice should conscientiously strive to ensure that certain prerequisites of information, skill, and attitude are met.

Necessary *information* includes a knowledge, first, of the physical factors in sexual functioning—anatomical, hormonal, and neurological—in normal and pathological conditions; second, knowledge of surgical or medical procedures likely to present iatrogenic complications of sexual performance; and third, an awareness of those diseases which themselves affect sexual functioning, *e.g.*, diabetes, chronic debilitating diseases, and emotional disorders.

In terms of *skill*, it is essential to minimize iatrogenic problems of sexual performance from medical and surgical procedures. Whenever procedures with sexual side effects must be used, it is only fair to prepare the patient ahead of time. Most of us are aware of the sexual side effects of our usual procedures and common prescriptions. Unfortunately, we do not often impart our information to the patient prior to treatment. This leaves him with a frightening and inexplicable onset of sexual dysfunction where none has existed previously. Lack of information, subsequent anxiety, and embarrassed reluctance to discuss the problem may turn mild impotence or dyspareunia into major symptomatology.

Lastly, but importantly, one's *attitude* regarding sexual disabilities requires assessment. I am not necessarily referring to undergoing "desensitization" by exposure to pornography or group discussions about sex, but rather to whether one can look upon sexual disorders as a legitimate medical concern—in other words, as a dysfunctional state with morbid influence. Included in this attitude is tolerance of a patient's frailties, regardless of one's own moral bent and state of function or dysfunction. Attitude is a personal decision. In general, however, it is better to recognize than to disregard limitations. Few skills in the physician's repertoire are more useful than a matter-of-fact attitude toward the patient with a sexual disability.

ASSESSMENT OF SEXUAL DISABILITIES

It is difficult to agree on what constitutes sexual adequacy. For example, should a woman who enjoys sexual intercourse but masturbates to climax be considered inadequate? And what about her partner? Perhaps the best response to the question "What is sexual adequacy?" is that there are no absolutes in the matter. Adequacy may be defined, following Lazarus (1969), "as the ability to obtain and maintain a sufficient degree of sexual arousal so as to derive pleasure from the sexual act and contribute to the enjoyment of one's partner, finally leading to orgasmic release. . . ." There is no specification of the type of sexual act or the means by which orgasm is reached. What is adequate performance for one individual with one partner, or in one set of circumstances, may be inadequate with another.

Misleading Presentation of Sexual Problems

Sexual problems present with various calling cards, such as headache, fatigability, back pain, being "run down," dysmenorrhea, and a gamut of other nonspecific complaints. For some people, it is easier to hurt physically than to acknowledge sexual malfunction. Only a detailed history defining the time of occurrence of the most severe symptomatology (for example, at bedtime, or when the spouse comes home in the evening) will give a clue to the sexual underpinning of the complaint.

The sexual problem, once uncovered, may represent little more than unrealistic romantic expectations or concerns about sexual propriety. A patient may feel inadequate and cheated despite acceptable levels of pleasure and fulfillment. Contrast is presented by a patient whose boundaries of acceptable behavior are narrow compared with a more adventuresome spouse and who views experimentation as less than proper. In general, there is no "abnormal" sexual behavior between consenting adults, although the line might be drawn at foreplay and intercourse substitutes involving physical abuse. Judging from their widespread occurrence, oral-genital connection and the whole range of coital positions are encompassed within "normal" sexual practice.

The basic tool in the assessment of sexual disability, as in any other area of medicine, is the history. Once a sexual disability has been brought into the consultation, it is important, if you do not plan to refer immediately, to set aside time to take an adequate history—even if it means rescheduling.

After taking the history, a physical examination, including genitals, is mandatory. A detailed outline of the history would be impossible here. There are, however, certain basic areas to be covered:

What Is the Problem, as Perceived by the Patient? The common introductory statement, "I don't enjoy sex!" from female patients may represent anything from fear of pregnancy to primary anorgasmia to severe neurosis. Women are often more willing than men to come forward with a complaint of sexual dysfunction and will occasionally do this service for their husbands. A woman complaining of not enjoying sex may be serving as the entree into treatment for an impotent husband.

What Is the Duration of the Problem? Were impotency problems, for example, intermittently noticed from the beginning of coital activity involving a partner, or have they developed after previously satisfactory performance? Has the problem been consistently present since it began, or has it been intermittent?

What Are the Concurrent Events? For example, when difficulties started, what else was happening in your life? Birth of children, debts, affairs, career failures, drinking, physical illness, etc. may be precipitating events. It will often be profitable to go over seemingly unrelated events coinciding with disability onset.

What, if Anything, Has the Patient Found That Will Temporarily improve Functioning? Temporary improvements can be occasioned by such occurrences as a fight with the husband, getting the children away, being taken out for dinner, using a tranquilizer, etc. All these modes of improvement will tend to help focus on the pathogenic agent.

What Does the Patient Feel Has Caused the Problem? And How Serious Does He [or She] Feel It Is? Patients often have clear perception of the etiology and seriousness of their difficulty, a realization that may be of great help in the ultimate recommendation for treatment.

What Are the Patient's Thoughts in Terms of Treatment? Suggestions from patients will run from hormones, to counseling, to psychotherapy. I do not believe that patient preference for a treatment modality should outweigh medical judgement, but it may be extremely helpful in gauging the introduction to the preferred treatment mode.

A rule of thumb in assessment of a sexual problem is, whenever possible, *see the spouse or partner*. The advantages are as follows: (1) *added history*—the spouse may be less shy about mentioning certain aspects of the history; (2) *minimization of the "paranoid position"*—when sex is being discussed solely with one member of a sexual partnership, the other may feel excluded or, worse, suspicious; even if the partner declines to come, he has at least been invited; (3) *contact with the more dysfunctional partner*—often the less dysfunctional partner, being less embarrassed, may seek consultation first, the more dysfunctional person requiring a specific invitation to participate; and (4) *collaboration and cooperation with counseling or referral*—whether direct counseling or referral is planned, cooperation of the partner is essential to its success.

COMMON SEXUAL DISORDERS

Common sexual complaints are outlined in Table 1.1, divided by male and female disorders. The common disorders for males are premature ejaculation, impotence, and retarded ejaculation; for females, dyspareunia, anorgasmia ("frigidity"), and vaginis-

TABLE 1.1
Common Sexual Complaints

Male	Female
Premature ejaculation	Dyspareunia
Impotence	Anorgasmia
Retarded ejaculation	Vaginismus
Sexual withdrawal	Sexual withdrawal

mus. Both sexes may exhibit a "nonspecific" sexual withdrawal, that is, decrease in sexual interest, frequency, or enjoyment without other specific symptoms such as premature ejaculation or dyspareunia.

The definitions of sexual disorders leave much to be desired and are subject to disagreement among reputable people. The definitions preferred by the Sexual Behaviors Consultation Unit of the Johns Hopkins Medical Institutions are outlined below.

Male Disorders

Premature Ejaculation. (1) Ejaculation during a process of foreplay understood by both partners to be leading toward intercourse; (2) ejaculation just before or during the act of penetration; or (3) ejaculation anytime during the first 15 penile thrusts after intromission.

Impotence. Inability to achieve or maintain an erection—prior to ejaculation—sufficient for penetration and completion of the sexual act. This definition includes loss of erection during coitus, but prior to ejaculation.

Retarded Ejaculation. Very slow ejaculation or virtual inability to ejaculate. This condition is usually limited to an essential inability to ejaculate intravaginally, with ejaculation by masturbation being spared.

Female Disorders

Dyspareunia. Vaginal or pelvic pain associated with penetration and coitus, very often leading to termination of the sexual encounter.

Anorgasmia. Episodic or relatively continuous inability to reach orgasm in situations judged to be appropriately stimulating. There may be anorgasmia with both coitus and masturbation or just with coitus.

Vaginismus. Spasm of the perivaginal musculature rendering penetration difficult or virtually impossible to accomplish.

Male and Female Disorders

Nonspecific Sexual Withdrawal. Withdrawal from sexual activities or decrease in sexual frequency by either or both partners without evidence of one of the specific disorders listed above. It is nonspecific in that sense only; psychologically, the causes of withdrawal may be quite specific.

In many ways these definitions are simplified and do not adequately represent clinical complexity. For example, a man who ejaculates prematurely may be paired with a woman who doesn't experience orgasm. It will not be clear initially whether she has a primary disorder or whether her difficulty is purely secondary to her husband's condition. In general, sexual disorders in men involve performance failures, while disabilities in women usually relate to failures of satisfaction.

DIFFERENTIAL DIAGNOSIS OF ORGANIC AND FUNCTIONAL DISORDERS

The definitions of the common disorders will provide a framework for considering the differential diagnoses of organic and functional etiologies.

Premature ejaculation is seldom primarily organic in etiology. It is usually related to anxiety in the sexual situation, which may be related to strife between sexual partners or unreasonable performance expectations. At a deeper level it may be related to unresolved resentment, rage, or fear growing out of the individual's past experiences, entirely unrelated to the current partner. Anxiety about physical conditions, however, may contribute to the development of premature ejaculation. For example, concern about angina or cardiac insufficiency may establish the necessary prerequisites of anxiety for premature ejaculation to occur. Physical problems related to premature ejaculation are few in number (Kaufman, 1967) as follows: local irritation of the skin of the glans or prepuce and inflammations of the urethra and prostate.

Impotence, on the other hand, may be the outcome of a number of physical disorders and requires careful evaluation for organic etiology. Organic disorders, however, affect erectile capacity usually in different ways from the functional. An organic disorder will often manifest *absolute* (perineal prostatectomy) or progressive (diabetes) interference with erection; functional disorders will show *intermittent* or *periodic*, *situational* interferences with potency. A functionally impotent man may be impotent with one woman, but not another, or impotent heterosexually but not in homosexual relationships. Organically impotent men will attempt masturbation or relations with various partners with no better results. When awakening at night, or before voiding in the morning, functionally impotent men will have full and firm erections; organically impotent men will continue to show compromised function. The presence of nocturnal or full bladder erections with complete tumescence indicates the capacity for physiological response and makes the diagnosis of organic impotence less tenable.

Retarded ejaculation, like premature ejaculation, is seldom based on organic pathology. The absence of an ejaculate, which may at times mimic retarded ejaculation, may be associated with urological procedures giving rise to retrograde ejaculation, or with psychotropic agents such as Thioridazine.

Anorgasmia in the female, like premature ejaculation in the male, is seldom associated with organic conditions as a primary etiology; rather, physical illness or compromised function may establish the preconditions of anxiety or withdrawal sufficient for psychological anorgasmia. The functional etiologies range from unwillingness to experiment with more effective techniques and interpersonal disharmony with the partner, to unresolved intrapsychic conflicts.

Dyspareunia, on the other hand, is commonly associated with physical etiology and a careful screening for such conditions as vulvovaginitis, endometriosis, or uterine ligament tear is indicated. Differential points again are the consistent nature of dyspareunia—for example, with gynecological exam and any and all partners (organic)—versus episodic or situational dyspareunia (functional). Dyspareunia may be primarily functional, with the underlying causes being related to the relationship and/or the psychic state of the individual. Self-limited dyspareunia after childbirth is a frequent occurrence, and expectant parents should be warned lest the new mother's withdrawal be interpreted by her spouse as a rejection. (See Masters and Johnson, 1970, for a more comprehensive outline of organic etiologies.)

Drug and alcohol ingestion and various medications in the pharmacopeia (psychotropic agents and antihypertensive agents, for example) may establish a physiological basis for sexual dysfunction, primarily in the male, so that a careful drug history is indicated.

Nonspecific sexual withdrawal is "nonspecific" only in the sense that there is no apparent primary sexual dysfunction, such as impotence or anorgasmia. All too often, the psychological causes for the withdrawal are quite specific and deep-seated. Fortunately, however, the causes may be connected with temporary disharmony among the partners related to disturbing life events. Physical illness in one or both partners may also contribute to the withdrawal, and the primary mode of treatment is correction or amelioration, where possible, of the physical disorder.

The differential diagnosis of organic versus functional sexual disorders is, in the final analysis, dependent upon thorough history, physical examination, and laboratory studies. In general, however, organic disorders will show an unremitting consistency or progressive decline in function that is not found in the more situationally related, intermittent functional disorders.

OFFICE AND SPECIAL TECHNIQUES FOR THE TREATMENT OF SEXUAL DISORDERS

Every practitioner has a variety of psychological, behavioral, medicinal, or surgical techniques customarily used in dealing with the commonplace sexual problems seen in his practice. These may range from reassurance to counselling to active treatment, medically, surgically, or psychiatrically. It is hoped that these familiar techniques may be complemented or expanded by the brief discussion that follows. The central theme of the material outlined here is geared toward psychological and behavioral techniques for those conditions characterized by a primary psychological etiology or significant psychological overlay.

Provision of Information

Misinformation about sexual functioning is extreme in some couples and contributes to the sexual disability in many. In such cases, it may be useful to provide information on the anatomy of the genital area, the physiology of arousal and orgasm, techniques of foreplay, coital positions, and the range of acceptable practice.

One means of providing information that some use is through the use of conjoint physical examinations (see Chapter 5). The term "conjoint" in the conjoint physical examination indicates that both individuals in a sexual partnership will be physically examined, one in the presence of the other. For example, the physical examination of the female partner may be utilized to point out to her spouse the location, function, and sexual response of the clitoris, labia majora, labia minora, introitus, and vaginal barrel. Breast responses to sexual stimulation may also be explained with the organ visible. Reversing the situation, examination of the male may be utilized to explain the location, function, and sexual response of the foreskin, glans, penile shaft, scrotum, testes, and internal organs. With the patients properly prepared, the physician comfortable, and with a confidential and supportive setting, a number of physicians have found this a productive and helpful procedure.

Patients may be selected for brief educational intervention when history indicates lack of information and experience and factual misconceptions together with an interest in having more data. This technique is usually appropriate in individuals just beginning sexual activity. Where the partnership has more longevity, there must be some question regarding their ability to communicate and use information from each other perhaps indicative of more deep-seated problems in the relationship and in the individuals. The primary effect of providing information in an understanding but matter-of-fact way is to take sexual functioning out of the realm of the mysterious and forbidden.

Counseling

To embark on a course of brief counseling implies not only the provision of factual information, as above, but also several sessions during which ongoing sexual activity can be verbally explored. At issue are when and how the sexual approach is made, whether arousal is experienced, how coitus is practiced, and what satisfactions are achieved. Suggestions may be made for practicing in weak areas: for example, if arousal seems insufficient during foreplay, one may advise the couple to share their individual preferences and to practice foreplay, relegating coitus for the moment to the background. If one partner has difficulty achieving adequate arousal, you may suggest that this partner be responsible for determining when coitus is to occur. If failure to achieve orgasm is the difficulty, instruction in afterplay techniques to achieve orgasm may be indicated.

The primary goal in brief counseling is to enable the individual, or couple, to be more aware of needs and to communicate them more freely, giving nature an opportunity to take its course. Individuals or couples are selected for brief counseling when there is a problem of some standing, but not ingrained, where neurotic aspects of the sexual difficulty are not immediately apparent, and where simple information lack is not primary.

Behavior Modification Work

Formal behavioral modification work is most frequently carried out with couples, roughly as outlined by Masters and Johnson (1970). (For work with individuals in other behavioral modification techniques, see Yates, 1970.) I will speak primarily of our use of the Masters and Johnson modality.

This technique requires participation by the couple in a series of sessions extending from 10 to 20 in which there is detailed attention to the sexual history, the personal history, the lovemaking techniques, and communication. A series of graded exercises are recommended excluding genital touching and coitus initially, gradually leading up to coital activity as foreplay and genital exploration are mastered. In general, this formal technique should not be attempted without previous experience and training.

Couples are selected for such a program as an initial choice when there is a more longstanding or more complete disability. In general, exclusions—and referral for psychotherapy—are based on the presence of "bankrupt" marriages (where the couple cannot cooperate in any of the basics of married life), high degrees of neurosis, psychosis, or the perversions.

Psychotherapy

Psychotherapy of sexual disabilities may be undertaken with either a couple or individuals. The primary goal is to elucidate the historical roots of the difficulty in development, together with the associated fantasies and emotions, conflicts, and inhibitions. This technique requires experience and training and implies an open-ended time commitment to the treatment program. The reason for this requirement is that pathogenic elements are sealed off from conscious knowledge and volition, and the length of time required to reach and then rework such material is not under the physician's direct control. The pathogenic material and fantasies have not simply been forgotten; they have been actively extruded from awareness, and any attempt to bring them to the fore will be resisted even by the most cooperative patient.

Couples are selected for this program when there is overriding anxiety regarding a more direct approach to sexual functioning; individuals, on the basis of high levels of neurotic, affective, or psychotic problems.

The techniques for treatment of patients with chronic disabling disease are covered in Chapter 10; for problems related to drug use or abuse, in Chapter 9; for problems amenable to interpersonal couples treatment, Chapters 5 and 6; for behavior therapy, Chapter 7; for the use of desensitization and graphic materials, Chapter 8; for surgical intervention, Chapter 11; and for the use of surgical prostheses, Chapter 12. Issues related to individual psychotherapy for sexual disorders are covered in Chapter 13.

SUMMARY—THE DOUBLE STANDARD

The various conditions, from disappointed romantic notions to impotence or frigidity, are clinical entities in their own right, but the important points are that one sexual dysfunction may progressively shade into another more serious disability, and the plight of one partner usually affects the other. Given their complexity and his limited time, what then is the role of the physician in dealing with these problems?

In some cases, I have seen excellent diagnosticians bypass the sexual history in dealing with genital problems and proceed directly on to the physical exam. They would have considered such a shortcut unthinkable in a patient with abdominal distress. In part, this double standard is carried over from medical training, in which sexual matters are passed over lightly, if they are presented at all. In addition, being part of the larger culture, physicians often suffer from the reluctance to discuss sexual matters that characterizes the general population. Often, however, counselling is avoided because sexual disabilities are considered to be either physically determined or the result of deep-seated psychopathology. Whether because of training gaps, personal reluctance, or black-and-white perspectives on etiology, the potential for helpful immediate counsel is often minimized.

Sexual difficulties may be brought about by physical pathology, emotional or relationship problems, and lack of education or experience, in pure culture, or in combination. Whatever the etiology, however, there are certain common steps in the development of most dysfunctions: the patient in the office has usually been through a progression of disappointing performance, withdrawal, frustration, increasing anxiety, and further failure. In view of his demonstrated vulnerability, potential iatrogenic complications must be avoided. If the history is bypassed or shortcut, the facts will not be apparent to the patient, and for him the disability will be even more mysterious and foreboding. If discussion of sexual matters is taboo in the physician/patient relationship, already present embarrassment and estrangement will be reinforced. Etiological insistence on either physical or serious emotional causation may unjustifiably preclude attempts at rehabilitation when habit, conditioning, and lack of experience or knowledge are, in reality, major factors.

Since sexual misinformation abounds despite the "sexual revolution," the physician may need to provide basic information to his patients. As an educator, however, he must be enlightened regarding his own ability to communicate information and understanding rather than embarrassment or a personal moral code. To talk about a problem with someone who can comfortably listen is a relief to the patient, and the chance to ventilate is sometimes sufficient to begin the process of change.

The major fear to combat in dealing with sexual inadequacy (to paraphrase a famous line) is fear itself—fear of inadequacy, fear of failure, and fear of helplessness. A basic step in intervention is to give the patient permission to relax rather than an order to perform. Permission delivered in the presence of both partners, to approach the sexual act gradually, stopping when anxiety threatens, and to explore a range of intimacies in stepwise fashion, will serve to defuse anxiety.

To simply reassure a patient that he is not hormonally or physically deficient begs the important steps of outlining the basic sexual problem, instilling hope for its resolution, and establishing a mutual working base with the spouse. In any case, sexual and genital problems are the product of a complex interaction of physiology, learning, and relationships; and, for many, referral for additional treatment is indicated. Even in these circumstances, the initial consultation may prevent additional deterioration and establish the basis for further work.

REFERENCES

Engel, R. 1974. Surgical construction of the male genitalia. Clin. Plastic Surg., *1*:229.

Horton, C., ed. 1973. *Plastic and Reconstructive Surgery of the Genital Area*. Little, Brown and Co., Boston.

Jones, H., Jr. 1974. Surgical construction of the female genitalia. Clin. Plastic Surg., *1*:255.

Jones, H., Jr., and Park, I. 1974. Differential diagnosis in intersex conditions. Clin. Plastic Surg., *1*:223.

Kaplan, H. 1974. *The New Sex Therapy*. Brunner/Mazel, New York.

Kaufman, J. 1967. Urologic factors in impotence and premature ejaculation. Med. Aspects Hum. Sexuality, *1*:43.

Lazarus, A. 1969. Modes of treatment for sexual inadequacies. Med. Aspects Hum. Sexuality, *3*:53.

Masters, W., and Johnson, V. 1966. *Human Sexual Response*. Little, Brown and Co., Boston.

Masters, W., and Johnson, V. 1970. *Human Sexual Inadequacy*. Little, Brown and Co., Boston.

Meyer, J. 1975. Individual treatment of sexual disorders. In: Freedman, A., Kaplan, H., and Sadock, B., eds., *Comprehensive Textbook of Psychiatry*, Ed. 2, p. 1544. Williams and Wilkins, Baltimore.

Meyer, J., Schmidt, C., Jr., Lucas, M. J., and Smith, E. 1975. Short-term treatment of sexual disorders: interim report. Am. J. Psychiatry, *132*:172.

Money, J. 1961. Sex hormones and other variables in human eroticism. In: Young, W., ed., *Sex and Internal Secretions*, Vol. II, p. 1383. Williams and Wilkins, Baltimore.

Yates, A. 1970. *Behavior Therapy*. Wiley, New York.

TWO

The Approach to the Patient

ROY M. WHITMAN, M.D.

This paper will describe the basic psychodynamic approach to the treatment of sexual disorders. Included will be some of the recent research in behavioral science and the psychophysiology and psychotherapy of sexual disorders from other than the dynamic therapies and how they influence current psychotherapeutic approaches. Finally, an attempt will be made to show how the two methods of approach, *i.e.*, the psychodynamic and the behavioral, are not incompatible and are especially useful in treating psychosexual disorders on an intensive basis.

When I was a medical student many years ago, I remember the Professor of Public Health giving the one lecture in medical school on sexual problems. His basic approach was that if you listened to the person or couple who was having a problem and then told them that many people had problems such as that and not to dwell on it too much, time would set the marriage right. A basic truth was communicated that I knew was somehow important: words and attitudes could change something as subtle and significant as the sexual function of human beings. Such observations would lead me to psychiatric residency, to analytic training, and to an abiding curiosity about the relationship and effects of verbal and affective interactions on human behavior. I felt that a relationship and understanding of the whole person, his psyche and his soma, a psychosomatic approach, made the most sense.

Many years later I still feel that approaching patients with sexual problems involves the basic medical approach of taking a history and doing a physical examination, along with whatever laboratory and specialized examinations seem to be indicated. Taking any type of history is always an exercise in tact and combines receptivity with aggressiveness whenever each seems appropriate. But taking a sexual history is an even more taxing undertaking inasmuch as it involves such a private area of human functioning and often may impinge upon the attitudes and values of the interviewer himself in a way that taking the history of, for example, a patient with peptic ulcer never could. A recent publication by the Group for the Advancement of Psychiatry (GAP, 1973) is the best guide that I know of for taking such a sexual history.

In this publication some of the typical pitfalls that the interviewer may fall into are noted. For example, he must be alert to imposing his own values on the patient by verbal and particularly nonverbal responses. The raising of an eyebrow has a great deal of impact on a patient who feels guilty disclosing his secrets. But there are problems that have to do not only with attitudes and values of the interviewer but also anxiety that may arise from his not knowing exactly what he is going after and what to do with it should he get it. This could be called competence anxiety and often is more basic than unresolved sexual or other values of his physician. The best antidotes for this anxiety are experience; supervision; courses, and reading in the physiology, psychology, and psychopathology of human sexual response (A. M. A., 1972; Kaplan, 1974; Katchadourian and Lunde, 1972; Kinsey and associates, 1948; Masters and Johnson, 1966, 1970).

Confidentiality is always an issue in taking a life history but particularly so in taking a sexual history. The physician should be alert to this almost universal concern and make appropriate comments about it. In terms of the hospital's records, a generalized terminology "for the chart" is often a necessary safeguard for the patient and in no way damages the usefulness of the record for most research or clinical purposes.

What has been most striking to all those who have engaged in history taking as it has been affected by the new research in sex therapy is that one may take a very complete sex history in the first few interviews or even the very first interview (Kinsey and associates, 1948). Provided one proceeds with respect and dignity, it is quite amazing how one may proceed to elicit the most private of behaviors and feelings. In general, questions about attitudes should precede those about actual behavior, however, and this is one of the useful bits of advice in the GAP report.

As for the rest of the medical examination, it is pertinent to note that the physical examination has become crucial not only for the elicitation of organic impairment but also as an introduction to the basic anatomy of the sexual apparatus. Though the controversy rages on between the various mental health disciplines as to the importance of medical training for doing psychological treatment, it behooves the sex therapist to be at least familiar with the major organic dysfunctions that must be remedied before undertaking psychotherapy. And some of the most intriguing theories of sexual function are often forthcoming during either history taking or physical examination by the sensitive clinician. One I remember from several patients was what one medical student called "the agricultural theory of sexuality." What he meant by this was that the patient literally accepted the idea that a seed was planted in the mother's stomach as had been told to him or her when quite small by a loving parent or teacher. We must always remind ourselves that there is a confusion of tongues between the adult and the child (Ferenczi, 1933) wherein the most well intentioned of phrases may be concretely or in some way distorted by the listener. Just yesterday my 3-year-old told me she had learned on TV a new way of making toast—click two glasses together! I blinked before I understood her distortion and whence it had come.

Fascinating studies in simultaneously doing a physical examination and taking a sexual history are being done by skilled obstetricians who do physical examinations on the woman with the husband present. They use this undertaking as a way of both exploring the female anatomy and also provoking the discussion and resolution of confusion about it which had contributed to frigidity, vaginal spasm, and other sexual difficulties.

Most standard texts on sexual dysfunction are extremely careful to mention many physical complaints which may hide sexual problems or occur simultaneously with them. But sexual problems may hide other problems as well, including physical disease or indeed more serious mental disease such as depression.

This brings us to attempt some way of organizing a psychiatric workup which can be applied to sexual problems. The recent findings in sexual physiology and psychology have affected my use of these categories especially when I am faced with what begins to emerge as a sexual problem early in the encounter with the patient or couple.

Levine (1952) in his chapter on the principles of psychiatric treatment in *Dynamic Psychiatry* has outlined the six basic considerations which should be considered in formulating the treatment of any psychiatric problem: (1) clinical diagnosis, (2) dynamic diagnosis, (3) genetic diagnosis, (4) transference, (5) countertransference, and (6) treatment possibilities.

This refers to the broad general category into which the patient's responses fall. The major diagnostic categories are important to consider inasmuch as homosexuality may be the early signs of organic brain disease or perverse sexual activity the precursor of a schizophrenic decompensation, for example. Clinical diagnosis has been justifiably attacked on the basis that it is not useful at best and dehumanizing at the worst. But it remains an area of some communication and understanding and combined with physical abnormality makes an over-all brief statement about the patient albeit with much omission and condensation. A particularly useful way of formulating this is in terms of problem areas which then keeps an eye on the therapeutic implications of diagnosis and paves the way for translation into effective action.

It becomes important in dealing with sexual disorders to differentiate between sexual disturbance based not only on the major psychological disorders but also on character disturbance. Thus, premature ejaculation on the basis of a severe narcissistic character disorder implies different treatment than the same symptom based on a simple reflex pattern which does not involve the whole character structure. I choose this symptom specifically because it has become so amenable to short term sex therapy using the squeeze technique that practitioners may forget that they have not discharged their total responsibility if they treat only the symptom, particularly when that symptom may represent a symbolic way of soiling women which is at the root of an entire developmental sequence. But the symptom may represent the physiological accompaniment of anxiety and not have a symbolic meaning such as the one just mentioned, as diarrhea may be the accompaniment of anxiety and not a manifestation of destructive rage.

DYNAMIC DIAGNOSIS

This form of diagnosis is much more defended by therapists as it has implied indications for action. It refers to the forces, internal and external, currently in operation in the patient's total life situation at the moment he appears for treatment. These forces are to be distinguished from genetic forces which in a sense were and are also dynamic but historically occurred earlier in the life of the person leading to the present situation.

Four general categories may be considered although they are by no means exhaustive. First is the person's current environmental situation which is important in either leading to the beginning of illness or keeping it going. In this scheme the most important environment of most patients with sexual disorders is their sex partner. In fact, this partner has been deemed of such importance by many of the workers in this field of counseling that they will not see a patient alone. Such phrases as, "there are no uninvolved partners in a sexual problem in marriage!" have led not only to the diagnostic interviewing of the couple as a couple but also requires that the marriage interaction and most exactly, the sexual relationship, be the focus of the treatment. It is worth noting that there is a two-way street between our usual psychotherapy and the current treatment of sexual disturbances with the emphasis on the marital dyad or marital unit as Masters and Johnson dryly call the couple. Thus I have been much more willing to see marital partners in the course of the therapy of one of them than I was in my earlier years of practice. I have never had one chance to regret this despite the dire warnings I had heard about it, but I have often had the chance to value such a content, and patients have been uniformly grateful for such flexibility.

Second to consider are the internal restrictive and standard setting aspects of the person which go under the over-all name of superego and ego ideal. While always important in understanding human beings, this area of the personality is of great importance in considering the treatment of sexual disorders inasmuch as the clinician can get a quick idea about what is acceptable and unacceptable to the person, get leads for outlining the direction of sexual exercises, give suggestions for pertinent reading, and get a plan for dealing with the so-called forbidden areas of sexual feeling and behavior. In recent years I have found considering the ego ideal as a separate entity very fruitful and have divided it off in my mind from the superego (considering the ideal to be what the organism strives *toward* and the superego as the internal *punishing* forces or restrictive forces). I mention the ideal particularly because it is such a negative but little considered influence on sexual behavior. Thus a man may see himself with a constant erection during sexual play and may become frightened and even more inhibited when it comes and goes. Or occasional sexual failure or lack of interest may be seen as incompatible with some unspoken ideal of a "push button man" always ready to go.

Third are the instinct derivatives which include the drives and impulses in the person including sexual, narcissistic, aggressive, and dependency drives. In usual psychiatric practice we seldom consider these in a quantitative way but in the treatment of sexual disturbance it is important to do just that. I have found that a good deal of the anguish in a marriage may be due to unequal sex instincts (Whitman, 1969). It is crucial to distinguish quantitative drives from inhibited or overstimulated drives and the best clue to this is the observation made by Kinsey and associates (1948) that the pattern of sexual expression is fairly consistent throughout the history of the person, although its expression may change with the different developmental sequences.

Fourth are the integrating and synthesizing forces in the person which go under the summary term, ego. Evaluation of this agency of mind is useful in assaying aptitude for psychological treatment and the ability to master various levels of abstraction and understanding. Defenses and therefore rigidity of response to treatment would be considered here.

The danger of such a shorthand summary is that even as with the clinical diagnosis this may become too theoretical and thus become an intellectual exercise for the clinician. A sensitive grasp of one dynamic formulation expressed in a feeling way is often more useful to both patient and clinician in the actual treatment. The self-image of the person as an ego attitude might be captured as one useful unifying concept. In one patient's conception of himself he appeared as a butler; it seemed that he way always serving people, an orientation that he brought into the sexual relationship with his partner and was destructive of free interaction between them.

Two processes in the therapist's understanding of the patient occur during interviews, the intellectual and the empathic. The intellectual has the therapist collating relevant data and sorting them out in a meaningful way; the empathic has him experiencing minute identifications with the person and asking himself such a question as "How would I feel if I were in his shoes and my wife laughed at *me* when I told about our difficulties together?" An especially fruitful way of asking oneself this query and sweeping away the adult rationalizing part of the personality is to phrase this question as, "How would a child feel in such a situation?" The transactional analysis school has caught this problem very well in considering three ego states, adult, parent, and child and questioning which is responding to what situation. While these seem equivalent to the id, superego, and ego mentioned above, they have the advantage of being personified and being considered ego states rather than abstract agencies of the mind.

Empathy is crucial in dealing with people and is different from sympathy. A sequence of empathy I have seen in its breakdown either under fatigue or a deteriorated therapeutic situation is from empathy to sympathy to antipathy to apathy. This, of course, applies to marriages as well as therapeutic contacts and is of great importance in determining where the marriage partners are with each other. One of the major contributions of Masters and Johnson is the dual therapist approach to treating another couple. In addition to certain dynamic advantages, it seems to protect (because of the checks and balances of the other therapist) the empathic process of minute identification without allowing it to become gross identification.

A dynamic diagnosis is often the key to a corrective emotional experience so that patients, for example, with overly ambitious parents and therefore parallel ego ideals can be encouraged to set much lower but still satisfying goals for themselves. It would seem that the main corrective emotional experience offered by the therapist with most of today's patients is that of a nonjudgmental attitude, which has overtones of permissiveness and acceptance in it. One could conceive in the future that stricter limit setting might be necessary to counterbalance an overly permissive unbringing and society.

The use of the patient's attitudes toward the therapist as compared to how the therapist is actually behaving may be fundamental in bringing about changes in behavior. However, the use of the responses to the therapist, while they should be carefully noted, seem to be of lesser importance in the intensive brief treatment of sexual disorders than in other forms of analytic psychotherapy. The reason for this is that the therapist encourages the major cathexis to be directed toward the sexual partner and transferences, if one uses that term, to that partner are more important than transferences to the therapist. By transference, I mean the carrying forward of personality constellations from the past into the present when they are no longer appropriate. If the man's mother expected him to be an achiever in school and business, that does not necessarily mean that his wife will expect him to be an achiever in bed (although he seems to be acting in just that way).

In the few examples I have given I have used performance anxiety on the part of the male (though it also may apply to the female) as a recurring problem. This is because some of the new sex therapies have implied that performance anxiety is a new discovery which psychoanalytic theory had overlooked. A probable reason for this is that the whole narcissistic area of the personality has been slighted by analysts in the past and is only now being given the prominence it deserves (Kohut, 1971; Offenkrantz and Tobin, 1974). I think that performance anxiety is a narcissistic need for approbation which is initially internal and becomes projected to the partner.

The concept of anxiety is central to understanding human

behavior, and anxiety is essentially an antisexual attitude. Schematically there is an outer layer of defense against the anxiety, the so-called defenses of reaction formation, projection, denial, etc. Levine (1952) also liked to think that there was a third layer underneath these two which often contained worthwhile assests of decency, compassion, and other qualities which we rate positively.

This three-layer concept underlines the importance of not taking the presentation behavior as the whole person, but rather recognizing that these are defenses against anxiety. Even the most skillful therapists occasionally fall into the trap of taking the patient's statements at face value such as the patient devaluing the treatment he is anxious about losing the support of the therapist because of some upcoming separation. A misbehaving child is often a frightened child, and this holds for aggressive children as well.

Responses to the second layer of anxiety also indicate to the patient that an empathic and compassionate adult with some competence in these matters will lend his strength and understanding to the resolution of such problems. Talking about sexuality and the nuances involved in taking a sexual history, in and of itself, is often anxiety-relieving, inasmuch as the patient invariably reports that a significant number of adults around him spoke rarely of sex and then with great anxiety and embarrassment. The patient is impressed that the therapist does not share his contempt, disgust, or ridicule of certain feelings which he finds anxiety-provoking even to tell.

GENETIC DIAGNOSIS

This term has been used in dynamic psychiatry to refer to early formative influences in later dynamic constellations of behavior. That these may include hereditary factors and constitutional elements is also true, but far more important are early life experiences. Thus we now know that the most common pattern of child beating and sadistic behavior on the part of an adult is not only related to being one partner in a young couple overwhelmed by too many pregnancies too close together but also that the beater as a child was the target of being beaten himself.

In this regard, early sexual influences are impressive by their staying power and exertion of influence right on to the present. Fetishistic behavior of all types or even a compulsive approach to foreplay are often patterns which have been laid down very early in life. If is often important to determine how much is regression and how much fixation inasmuch as each formulation leads to a different dynamic pattern and a different therapeutic approach. Thus, a fixation to a dependency position with avoidance of any adult sexuality which might jeopardize such a position is different from sexuality which became frightening or difficult because of some current situation that caused regression to an infantile-dependent position. Emphasis on fixation often leads to longer periods of therapy; for example, primary impotence might well be correlated with fixation and secondary impotence with regression.

It is in this area that we once again meet infantile theories of sexuality. The fantasy life of the child is based on the level of cognitive and emotional comprehension that he has attained at the time that he makes certain significant observations. Thus if he sees the parents making love, he may conceive of this in terms of an attack by the man on the woman. If the girl has no concept of the vagina, then she may assume the impregnation takes place via the mouth and the child is born via the anus. Familiarity with some of the basic misconceptions and sex theories of childhood is extrememly helpful if not essential in understanding some of the problems that adults have with their sexuality. And a clear comprehension of the concept of psychosexual development, which may be subdivided into zones (oral, anal, phallic) and modes (receptive, retentive, and extrusive) such as Erikson (1950) has done so neatly in his book is often indispensable to understand neuroses and perversions and the relentless fascination they have for so many people.

Genetic considerations might determine the sex of the therapist recommended. In the dual therapist approach this problem is automatically resolved, but members of the couple will often seek further therapy for interpersonal problems after the sexual one is helped, and then the patient's ability to work with a man or a woman based on some understanding of the degree of conflict with the corresponding partner is useful in making an appropriate recommendation.

TRANSFERENCE

The concept of transference is central to that of psychoanalysis, and creating the conditions for the appearance of a transference neurosis and its resolution is one way of demarcating analysis from all other forms of therapy. By transference neurosis is meant that the early genetic and current dynamic constellations become activated and focused in the analytic situation, and much of the therapeutic work is directed toward the differentiation of past and present and how the present intrudes on the current relationship with the analyst. When other practical aspects are favorable such as psychological mindedness; the capacity and willingness to invest time, energy, and money in a prolonged enterprise; a positive or at least neutral life situation, etc., this is the treatment of choice for neuroses accompanied by sexual disturbance. It is sometimes a useful forerunner for intensive sex therapy and saves a great deal of time and energy in an intensive sex therapy program. It may even proceed simultaneously with sex therapy, but my preference is that this should be a sequence. Otherwise conflicting loyalties, jurisdictional disputes, and even envious sabotage by the "back home" therapist may undermine the sex therapy.

And this is where transference is so important. There is nothing more frustrating than coming head on with a well developed transference reaction or neurosis to an idealized therapist. All sorts of primitive reactions such as having "mother and father fight over me" or "my father is better than your father" come into play and play havoc with both therapies.

If we consider that 4-times-a-week recumbent interviews, and 2 weeks of daily prolonged interviews are the two paradigms for classical psychoanalysis and Masters-Johnson sex therapy, respectively, then we see that in actual practice these comprise the minority of the cases. We recognize that in the person's own city often less intensive therapy both for analytic and sex purposes will be the rule and this has been most cogently described in Helen Singer Kaplan's (1974) new book where the exigencies of a low and middle income setting influenced the therapy offered.

In the actuality of these local settings, transference interpretation and clarification is the exception, although it is important that the therapist recognize that the reactions to him are the characteristic reactions of the patient in a relatively unstructured setting. As I said earlier, the really crucial transferences occur toward the sex partner and, whether one works with the individual patient or the marital pair, this is the most important area for scrutiny. To divert intense reactions to the spouse away from the spouse to the therapist risks not only an intense but eventually unrealistic involvement. Seducing one member of the pair away from the other leads to such fantasies as "only the therapist can give me an orgasm"; though more therapists than we would like to admit respond with realistic gratification of such a wish, most therapists do not and then must help the patient in his tortuous return to a realistic sex partner.

Transference gives one very important clue to the patient's reactions: how justified are the patient's complaints about his spouse? Though in general one attempts to have an even-handed approach to a couple, the impulse is very strong to determine who is the instigator or perpetuator of the difficulties in the marriage. For example, after I had seen a man for a while who bitterly complained about his wife's constant criticism of him and also of her compulsiveness, I asked the wife to come to a conjoint interview. Her first remark as she entered my office was: "Dr. Whitman, don't you ever clean your windows here?"

COUNTERTRANSFERENCE

The last example given is a good one with which to begin the section on countertransference. The natural response on the part of the therapist at this point is to respond not only with annoyance at this criticism of him but also to say to himself that this initial remark verifies the patient's statements that his wife is difficult to live with. It is easy to fall into a blame-assigning orientation. The therapist then becomes identified with the husband and no longer is able to take a position approximately equidistant between husband and wife.

A simple division of countertransference is (1) a response to the patient's transference, and (2) a response to the patient because of unresolved areas of functioning and feeling in the therapist's own life. In the first instance, almost any therapist would respond with similar feelings, whereas in the second, it is a highly individual response by the therapist. In the first instance, the therapist can use the data for understanding how the patient affects all people; in the second, the response is only useful for some self-analysis by the therapist.

Sexual material is stimulating to all members of our society. It is therefore evocative of countertransference feelings of both types. If the woman seems particularly unattractive in the therapeutic situation, the therapist might wonder why she is underplaying her femininity; a similar situation would hold for the man. Perverse sexual experiences, unusual behaviour such as threesomes, group sex, sex with prostitutes, etc. may all stimulate fantasies within the therapist which produce disgust or excitement. Prejudices about homosexuality, crossdressing, bisexuality, and adultery are all situations that must be dealt with in the same objective way without imposing the value systems of the therapist on the individual or couple. In fact, a recent publication (Smith and Smith, 1974) documents certain changing mores toward extramarital sex, in much the same way Kinsey and his associates (1948) documented that premarital sex was part of the unspoken morality.

One particular countertransference mistake quoted by Levine (1952) as a general one and which is totally destructive of successful sex therapy is that of excessive therapeutic ambition. In such a situation, need for success on the part of the therapist coincides with need for achievement on the part of the couple, and the result is inhibition. Sex thrives where the goal is pleasure not performance!

There are three major safeguards against both types of countertransference: (1) adequate supervision over an extended period of time; (2) strict and honest self-scrutiny and self-analysis; and (3) some form of psychotherapy of the therapist. Similar to what Freud observed about the transference, countertransference can become a facilitating as well as inhibiting force in the therapy, and the successfuly analyzed or treated therapist is not afraid to use his own responses freely as clues as to what the patient is trying to stimulate in him.

TREATMENT POSSIBILITIES

We may state that learning occurs by three modes in psychotherapy: by identification, by conditioning, and by insight. It is usually considered that analytic psychotherapy succeeds via insight, but this is insufficient recognition of the importance of identification and conditioning (Offenkrantz and Tobin, 1974).

Levine (1952) listed the following groups of therapeutic procedures: procedures for the general care and protection of the patient and society such as hospitalization; procedures aimed at correcting structural pathological processes such as surgery for a tear in the uterosacral ligament; procedures aimed at correcting physiological problems such as postmenopausal tissue atrophy; medical treatment of physiological problems such as the use of Mellaril for premature ejaculation; physical therapies such as electric shock in severe depressions; and finally, psychotherapy.

Early decisions that must be made in planning a psychotherapeutic approach include a genetic-dynamic formulation as outlined in the earlier sections. That does not mean that this will be an inclusive formulation because all the data may take some time to gather. But the therapist must force himself into some sort of working hypothesis which can be altered as treatment progresses.

But an even earlier decision would be whether the spouse should be seen alone or the couple together. I usually make this decision on the basis of the expressed need of the presenting marital partner. Thus, if a wife calls up and indicates that her gynecologist has referred her to me for a sexual problem and that her husband is very doubtful about the whole business, I will immediately say, come on in and let's talk about the situation and where you are at the present time. However, if she calls up and says that she and her husband are both upset about her frigidity, and they want to come in, I will make a time to see both of them for the initial interview.

After the initial interview, I may decide to treat just one member of the couple although I find it useful to see the other partner at least once, sometimes at regular intervals. Sometimes after a period of psychotherapy with one partner, I will then call upon my cotherapist to join me and involve both husband and wife in an intensive Masters-Johnson form of graduated exercises and therapy after we have gone through a similar but abbreviated format of dual history taking, single history taking, switching interviewers, and a round table discussion (Masters and Johnson, 1970). Another possibility of which I availed myself recently was to refer each of the members of the marriage to long term individual therapy holding out the promise of intensive sex therapy for the time when the other therapist and I deemed this appropriate.

The next major decision has to do with whether the sexual disability is a manifestation of a deeper lying problem or whether it exists in an intact personality and is somewhat removed from the main thrust of the person. This is an extremely important decision to make and really dictates the whole therapeutic intervention.

What seems to be increasingly true is that there can be sexual dysfunction *without* major personality damage, and there can also be sexual dysfunction *with* major personality damage. There can be secondary responses to sexual dysfunction as well, which can easily be confused with total personality maladaptation. Recently, I saw a couple in which the man suffered from secondary impotence and he became so depressed and preoccupied with the symptom that be began to fail in general social and working situations. But the main goal was the alleviation of the sexual problems and this quickly led to a resolution of the other problems as well.

Homosexuality would seem to me to be an example of a symptom where the personality might or might not be engulfed by the sexual orientation. This is probably the explanation of the contradictory findings about this illness; in some instances it seems to exist apart from the rest of the personality, and in some instances the whole orientation of fear of women and their genitalia and a wish to take a passive role toward men not only in sex but totally would seem to be the situation. Then, with a properly motivated person his whole genetic-dynamic pattern can be examined with profit. In fact, it is my experience that diverting the discussion to other interpersonal concerns often is more effective in understanding the sexual concerns than dealing with the sexual problems directly. This would be true in all those disturbances which are truly *psycho*sexual, *i.e.*, where the psychosexual developmental sequences are the central personality core.

AN INTEGRATED APPROACH TO TREATMENT

Much of the literature on the topic of sexual disturbances would imply an either-or approach to the treatment of sexual dysfunction. Either the patient enters into psychoanalysis or psychoanalytic therapy, or he goes into a Masters-Johnson type of behaviour therapy approach. But analysts use reward and punishment techniques throughout the analysis, and behavior therapists use insight and unconscious understanding all the time, not to mention identification often stimulated by modeling by the therapist.

It seems to me that the crucial element is that there be a constant feedback process into the treatment which is composed of practice and careful reporting of both success and failure. The cooperation of a partner is central for the success of such a program, but the partner may be wittingly or unwittingly cooperative.

The function of the therapist in dealing with the conscious aspects of the problem is to break down the step-by-step elements of the sexual relationship and examine microscopically (from the past as well as the present) the ingredients that go into it.

A joke comes to mind that illustrates this very well. A young groom in a stable frequently fantasized about a beautiful young girl who often came to ride but hardly seemed to notice that he existed. His fantasy took the form of gaining her attention in a dramatic way and then taking her for a ride near a cool stream he knew of in the forest, then kissing her, gently removing her clothes and proceeding gradually to a beautiful seduction. He hit upon the unique means of painting one of the horses green so that she would say, "Look at that green horse!" He would respond to her exclamation, and they would talk, and he would suggest a ride together, and the fantasy would go its pleasant dreamy way. Finally, one day he got enough courage to paint the horse green and just as he fantasized, the girl remarked about the green horse. He blurted out, "Let's screw!" and that was the end of the daydream and his hopes with that girl!

The therapist must take over control from the couple of the amount and rate of sexuality that they can engage in else they will be rushing ahead with great anxiety to the "let's screw" stage. Pleasuring, caressing, massaging, and all the forms of foreplay must be engaged in for their own sake with a strict recommendation that genital sexuality be postponed. Constant reporting allows the therapist or therapists to guide the person to the next step. Simultaneously, however, the therapist is also attending to the unconscious aspects of the treatment. He listens to the associations of the patient, watches his nonverbal behavior, and asks about dreams and fantasies.

An example of this combined treatment came up lately. A couple we were treating jointly were at the stage of masturbation of themselves which they had never before been able to do without guilt and shame. The man told about looking for Japanese girls when he was in Tokyo rather than "beating himself off" as the other guys in the barracks did (said with much contempt). He then talked about wanting to hurry on to the next sequence of the sexual pattern, mounting and entry. It was clear to me that he had more shame about masturbation than he had anxiety about intercourse and indeed used heterosexuality as a defense against masturbation. I used this insight to postpone the next step in the sexual sequence until he felt completely at ease with masturbation.

A patient referred by Masters and Johnson to me with secondary impotence of 3 years' duration had difficulty with premature ejaculation which began after a severely mentally deficient son was born to them. Consciously, he wanted quickly to undo the damage by having another child who was healthy, but unconsciously he felt that they would have the same terrible result. The symptom was a good contraceptive. He had a dream that he was fighting in Viet Nam with one of the new plastic submachine guns that had been introduced there. The bullets he was firing were defective although the machine gun was all right. Discussion of the dream produced the sequence that he was responsible for the defective child because of some defect in his sperm. This was his unconscious conviction despite two previously healthy children and despite the fact that the obstetrician had tied the defective child to an illness that the wife had had in the early months of the pregnancy. Discussion of the dream reassured him that his genital apparatus was undamaged, which had been his further fear when he began to suffer from impotence along with the premature ejaculation. Zeroing in on the fantasy of the defective sperm, which had no truth in current fact but related to some adolescent fears he had had about his inability to father a child at all, produced a rapid resolution of the whole sexual dysfunction. The wife whom I saw just twice conceived, and I heard from him a year later that he had been transferred away from Cincinnati and they had a completely normal baby boy born soon after the transfer.

These two examples illustrate that insights into the patient's unconscious are often the most dramatic help that we can give. But guided sexual behavior with reference to the unconscious with the therapist(s) acting as a model for the patient or couple can be equally rewarding in the amount of gratitude and relief of suffering experienced. It therefore behooves the complete therapist to be familiar with both analytic insights and behavioral sequences with reported feedback in order to help the patient most effectively within the shortest period of time. A clear dynamic-genetic working formulation is essential no matter what technique is employed and leads to increasing rationality of therapy.

REFERENCES

American Medical Association. 1972. *Human Sexuality*. Chicago.

Erikson, E. 1950, *Childhood and Society*, Ed. 2, p. 71. W. W. Norton, New York.

Ferenczi, S. 1933. Confusion of tongues between the adults and the children (translation). Int. J. Psychoanal. V30: 5.

Group for the Advancement of Psychiatry (GAP) Report No. 88. 1973. Assessment of Sexual Function: A Guide to Interviewing. Committee on Medical Education, Vol. VIII, p. 756.

Kaplan, H. S. 1974. *The New Sex Therapy*. Brunner/Mazel, New York.

Katchadourian, H. A., and Lunde, D. T. 1972. *Fundamentals of Human Sexuality*. Holt, Reinhart and Winston, New York.

Kinsey, A. C., Pomeroy, W. B., and Martin, C. S. 1948. *Sexual Behavior in the Human Male*. W. B. Saunders, Philadelphia.

Kohut, H. 1971. *The Analysis of the Self*. International Universities Press, New York.

Levine, M. 1952. Principles of psychiatric treatment. In: Alexander, F., and Ross, H., eds., *Dynamic Psychiatry*. University of Chicago Press, Chicago.

Masters, W. H., and Johnson, V. E. 1966. *Human Sexual Response*. Little, Brown & Co., Boston.

Masters, W. H., and Johnson, V. E. 1970. *Human Sexual Inadequacy*. Little Brown & Co., Boston.

Offenkrantz, W., and Tobin, A. 1974, Psychoanalytic psychotherapy. Arch. Gen. Psychiatry, 30: 593.

Smith, J. R., and Smith, L. G., eds. 1974., *Beyond Monogamy: Recent Studies of Sexual Alternatives in Marriage*. Johns Hopkins Press, Baltimore.

Whitman, R. M. 1969. Multiple organisms. Med. Aspects Hum. Sexuality, 3: 52.

Psychological Assessment of Sexual Disorders

THREE

LEONARD R. DEROGATIS, Ph.D.

The present essay is directed to the issue of clinical assessment of psychological processes in the sexual disabilities. The tone is conceptual rather than procedural, and the report attempts to outline a rational framework to provide a conceptual basis for this essential clinical enterprise. Eight major aspects of psychological functioning—sexual experience, attitudes, information, symptoms, affects, gender role definition, fantasy, and erotic drive—are instated as principal dimensions along which assessment should be conducted. Each dimension is appraised concerning the manner in which it contributes etiologically in the sexual dysfunctions, and relevant clinical research on each factor is briefly reviewed. Part of the report is also given over to the influence of "mediating variables"—gender, age, health status, social class—on the clinical appearance of sexual disorders, and their role in psychological assessment is discussed. A final section of the essay is devoted to instilling the notion that psychological clinical assessment is clearly an aspect of "clinical science" and, as such, must be performed within the context of rational, analytic, scientific operations and decisions.

As is the case in all areas of clinical assessment, effective evaluation is possible only if the clinician remains aware that disorders occur in total persons and are not merely limited to organ systems. This is also true in the psychological assessment of sexual disabilities. Each individual carries with him a personal life history and profile of attributes that tend to render him unique, and this uniqueness requires the incorporation of information on the individual's particular "personalized context," if accurate assessment of his sexual disability is to result.

The principal responsibility of the clinician-assessor is to evaluate current and past functioning and arrive at an accurate prediction of future behavior potential. In this context it is the "commonality" rather than the uniqueness of the individual's behavior that temporarily becomes the focus of attention. The extent to which an individual's profile of characteristics matches other profiles with known outcomes is of prime concern. This suggests that information relating to the individual's psychological status should be assessed within a *normative* framework. The normative approach allows shared characteristics with predictive value to be highlighted and utilized so that accurate clinical judgements concerning the nature of the problem and its most efficient treatment can be maximized.

Although psychological processes actually function in an integrated and continuous manner, it aids assessment to view them through a scheme which dissects behavior into discrete functional categories. A framework of this kind is also consistent with the assessment process at the clinical level, where it functions naturally in an analytic fashion.

In appraising sexual disabilities, we have come to utilize a conceptual scheme which distinguishes eight interrelated categories of psychological functioning. These are *attitudes*, *information*, *experience*, *symptoms*, *role definition*, *affects*, *fantasy*, and *erotic drive*. Each of these categories represents an area of psychological functioning that has an important role in the development and maintenance of normal sexual behavior. This being so, clues to the nature, causes, and scope of sexual dysfunctions may be gleaned from a careful evaluation of the quality of functioning in each area. By building our psychological assessments around these fundamental categories we have found that the accuracy and comprehensiveness of our evaluations has been noticeably enhanced. In addition, this framework also serves as a basis for the Sexual Functioning Inventory (SFI), a psychological scale presently under development, designed to assess the nature and magnitude of sexual dysfunctions.

Beyond information from the areas above, evaluation of sexual disabilities also involves information about certain key "mediating" variables. *Gender* of the patient, *social class*, *age*, *health status*, and a number of other variables have been repeatedly observed to play a modifying role in determining the nature and course of these disorders. Assessments can be sharpened only by taking these factors into account, and evaluations which fail to do so may introduce serious distortions into the assessment process.

It is our purpose in this communication to present a conceptual scheme for the psychological assessment of sexual dysfunctions and to touch upon other patient parameters observed to be relevant to the etiology, diagnosis, and quality of treatment-response in these conditions. Although it is not intended to be comprehensive, it is hoped that the ideas presented here will provide the reader with a thoughtful and stimulating review of the problems and issues attendant upon this important and challenging task.

SEXUAL EXPERIENCE

Perhaps nowhere more clearly than in sexual behavior is confirmation found for the adage "you must learn to walk before you can run." Sexual experiences, regardless of how early or late they are initiated, seem to progress through a required hierarchical sequence reminiscent of the "by the numbers" algorithm so cherished by the cadre of the armed services.

The postulation of a hierarchical pattern of sexual exploration has been suggested for some time now (Kinsey, Pomeroy, and Martin, 1948); however, a recent series of thoughtfully done studies have provided us with a consistent picture of sexual behavior as a set of experiences with a highly prescribed order. Starting with the work of Podell and Perkins (1957), a series of investigators (Bentler, 1967a,b; Brady and Levitt, 1965; Zuckerman, 1973) have demonstrated the capability of ordering heterosexual activities on a unidimensional cumulative scale of the Guttman (1950) type. Essentially this means that sexual behaviors can be arranged in a sequence on a scale such that the positive endorsement of a specific item on the scale carries with it the implication of having experienced all activities listed previously. Table 3.1 gives a hierarchy of sexual experiences for males and females which represents a consensus of the findings from the studies listed above. As is apparent from these data, the range of an individual's sexual experiences may be determined quite reliably by ascertaining which item in the hierarchy he fails to endorse. Also, it is important to note that the hierarchies for males and females are highly similar; Zuckerman (1973) reported a rank-order correlation coefficient of 0.95 between them.

Obviously, knowledge concerning the range of an individual's sexual experience is highly relevant to the assessment of disabilities in this area (Athanasiou and Sarkin, 1974; Gebhard, 1965; Shope and Brodrick, 1967). Details concerning the initiation, frequency, and comprehensiveness of sexual activities represent significant characteristics that should be taken into account in any accurate evaluation of dysfunction. Problems with impotence in a man who has experienced most or all of the "advanced" items on the scale should be interpreted from a

TABLE 3.1

Hierarchy of Male and Female Sexual Experiences

Males		Females	
Scale Position[a]	Sexual Behavior	Scale Position[a]	Sexual Behavior
1	Kissing on the lips	1	Kissing on the lips
2	Caressing breasts	2	Having breasts caressed
3	Caressing nude breasts	3	Male prone on female
4	Lying prone on female	4	Having nude breasts caressed
5	Kissing nude breasts	5	Having nude breasts kissed
6	Female stroking penis	6	Male stroking vagina
7	Stroking female vagina	7	Stroking male penis
8	Intercourse—male superior position	8	Male oral stimulation of vagina
9	Female oral stimulation of penis	9	Oral stimulation of male penis
10	Oral stimulation of female vagina	10	Intercourse—male superior position
11	Intercourse—female superior position	11	Intercourse—female superior position
12	Intercourse—ventral-dorsal position	12	Intercourse—ventral-dorsal position
13	Mutual oral stimulation of genitals to orgasm	13	Mutual oral stimulation of genitals to orgasm

[a] In a number of cases, for example, Scale Positions No. 5, 6, 7 for the males and 8, 9 for the females, only a 1% difference in endorsement rates determined the ranks.

different perspective than a similar problem in an individual who has never experienced coitus with a female. The discovery of a reliable hierarchy of sexual experiences helps in the interpretation of the patient's sexual history and simultaneously argues for obtaining as complete a history as possible. These data will enable the clinician to know whether the dysfunction with which he is confronted represents interference in a preexisting behavior pattern, or failure to attain initial mastery in critical aspects of sexual functioning.

ATTITUDES AND INFORMATION

Closely related to the sexual experiences of the individual are his beliefs and attitudes about sex. These aspects of sexuality function in an integrated complementary fashion and represent the cognitive components of sexual behavior. The experiences the individual chooses to engage in, as well as the success he has with them, are very much a function of the information he has about sexual matters and the positive and negative valences he assigns the various aspects of sexuality. The relationship is also reciprocal, in that behavior or experience will often serve to modify or sustain preexisting attitudes and belief systems.

Sexual attitudes are acquired through a complex series of encounters with various agents of the socialization process: parents, family, institutional authorities, and peers all make contributions. As is the case with attitudes in general, sexual attitudes serve a function of enabling the individual to give rational expression to his *feelings*, in this case, concerning sexual matters. Because of this function, attitudes may serve clinically as an indicator of the prevailing affective tenor of the patient regarding sex.

A substantial amount of research has shown that attitudes once established have a marked effect on receptivity to new information. Prevailing attitudes tend to govern selectively the accessibility of the individual to new knowledge. Information which tends to support incumbent attitudes is sought out and readily incorporated in the prevailing belief system, while data which are contrary to prevailing beliefs are usually avoided. In situations where confrontation is inevitable, the individual will often employ defense mechanisms such as rationalization or denial to avoid assimilation, a use which Athanasiou (1973) termed the "ego-defensive" function of attitudes.

Another utilization of attitudes has to do with their "value-expressive" function (Katz, 1960). It is this function that relates attitudes to affects and helps explain the extraordinary resistance to modification of many nonadaptive attitudes and beliefs. As mentioned earlier, attitudes are in part developed through interactions with significant agents of the culture. To this degree they reflect how well the individual fits the cultural "ideal." This rather global prototype is translated into specific normative terms by the various primary reference groups (*e.g.*, family, ethnic, religious, etc.) of the individual. The usual result of deviation from primary group standards is the experience of a certain level of "cognitive dissonance," given additional emphasis by the concurrent experience of the strong negative affects, anxiety, and guilt. Since under most conditions the individual will seek to reduce dissonance and avoid unpleasant emotion, contradictory information tends to be "gated out." In this manner, belief systems, often highly nonadaptive in nature, tend to be perpetuated by selective inattention to new information that would threaten to invalidate their basic tenets (see Salzman, 1967).

Attitudes tend to be related to behavior in rather predictable fashion in some areas. Fortunately, sexual behavior is one of the areas of psychological functioning where this is true. A number of studies have evaluated the relationship between a general "conservativism" dimension and the arousal value of pornography (Athanasiou and Shaver, 1971; Wallace, Wehmer, and Podany, 1970). The results of these investigations consistently show that those who score high on liberalism also tend to indicate high arousal value for sexually explicit material. They tend to be younger, better educated, and less religious than those who score on the conservative end of the scale. The latter group tend to react with revulsion and disgust to pornography and have a tendency to experience higher levels of guilt about sex (Mosher and Greenberg, 1969).

Athanasiou (1973) also indicated a high level of relationship between attitudes toward premarital sex relations and the tendency to engage in that behavior. His data show that more than 50% of those subjects who had a negative attitude toward premarital sex actually avoided intercourse until marriage. Approximately 45% of those who endorsed the idea that sexual intercourse was acceptable behavior for engaged couples first experienced coitus with their fiances.

It seems undeniable that attitudes do have predictive value regarding both the sexual experiences of the individual in the past and his orientation toward sexual behavior in the future. Attitudes are very strongly linked to dominant affective themes and reflect the level of sophistication the person possesses. In their ego-defensive function they allow some insight into the conflicted areas of the individual's sexuality; in their value-expressive role they provide a window to the person's immediate cultural background.

The clinician in making his assessment should attempt to elicit as much information as possible from the patient concerning both his *present* and *past* attitudes about sexual matters. He should also have some appreciation concerning the patient's knowledge about sexual functions. Since attitudes (usually value-expressive) are often substituted for factual information, the assessor must also be aware of this possibility and be cognizant of the extent to which this mechanism is employed. Accurate evaluation of the major belief systems of the sexually dysfunctional patient is not only important for the assessment *per se;* it is also invaluable in providing guides for therapeutic efforts to modify dysfunctional behavior patterns.

PSYCHOLOGICAL SYMPTOMS

There hardly seems a need to communicate the idea that a crucial aspect of clinical evaluation involves documenting the signs and symptoms of pathology exhibited by the patient. When assessing the sexual disabilities, the clinician has an additional task: he must separate those symptoms that are subsumed by the sexual disorder from those manifestations of disturbance that are reflections of a coincident psychological disorder (*e.g.*, neurosis, psychosis, personality disorder). As a related issue in his assessment, the clinician must also decide the question of *primacy*. That is to say, he must decide whether the patient is presenting with a primary sexual disorder plus concomitant symptoms or whether, in fact, the sexual disturbance is a secondary manifestation of a primary disorder of thought, affect, or personality.

The clinician should also be aware of frequent "masked" manifestations of sexual disturbance that present as unelaborated physical symptoms. Hansen (1967) contended that a majority of physicians markedly underestimate the impact that sexual conflict exerts on the clinical appearance of many disease processes. He believed that the physical symptom should " . . . " be regarded as a composite communicative phenomenon . . . that always has the potential to operate as a symbolic representation of a sexual conflict. Hansen further estimated that one out of every three patients seen in the internists' practice will eventually manifest a sexual disturbance in one of its symptomatic forms. He has compiled an inventory of the more common symptomatic equivalents and noted that *chronic fatigue* is at the top of the list.

In documenting those symptoms that clearly arise from the sexual disorder, the clinician should develop an explicit, deliberate style to his anamnesis. The detailed nature of the disorder, frequency of the problem, duration of the difficulty (regarding both time elapsed since its intial appearance and the average length of one attack), as well as an appreciation of the subjective degree of distress experienced by the patient, should all be carefully noted. Beyond these details, it is also important to obtain data concerning the situational aspects (*e.g.*, where, when, and with whom) of the dysfunction. Gebhard (1965) has clearly indicated that situational factors often have a marked influence on the disorder and can provide important insights into etiology and treatment strategy.

A major issue surrounding the symptomatology of the sexual disabilities involves the question of just how profound a level of disturbance this group of disorders represent. Traditional psychoanalytic writers (Fenichel, 1946; Ferenczi, 1950; Moore, 1964) have often portrayed sexual dysfunctions such as impotence and anorgasmia as serious disturbances reflecting deep-rooted, pervasive neurotic conflicts. In opposition to this view, Masters and

Johnson (1970) have described a majority of patients with sexual dysfunction as being free from the symptoms of formal psychiatric disorder.

Meyer (1975), in his excellent review of therapeutic approaches to the sexual disabilities, has addressed this issue in part under the heading of "the symptom-disease controversy." He described the issue as, "... a point of controversy, or less benignly, an area of warfare ...," which has become of great moment in the ongoing debate between the psychodynamic therapists and those who endorse direct intervention techniques. The issue is one of both theoretical and practical consequence. Dynamic formulations are based in large measure on psychoanalytic theory and rely heavily on the construct of "unconscious process." Psychodynamic therapies are analytically oriented and tend to deal with the total personality. Direct intervention approaches shun dealing with the personality of the individual, are based on various formulations of learning theory, and tend to view "the symptom as the disorder" (Ullmann and Krasner, 1969; Wolpe and Lazarus, 1966). In these techniques therapeutic focus is narrowed specifically to the sexual dysfunction and has a strong remedial flavor.

With the recent surge of research in the area of sexual disabilities, there have been numerous investigations attesting to the fact that these conditions *need not* be strictly limited to individuals with severe neurotic or character pathology. In addition to Masters and Johnson (1970, 1973), Faulk (1973) has recently reviewed the literature on female disorders (frigidity) and cited numerous studies that have failed to uncover a positive relationship between frigidity and the presence of neurosis. Cooper (1968a,b, 1969) has performed a similar evaluation focusing on the male problem of impotence and concluded that only a minority of patients were observed to be suffering from neurotic conditions. More recently, Lidberg (1972) has confirmed this finding in a study that focused on the background factors of men with potency disorders. Lazarus (1969, 1972) concurred with the idea that many cases of sexual disability are free of serious neurotic concomitants; however, he made the observation that sexual disabilities frequently accompany severe neurotic conflicts.

Part of the inconsistency concerning the status of coexisting psychopathology in cases of sexual disability stems from the present nosological obscurity regarding definitions of clinical states (Panzetta, 1974). Although there are definite signs of renewed interest in diagnostic processes in psychiatry (Feighner, Robins, Guze, Woodruff, Winokur, and Munoz, 1972), recent evaluations still indicate a persistent lack of agreement in making diagnostic assignments (Kendell, 1974; Ley, 1972). This is particularly true of the neurotic and personality disorders where agreement is lowest. The problem is compounded by the fact that the sexual disorders themselves are in a poorly defined nosological position (*e.g.*, Hoenig and Kenna, 1974).

As an alternative to the categorization procedures which form the basis for diagnosis, one can opt to assess psychopathology according to a *dimensional* model. Rather than assign individuals to categories, dimensional approaches portray an individual relative to his position on a series of major symptom (or trait) dimensions. The nature of the dimensions employed is determined by the area of behavior being assessed. The areas of psychopathology (Lorr, 1963, 1969, 1970) and personality (Cattell, 1970; Eysenck, 1970) have been particularly fruitful in the application of dimensional procedures.

A *dimension* is best understood as a collection of items (symptoms, stimuli, tests, etc.) that have in common the fact that they are all measures of some superordinate concept. In psychopathology, dimensions may be considered analogous to *syndromes* (*e.g.*, depression), while in the area of personality, a dimension might be analogous to a trait (*e.g.*, authoritarianism). Dimensional methods need not be seen as being in competition with categorical models, for as Torgerson (1968) had the foresight to point out, an ultimately useful psychiatric nosology will probably combine concepts from both models.

At the Sexual Behaviors Consultation Unit (SBCU) we have recently introduced preliminary symptomatic screening procedures as part of our standard assessment methodology. One aspect of our screening involves having all patients presenting with sexual disabilities complete a self-report system inventory. The inventory requires 15 to 20 min of the patient's time, and, since this group of patients has typically shown high levels of personal motivation, the quality of the self-report is usually highly valid.

The screening inventory we employ is the SCL-90 (Derogatis, Lipman, and Covi, 1973), a recently extended version of the Hopkins Symptom Checklist (Derogatis, Lipman, Rickels, Uhlenhuth, and Covi, 1974). The SCL-90 is comprised of 90 items, each rated on a 5-point scale of distress, that represent a broad spectrum of outpatient psychopathology. The scale is scored on nine underlying symptom dimensions: somatization, obsessive-compulsive, interpersonal sensitivity, depression, anxiety, hostility, phobic anxiety, paranoid ideation, and psychoticism. In addition, three global measures of pathology, each addressed to different reflections of psychological disorder, are scored (Derogatis, Yevzeroff, and Wittelsberger, 1975).

Below we have presented an analysis of the symptomatic status of the first cohort of patients evaluated via our screening procedure at the SBCU. This has been done both for descriptive purposes and also to provide some objective commentary on the question of coexisting symptomatology in the sexual disabilities. The generalizability of our findings is clearly limited; nonetheless, we believe that the data will make a needed contribution to the objective assessment of psychological symptoms in this important class of patients.

Descriptively, the patients we are reporting on were young, white, and of middle to upper social class status. The mean age was 32.4 with a standard deviation (SD) of 10.1; approximately 60% of the sample were in social classes I to III; and males comprised 58% of the group. The mean symptom profiles for both males and females are presented below.

The mean profile for the 26 males in the sample is given in Figure 3.1, where it is plotted against a norm developed from psychiatric outpatients. In general, the profile fluctuates between 0.5 and 1.0 standard deviation below the outpatient mean. The pattern of the profile shows elevations on *hostility*, *paranoid ideation*, and *somatization*, though none of them reach the average level of the outpatients. The global indices of pathology are quite consistent, with all three of them having scores 0.9 standard deviation below the mean. In terms of over-all pathol-

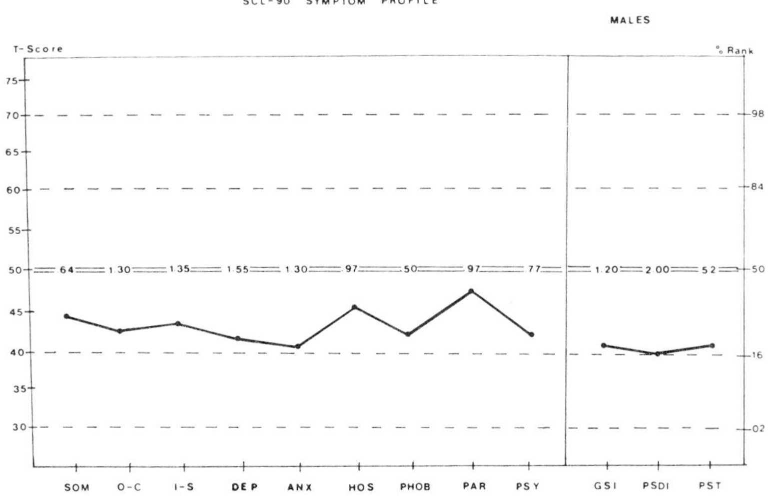

Fig. 3.1. Mean SCL-90 symptom profile for male sexual dysfunctions compared to norms for male psychiatric outpatients.

ogy, this places the males in approximately the 20th percentile of the distribution of psychiatric outpatients.

A similar profile for the 19 female patients is presented in Figure 3.2. This profile is plotted against a norm for female psychiatric outpatients. As is the case with the males, the profile is within a standard deviation below the mean; however, on several dimensions the females closely approach the outpatient average. Dysfunctional females show peaks on *hostility*, *paranoid ideation*, *somatization*, and *phobic anxiety*, with the hostility score being very close to the mean for outpatients. The finding concerning hostility is of particular interest, since Fisher and Osofsky (1967) observed that orgastic consistency was inversely related to level of hostility, the latter being measured through various psychological instruments. On the global measures there is again consistency among the indices with average scores falling in approximately the 20th percentile for outpatients.

These figures are addressed to *level* comparisons with the outpatient sample; another important facet of the comparison has to do with similarity of symptom *patterns*. In order to accomplish this contrast, the raw score profiles for the SBCU patients and the psychiatric outpatients were correlated using both Pearson and Spearman coefficients. The correlations were 0.89 and 0.90, respectively, both highly significant, indicating substantial similarity between the general symptomatic profiles of these two groups.

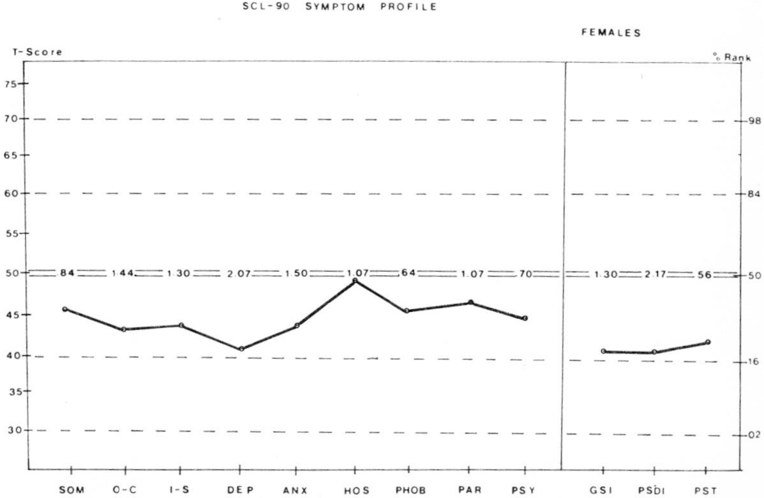

Fig. 3.2. Mean SCL-90 symptom profile for female sexual dysfunctions compared to norms for female psychiatric outpatients.

A more detailed analysis of the psychopathology in this sample can be obtained by shifting interpretive focus to the discrete symptom level. In comparison with the outpatients the sexual disabilities group tend to have significantly lower proportions of endorsement for most symptoms on the SCL-90. With certain symptoms, however, the SBCU patients show higher levels of endorsement or show no significant difference, in comparison to the outpatients. These select symptoms, along with the proportions of patients reporting distress from them, are given in Table 3.2. Summarizing the data in Table 3.2, it becomes clear that on a fair number of symptoms the proportion of SBCU patients reporting distress was not substantially different from the proportion for psychiatric outpatients. On a number of symptoms (those with footnote symbol a), the dysfunction patients

TABLE 3.2

Selected Symptoms and Rates of Endorsement for a Sample of Patients with Sexual Dysfunctions versus a Sample of Heterogeneous Psychiatric Outpatients

No.	Symptom	% Sexual Dysfunctions ($N = 45$)	% Psychiatric Outpatients ($N = 565$)
5[a]	Loss of sexual interest or pleasure	62.2	54.1
6[a]	Feeling critical of others	82.2	75.6
11	Feeling easily annoyed or irritated	82.2	88.3
21	Feeling shy or uneasy with the opposite sex	51.9	52.0
26	Blaming yourself for things	81.1	82.2
42	Soreness of your muscles	55.6	53.8
52	Numbness or tingling in parts of your body	37.8	42.9
57	Feeling tense or keyed up	84.4	91.3
60[a]	Overeating	55.6	45.0
63[a]	Having urges to beat, injure or harm someone	35.6	34.6
67	Having urges to break or smash things	40.0	40.7
68	Having ideas or beliefs others do not share	57.8	59.0
76	Others not giving you credit for achievements	51.1	54.6
84[b]	Having thoughts about sex that bother you a lot	68.9	43.5
86[a]	Feeling pushed to get things done	75.6	69.5
89	Feelings of guilt	64.4	67.4

[a] Proportion endorsing the symptom higher for the sexual dysfunctions sample.

[b] Proportion endorsing the symptom significantly higher for sexual dysfunction sample.

actually had higher endorsement proportions. And, on one system ("having thoughts about sex that bother you a lot"), the SBCU group manifested significantly higher proportions than the outpatient sample.

The patients with sexual disabilities showed high levels of endorsement for explicitly sexual items, as would be expected. Beyond that, however, they also showed high symptomatic levels of hostility and frustration, guilt and self-blame, and somatic concern. Additionally, they reported disproportionate distress arising from tension states and from overeating.

To conclude our brief analysis, I believe it is accurate to say that, although patients presenting with sexual disabilities did not show marked degrees of symptomatology, their symptom levels were in the clinical range. While global levels of psychopathology were generally lower than those of psychiatric outpatients, on selected symptoms, these patients actually reported more distress than the outpatient group. Over-all profile patterns were quite analogous between the two samples; and, although the mean number of symptoms reported (*i.e.*, 30) was a full standard deviation below the outpatient mean (*i.e.*, 52), these patients could hardly qualify as being asymptomatic.

In making psychological assessments of patients with sexual disabilities, coincident symptoms provide an extremely important "context" within which to evaluate the probable etiology and meaning of the sexual disorder. In spite of the nosological obscurities and difficult clinical judgements involved, it will continue to serve this valuable function for those clinicians who are willing to make the effort to ascertain the information.

ROLE CONFLICTS

There is little doubt that the manner in which a person defines the collection of behaviors, attitudes, feelings, and beliefs that represent his or her like-sex stereotype has a great impact on the nature of that person's interpersonal relations. Since sexual relations involve intensely intimate interactions, heavily imbued with emotions and personal needs, greater than normal pressure is placed on an individual's role definition in the sexual sphere.

A number of contemporary investigators have advanced the notion that conflicts arising from recent "liberal" modifications in traditional role models have resulted in an increase in certain types of sexual disabilities (Ginsberg, Frosch, and Shapiro, 1972). A prominent example is the increase in cases of "fear-of-failure" impotence, ostensibly occasioned by sexually liberated women making explicit comparisons of present and past partners

(Lazarus, 1972). Greene (1970) has pointed out another role-induced sexual casualty in the form of the contemporary female who, now that she has been given "cultural permission" to enjoy sex, feels a sense of failure if she does not experience orgasm at each occasion. Needless to say, this also has an effect on the male's role definition since he must perform at a level to bring the female satisfaction.

In examining the influence that role conflicts have in contributing to sexual disabilities, I believe there are several important issues that should be documented. The first of these has to do with the distinction between *role definition*, which is the stereotype one develops for oneself, and *role expectancy*, which is the characteristic posture that one anticipates for another. Distortions arising from either or both sets of role assignments can produce conflicts that will have a marked effect on sexual functioning.

If the individual is unable to approximate his or her own role ideal, then feelings of inadequacy accompanied by the negative emotions of guilt, anxiety, and depression will often develop. If one's partner fails to accommodate major dimensions of the role expected of him or her, then feelings of rejection and disappointment accompanied by anger and resentment usually follow.

Using this rather unadorned framework (see Steinmann, 1972, for a more complex analysis of role conflicts) there are essentially four areas of potential role discrepancy that require assessment: *male experiential* versus *male stereotype*, *female experiential* versus *female stereotype*, *male experiential* versus *female expectancy*, and *female experiential* versus *male expectancy*. It often happens that sexual partners meet the demands of their own idealized role definitions but fail to measure up to each other's role expectancies. Conversely, some individuals match their partner's anticipations very well but fail to satisfy their idealized images of themselves. Most often, however, the clinician will be able to uncover significant discrepancies in both role definitions and expectancies in cases of sexual disability.

A related issue which also has import in assessing role conflicts has to do with whether distortions exist in *experiential* or *idealized* roles. This gets at the question of whether the quality of actual functioning or unrealistic expectancies regarding functioning are at the basis of the disorder. A male who is able to achieve erection and normal orgasm, but whose refractory period is such that he can only perform once in an evening, may feel great distress if his image of a man is someone who "can go all night." Similarly, if a female's role expectancy for a man stresses tenderness, protection, and love to the exclusion of normal healthy passion, she may perceive herself as being "ravaged" when, in fact, her partner may be merely manifesting normal masculine desire.

In most instances of disability, the actual experiential role of the individual will contribute to the problem whether idealized images contribute or not. Frequently the difficulty will pivot on the dominance-submission axis. The traditional male-dominant, female-submissive, role set can become crystallized in a rigid stylized manner, with deviation becoming associated with psychic threat to one or both parties. Rigid adherence to stylized roles frequently leads to sexual dysfunction (Lewis, 1969) in that healthy sexual relationships require both gender role definitions to be sufficiently flexible to accommodate gender-major and gender-minor sexual themes. The opportunity for males to give vent to passive-dependent needs and females to assume a dominant-assertive posture is provided uniquely by sexual intimacy. Those relationships that are deprived of this opportunity through rigid, narrow role definitions are at much higher risk for the development of sexual disabilities.

Obviously, a great deal more can be written about the influence of sexual role conflicts on the development of sexual disabilities. Unfortunately, the present format does not allow an expanded review here. For the interested reader, a bibliography of male-female role research has been distributed by Steinmann (1971), and a thorough review of sex role research was recently published by Hochschild (1974).

AFFECTS

Probably the most pervasive influence in all forms of psychological disorder stems from the negative emotional states that accompany these conditions. This is no less true in the sexual dysfunctions where disruptive affects have been cited as etiological, coincident, or resultant factors in almost all forms of sexual disability. Cooper (1969) has thoughtfully cautioned that much of the work assigning causal status to the negative affects is clinical-anecdotal in nature; however, there still remains an overwhelming body of evidence to suggest that emotions play a key role in the development of sexual disorders. Lazarus (1972), writing on the psychological causes of impotence, stated "... they all boil down to one single basic cause—negative emotions."

Most serious students of emotion agree that the negative affects may be subdivided into primary and secondary classes, the latter representing subtle shadings and complex combinations of the former (Arnold, 1960; Tomkins, 1963). Our present essay will address itself only to the primary emotions, however, since a thorough assessment of the presence and quality of the major negative affects should provide the degree of information necessary for accurate clinical judgement.

There can be little doubt that the cardinal negative affect of the sexual disabilities is perceived by most experts to be *anxiety*. In part, this reflects the influence of Freud who initiated much of the modern work on sexual disabilities and also gave anxiety a central place in his dynamic formulations. Nearly all authors on the topic assign some conceptualization of anxiety to a central role in the etiology of the sexual disorders. At the very least, anxiety is accorded the status of a significant concomitant in those cases where it is not assigned causal status.

Kaufman (1967), who believes that 90% of male impotence is due to psychogenic factors, listed anxiety over pregnancy, injury (by some disapproving person, *e.g.*, husband, father, etc.), and criticism or rejection by the partner as major contributors to this form of sexual dysfunction. Cooper (1969) reviewed a broad spectrum of authors who invoke various constructs ranging from the psychoanalytic "castration anxiety" to anxiety about the morality of the act to account for potency disorders. Anxiety over venereal disease, commitment (*i.e.*, through subsequent marriage), and the responsibilities of fatherhood have frequently been cited as being causal influences. In a somewhat different vein, men with certain physical disabilities, particularly of the cardiovascular type, may sometimes develop impotence as a "protective response" to anxiety about death.

Kaplan (1974) made the useful distinction that, although deep and pervasive origins may exist for sexually disruptive anxiety, quite frequently, rather common "surface" sources of anxiety may account for sexual disturbances. In a sense, the "trigger" paradigm is applicable here: just as the velocity of a bullet is independent of the amount of force applied to the trigger once the critical level is attained, so the degree of impotence may be independent of the nature of the source-conflict once it has reached a magnitude to incur certain vasocongestive inhibitors in the nervous system.

Another interesting observation concerning the role of anxiety in the sexual disabilities has to do with the relationship between sexual disturbances and *anxiety neurosis*. Lidberg (1972) reported this diagnosis as having the highest incidence (11%) in his sample of male potency disorders. Ambrosino (1973), in his discussion of the phobic anxiety-depersonalization syndrome, indicated the dynamics of this disorder often " . . . produce frigid, unresponsive females." Martin (1971), in his review of anxiety and neurotic conditions, noted a high frequency of sexual disturbance associated with these disorders. It would seem that the frequent and chronic exposure to disruptive anxiety and tension may serve to inhibit natural sexual functioning in this group through a combination of fatigue, hyperarousal (producing an inability to relax conscious control), and deprecating self-perceptions (experiential role), arising from the constant affective tenor of fear. Systematic studies of the relationship remain to be done; however, it does provide a stimulating provisional hypothesis.

In patients suffering from sexual disabilities the experience of *guilt* is almost coincident with the experience of anxiety. The first step the clinician must undertake in his assessment of the influence of this powerful emotion in the disorder is to determine whether it is functioning in a *precipitant* or a *consequent* manner.

Lazarus (1972) has made note of the fact that our society naturally instills a substantial degree of guilt in its members concerning sexuality. In a broad sense one could conceivably indict society as the principal causative agent in the sexual disabilities because of its conflicted sexual standards. As research stemming from learning theory has clearly demonstrated, conditioned emotional responses are relatively easy to acquire and often extremely difficult to extinguish. It follows, then, that an environment which prescribes the experience of guilt as the "correct" response to stimuli of a sexual nature will almost certainly produce large numbers of individuals with dysfunctions in sexual performance.

Guilt can function as a precipitant in the sexual disorders in numerous ways. In addition to its instigation through cultural standards, guilt may be responsible for sexual dysfunction through a variety of themes. A common example may be found in males who are unable to reconcile their affection for the female partner with the sexual passion they feel toward her. The thought of "inflicting" carnal desire on the female love object produces acute feelings of guilt which, in turn, preclude any effective performance on the male's part. A similar phenomenon was described by Freud (1912), who believed the difficulty represented a failure to work through certain aspects of the oedipal situation. In these instances the male, according to Freud, has not matured sufficiently (sexually) to disengage preexisting feelings of affection from the original focus (the forbidden mother image). The normal developmental course involves detaching the long standing feelings of affection from the mother, fusing them with more recently emergent sexual feelings, and redirecting the resulting feelings toward a new sexual object. Disorders of this type essentially involve guilt arising from the equating of sexual impulses with aggression; in addition, analytic theorists believe oedipal guilt is also involved in the process.

Psychoanalytic theory also postulates a mechanism whereby guilt may operate to effect sexual dysfunction in the female. The source is again the oedipal conflict. According to theory, normal psychosexual development for the female child involves a transition of investment of love from the mother to the father. Simultaneously, the mother is perceived as a rival by the child who experiences jealous fantasies about eliminating her mother. Since society places strong sanctions against this form of aggressive behavior, the child experiences guilt over these feelings. If the female responds to the oedipal conflict by transferring her original feelings about the father onto another man, then a healthy resolution takes place. If the girl is unable to totally abjure her original feelings for the father, adult sexual encounters will renew the rivalry with mother and its attendant guilt (Moore, 1964).

A sex-specific source of guilt for females which almost certainly acts to diminish sexual responsiveness is culturally induced and centers on the unique physical and physiological characteristics of the female sex. The physical appearance of female genitalia have always engendered a certain amount of anxiety among males ("castration anxiety," for those with a psychoanalytic orientation), and the process of menstruation has universally been abhorred and misunderstood by men. In societies where male dominance is strongly reflected in cultural standards, the female learns that she is physically "inferior," that her body is "unclean," and that her very femininity is a primary source of potential rejection. Needless to say, this attitude provides a rich basis for the growth of disruptive guilt feelings, a postulation empirically confirmed by Fisher's (1973) fascinating studies on the relationship between body image and sexual responsiveness.

Guilt as a consequent emotion in sexual disabilities is usually easier to deal with. In these instances its appearance is secondary to some primary factor and, in most cases, dissipates once the primary influence has been dealt with therapeutically. Cases such as this arise when sexual disturbance is related to hostile feelings toward the partner or to loss of emotional investment. In such instances, sentiments of this nature will often precipitate feelings of guilt in the person harboring them. Alternatively, the experience of guilt may be linked to an individual's inability to match idealized role images because of sexual dysfunction. In these cases the individual perceives that he has failed himself as well as his partner's role expectancy of him. Guilt, often accompanied by anxiety and depression, is a typical concomitant of this experience.

The achievement of satisfying sexual relations is dependent in large measure upon a person's ability to relinquish a certain degree of conscious control over phenomenal experience and cognitive functions and abandon himself to the pleasure inherent in sex. This state of mind is most readily facilitated by a relaxed posture and an absence of negative feelings. It is disrupted most effectively by an emotion which, considering its various forms, may be the most culpable of the negative affects in the sexual disabilities: *anger*.

As was mentioned previously, hostile affect has been clearly linked to a reduction in sexual responsivity in women (Fisher, 1967), and our own findings at the SBCU tend to provide further empirical confirmation for this notion (see section on SYMPTOMS). Psychoanalytic theory has traditionally postulated a hostile "retaliatory" theme behind certain female dysfunctions (*e.g.*, vaginismus, anorgasmia), with the primary (unconscious) motivation being to embarrass or humiliate the male. In addition, an interesting related finding has recently been communicated by Mellan (1971), who used Leary's (1957) interpersonal method to assess female sexual disturbances. He reported that frigid women accentuated dominance and hostility in their constructions of ideal role images.

There is also ample evidence suggesting that hostile affect has etiological significance in the male potency disorders as well. Lewis (1969), in a review of disruptive marital interactions contributing to impotence wrote, "The central clinical finding was that of considerable unconscious marital pathology having to do with passivity and aggression." Abraham (1949), representing a traditional psychoanalytic stance, related hostility arising from unresolved oedipal conflicts to male sexual disorders, in particular, premature ejaculation. Gutheil (1959a) cited hostility and resentment generated by the natural competition between the sexes as having etiological significance in the dysfunctions. This mechanism has been observed particularly among couples whose marriages have endured for substantial periods, and it is often the dynamic underlying "wife only" forms of impotence. Numerous other writers (Hastings, 1963; Lazarus, 1972) have also identified various shadings of anger and hostility as being responsible for disturbances in sexual functioning. Cooper (1968b) has confirmed some of Fisher's (1967) findings with psychological tests in establishing significantly higher hostility responses in a sexually dysfunctional sample.

Systematic research on the etiological impact of hostile affect in the sexual dysfunctions has been sparse in the past. The persistent observations of astute clinicians, however, have continued to assign etiological significance to this negative feeling state. In response, more recent investigators have applied a series of imaginative research designs to the questions emerging from this issue, and a consistent, empirically sound picture is emerging showing hostile emotion to be of central importance in the formation of sexual dysfunctions.

The final negative affect included in the present discussion is *depression*. The relationship between depression and sexual dysfunction has been noted since antiquity and is sufficiently integral that sexual disinterest or disorder is often interpreted as one of the cardinal symptoms of a depressive syndrome (Arieti, 1959; Gutheil, 1959b). Before advancing too far with the discussion, however, I believe it is important to clarify some of the confusion surrounding the concept of depression. The term, depression, as it is currently used may refer to an *affect*, a *symptom*, a *syndrome*, or a *diagnostic entity*, with only the semantic context within which it is used to convey the distinction (Derogatis, Klerman, and Lipman, 1972). This semantic difficulty has been the source of a great deal of confusion and inconsistency in work on depression, and it requires explicit documentation if it is to be avoided.

Kaplan (1974) noted that depression may be commonly seen in patients who present with sexual dysfunctions. Regardless of whether it is an emotional consequence of the dysfunction or a symptom of a formal affective disorder that has precipitated the sexual problem, a sad and dysphoric mood is very frequently attendant upon sexual disorders.

As is the case with any chronic assault on the individual's self-concept (*e.g.*, anxiety, pain, disease), the affective response to persistent sexual inadequacy is often depression. The individual may be otherwise psychologically normal or he may be characteristically "depressive" (Klein, 1973). Neither of these conditions contraindicates initiating treatment of the sexual difficulty. In the "reactive" depression, alleviation of the sexual disturbance usually will be followed by a rapid remission of the dysphoric affect and a return to normalcy. In the "neurotic" depression, relief from the problems of sexual dysfunction usually provides transient alleviation from depressive affect until the next disappointment or life trauma comes along.

If the depression antedates the sexual disorder and is an

etiological factor in its appearance, a different clinical situation exists. Under these circumstances, the affective disorder is more likely to be of the serious "endogenous" type (Klein, 1973; Klerman and Barrett, 1974). In these depressions, which characteristically occur independent of dramatic precipitating events, sexual processes become a casualty of a generalized retardation of functioning that affects all bodily systems. Sensory, motor, perceptual, and cognitive systems can all become markedly slowed and impaired, and in most cases libido is drastically reduced. Klein (1973) cited a "deranged pleasure center" as the etiological core of the endogenous depressions and believed that the central mechanism involves, ". . . a sharp, unreactive, pervasive impairment of the capacity to experience pleasure or to respond affectively to the anticipation of pleasure."

Kaplan (1974) counseled against initiating therapy explicitly for the sexual disorder while the individual is still manifesting clinical signs of a serious depression. In large part this is because interest in the environment in general, and sex in particular, is often still diminished by the influence of the depression. Other disruptive affects such as guilt (Harrow and Amdur, 1971), hostility (Weisman, Klerman, and Payke, 1971), and anxiety (Derogatis and associates, 1972) are often highly manifest during depressive episodes and could serve to negate therapeutic efforts. It must also be remembered that as most other symptoms of clinical depressions are capable of remission, so related sexual disturbances are also likely to remit with successful treatment of the primary depression.

Emotion is an aspect of human experience that adds dimensionality to our existence. It is the affective component that "fills out" the personality and transforms it from a two-dimensional sensory-cognitive construction into a three-dimensional truly human phenomenon. In both normal and disordered states of behavior, affects serve as sensitive indicators of the state of the individual. This is no less true of the sexual disabilities where an intelligent assessment of the patient's emotions can provide important cues concerning etiology, course of illness, prognosis, and treatment relevance. Evaluation of the nature of the patient's affective status is essential to accurate psychological assessment.

FANTASY

May (1969) wrote, "Fantasy is the language of the total self, communicating, offering itself, trying on for size. It is the language of 'I wish/I will'—the projection in imagination of the self into the situation. And if one cannot do this, *he* will not be present in the situation, sexual or other, whether his body is there or not. Fantasy assimilates reality and then pushes reality to a new depth" (p. 281).

There is little doubt that fantasy is a key function in sexuality, not to mention the rest of human experience. As May so aptly described, it provides the individual a means of rehearsing life events, both those that are yet to come and those that may have already taken place. Role behaviors are modeled and tested in fantasy before they are introduced in behavior; after empirical trial they are further shaped and polished in imagination prior to formal integration into the individual's behavioral repertoire.

From the clinician's viewpoint fantasy serves another purpose: it provides a window to the needs, wishes, and desires of the individual, both those that are represented by behavioral analogs, and others that are restricted to the realm of reverie. Extremely valuable insights into the motive structure of the individual can be gained by an appreciation of his dominant fantasy themes. Frustrations, fears, aspirations, and treasured ideals may all be made available to the clinical observer if he can gain a clear focus on the patient's theater of fantasy.

Several key aspects of fantasy should be emphasized in any thorough clinical assessment of a sexual disorder. First, the *presence* or *absence* of erotic fantasies, both within and beyond the context of explicitly sexual activities should be established. Second, the *frequency* of such fantasy episodes should be noted. Third, a detailed appreciation of the *nature* of sexual fantasies must be obtained by the clinician. Although patients may be reluctant and embarrassed to communicate such information, they should be encouraged to provide as many particulars as possible about erotic imagery. Freud (1913), in his classic work on dreams, explicitly reminded us of the critical nature of details in the interpretation of fantasy productions. This remains true of conscious erotic fantasies, even though the "dream work" has not obscured the meaning and significance of the imagery as it does in dreams.

The specific *situation* in which fantasy occurs is also of clinical significance. Is it a masturbation fantasy? Does it occur only with the marital partner? Is it experienced immediately prior to orgasm? Does it occur after coitus? This information serves to reveal more clearly the needs of the individual as well as the nature of interactions between sexual partners. *Recurrent* fantasies are particularly informative in this regard. They often reveal chronic unresolved conflicts or unfulfilled needs and suggest dominant affective factors in the patient's psychic experience.

Fantasies fulfill a number of important functions in intrapsychic processes. As previously mentioned, there is the "rehearsal" function which allows the individual an opportunity to choreograph situations in imagination before having to deal with them in reality. Secondly, fantasy provides a mechanism for "vicarious fulfillment" of those wishes and desires that cannot be satisfied in reality. In some cases there are marginally unconscious, forbidden wishes that cannot be acted upon; in other instances they are wishes of an idealized nature that cannot be achieved or attained in reality. Regardless of the theme, the "self-in-fantasy" substitutes for the real self, and while gratification has a somewhat ephemeral quality, accomplishments are limited only by the creative potential of the person's mind.

Fantasy serves yet another purpose in its "hedonistic" function. Here I am referring to the fundamental pleasure that people derive from fantasy activities. Particularly in the case of erotic imagery, a great deal of enjoyment may be obtained from these reveries, beyond any wish-fulfilling or anxiety-reducing functions this activity may involve.

Clinical research has provided us with some empirical evidence about erotic fantasy processes to accompany the wealth of clinical data available. Kinsey (1948) reported a greater incidence of fantasy activity accompanying explicit sexual behavior in males as opposed to females, and in persons from upper versus lower socioeconomic groups. In spite of the contention that males experience more sexual fantasy, most of the research has been on the erotic imagery of women.

Fisher and Osofsky (1967), reporting on a female sample, found a significant positive relationship between sexual responsiveness and degree of oral fantasy and pleasure derived from eating. This is interesting in light of the recent observation with our SBCU patients of an elevated level of distress associated with overeating (see Table 3.2). Also, there has been a supportive trend in the psychoanalytic literature (Lorand, 1939; Jones, 1966) relating female sexuality to dominant oral themes. Further support is derived from evidence that food and the act of eating may function as symbolic equivalents of sexual content (Hamburger, 1958).

In a more recent study (Fisher, 1973), the frequency of coital fantasies was evaluated in a sample of normal women. Results indicated that about 75% of the sample experienced imagery during intercourse, and the most accurate descriptive term that could be applied regarding frequency was "occasionally." A few women reported always experiencing coital imagery, while others indicated they never experienced the phenomenon. Hariton and Singer (1974) reported 65% of their sample as experiencing fantasies during intercourse at some time, with 37% having such fantasies "very often." DeMartino (1969) reported 44% of his sample as experiencing coital imagery.

A critical question regarding coital fantasy (more strongly directed toward women than toward men) has had to do with its evaluation as a positive or negative indicator regarding psychological health. A traditional psychoanalytic view concerning this issue holds that female coital fantasies are pathological indicators which reflect "distancing" mechanisms and a lack of mature emotional investment in the relationship. The actual experience of intercourse is hypothesized to be conflict-ridden and deficient in gratification, with the female turning to fantasy to escape the untenable reality (Shainess and Greenwald, 1971). Other theoretical formulations place a more positive valence on female sexual fantasies. Singer and Antrobus (1972) suggested an "adaptive" hypothesis for sexual imagery, which essentially posits enhancement of the coital experience through embellishments arising from imagery.

Hariton and Singer (1974) postulated a "cognitive style" hypothesis to interpret female sexual fantasies. The central concept here is that certain females utilize imagery to provide a "creative enrichment" throughout the spectrum of their life activities, and that, quite naturally, this style is carried over into the realm of sexual activities. In a creative and methodologically rigorous study, these authors evaluated the major hypothesis discussed above as to which did the most satisfactory job of explaining their data. They reported their findings to be in support of both *drive enhancement* and *cognitive style* theories but inconsistent with the analytic *deficiency* hypothesis.

The quality of erotic fantasies is a topic of major interest concerning both sexes. Typically, male fantasies have been represented as reflecting themes of "conquest," either of a direct physically aggressive nature or of the more seductive Don Juan type. Female fantasies, as they have been related through clinical literature, tend to dwell on themes of submission (forced or voluntary) and masochism. Although small, there is a body of clinical research literature that represents more systematic attempts at delineating this very significant aspect of sexual behavior.

In his systematic study of the factors affecting female orgasm, Fisher (1973) observed that the themes of many coital fantasies were of the "forbidden lover" type: ". . . about 40% involved scenes in which the woman was having a sexual contact or interchange with someone other than her husband" (p. 213). He further noted that in approximately 50% of these instances the imagery involved the female being forced to submit to the sexual act or some form of sexual humiliation or degradation. He stated, "Masochistic and exhibitionistic elements were strongly prominent in the fantasies that were collected."

About 30% of the imagery reported in Fisher's study involved unelaborated sensory experiences, such as flashes of light, the sound of water rushing past, etc. An additional 10% revolved around the theme of royalty or a personage imbued with special powers (*e.g.*, princess, goddess).

While these observations are consistent with the findings of other clinicians and researchers (*e.g.*, DeMartino, 1969), a significant question remains concerning whether fantasies of this nature are "normal" or represent conflicted neurotic processes. Hariton and Singer (1974) addressed themselves to this question in their excellent study. Their results showed that "thoughts of an imaginary lover" was the most frequent fantasy (56%), followed by a fantasy of "being overwhelmed and forced to surrender" (49%). In interpreting these findings the authors wrote, "Rather than being manifestations of problems found in a few neurotic women, they emerged as phenomena typical of a majority of a sample of presumably normal women. . . . It is unreasonable to hold to theories that link these fantasies only to neurosis" (p. 316).

It would be most excellent clinically if certain specific fantasies or themes were pathognomonic of disturbed sexuality, or if frequency or situational aspects of erotic fantasy gave unerring clues as to the presence of sexual disorder. Unfortunately, such is not the case. Degree of subjective distress associated with imagery is also far from an infallible indicator, since some individuals are able to entertain grotesque imagery without distress, while others find even the slightest fantasized impropriety difficult to endure.

The appraisal of erotic imagery in the mosaic of psychosexual functioning may be one of the most complex and demanding of the assessment tasks discussed here. It is probably also one of the most potentially informative and rewarding for the persistent clinician able to tolerate a certain degree of ambiquity.

EROTIC DRIVE

Kinsey (1948, 1953) utilized the composite concept of *total sexual outlet* to represent various manifestations of the sex drive that an individual might experience. Autoerotic, heterosexual, and homosexual activities all contributed to this collective index of erotic drive. His data indicated that the mean number of orgasms for males (across all age groups) was approximately three per week. The distribution of sexual activity was notably skewed, however, as may be appreciated from the observation that the modal frequency in this sample of males was *one* orgasm per week.

Information on levels of female erotic drive are not reported in the same format by Kinsey, since social constraints, role specificity (*i.e.*, single, married), a. d natural variability in response produce obvious distortions. Also, it is probable that the "orgasm" as a definitive unit of sexual experience is probably much less meaningful for females. The subgroup of females most comparable to the general male population in this context is usually considered to be "married women," and most comparisons have been made with this group.

During their most active sexual period (*i.e.*, the 3rd decade), the women in Kinsey's sample experienced a mean number of orgasms of approximately two per week. There was large variability in the female data, however, which suggested that this figure may not be an accurate representation of the "typical" female's sexual experience.

Fisher (1973), in his systematic study, reported a median frequency of intercourse of 3.4 times per week for his females. The medians in his seven samples ranged from 2.8 at the low extreme to 4.8 at the high. Of these women, the median number "always" or "nearly always" attaining orgasm was 38%, with a range of median values of from 31 to 50%. Analogous findings from Kinsey's study (1953) placed the proportion of women usually attaining orgasm at 42%.

The importance of obtaining information concerning drive level in the sexual disabilities is directly related to its potential for misinterpretation by patients as "pathological." Individuals will often conclude that their sex drive, or that of their partner, is pathologically high or low, based on subjective impressions or misinformation available from a multitude of sources. Since peak levels of erotic drive are distributed in a distinctly different manner across age in the two sexes (see section on AGE), the groundwork is laid for some fairly disruptive misperceptions and misinterpretations. Couples whose sexual needs may seem disproportionate may, in reality, be merely reflecting typical, but disparate, levels of erotic drive.

It should be emphasized that most research reported thus far has depicted sexual drive to be normally and continuously distributed characteristic for males and females. At any given chronological age there will be individuals with very high levels of sexual activity and others with relatively low frequencies of sexual interest. All of these fall within the normal range. There are no easily identifiable discontinuities in the pattern of erotic activity that demarcate normalcy from dysfunction; this distinction must be based on complementary information from other sources in addition to knowledge concerning drive.

Lazarus (1969) succinctly pointed out that defining "sexual adequacy" is a much more demanding task than it appears to be on the surface, with myriad circumstances serving to qualify and obscure the issue. Adequacy is most immediately related to drive level by the majority of people, with high drive people presumed also to be highly adequate. It is interesting to entertain the question whether the man who has daily intercourse with his wife, but fails to bring her to orgasm in any of their interactions, is more or less sexually adequate than the man who has coitus only once per week, but whose lovemaking allows his wife to experience profound levels of satisfaction.

The answer is, of course, "it depends on the wife!" It is the phenomenal experience of the two as "couple," rather than the independent experience of either one that defines adequacy. Regardless of how divergent an individual's needs are from the norm, he will not be judged inadequate so long as his drive level matches that of his partner. By the same token, the prototypic man may be judged inadequate by a woman whose erotic drive is simply somewhat more intense.

The clinical appraisal of erotic drive is a critical step in the complete psychological assessment of the sexual disabilities. In regard to both historical levels for the patient and typical levels for the partner, it creates a meaningful perspective from which to view the whole of the individual's sexual functioning.

MEDIATING VARIABLES IN ASSESSING THE SEXUAL DISABILITIES

As indicated in the introductory remarks of the present essay, there are a number of variables that act to mediate the effects of the various psychological processes in the sexual disabilities. Without giving due consideration to these parameters, accurate clinical assessment of the sexual disorders is held as improbable. The decision here has been to discuss only the more fundamental of these influences even though many others undoubtedly can be discerned. In part, this decision was motivated by a desire to avoid undue complexity; another facet of the rationale had to do with the "explanatory power" of the various factors. Those variables that were judged to have practical clinical import were included in the discussion; those that were seen as being principally of theoretical or academic interest were reserved for another discourse.

Gender Distinctions in Sexual Disabilities

It is a foregone conclusion for most people that there are "differences" between the sexes. For many years expectancies concerning these differences extended to the actual experience of the sex act itself. Generally, although often for grossly inaccurate reasons, it was presumed that the female's appreciation of sexuality was distinct from that of the male. More recently, however, as a result of contemporary social events, in particular the establishment of a "new identity" for women, the issue of distinctiveness has been clouded over. I believe it is important in assessing and treating the sexual disabilities to bear certain gender-related distinctions clearly in mind.

To begin with, it is probably true that while unelaborated performance of the sexual act by the female requires little in the way of acquired skills, a substantial amount of learning is necessary for her to achieve gratification or pleasure from intercourse. On the other hand, most males derive pleasure from sex almost automatically; however, there is a large learned component to male sexual behavior that centers in the "performance" aspect of the sexual act. These distinctions are reflected in the nature and incidence of sexual disabilities in males and females.

Meyer (1975), in his review of treatment approaches to the sexual dysfunctions, pointed out that disorders of satisfaction are much more typical of the female (*i.e.*, anorgasmia), while disorders of performance (*i.e.*, impotence) are more frequent among males. This suggests that for both males and females the learned components of sexuality are much more vulnerable to disturbance, primarily through conditioning to negative affects. Kaplan (1974) also viewed failure to achieve orgasm as ". . . the most common sexual complaint among women," and noted that probably half the male population experience a transient form of impotence at some time in their lives.

Relevant distinctions between male and female sexuality are also evident in other spheres. Gebhard (1973) has provided an interesting discussion concerning the differential reaction time between males and females in response to erotic stimuli. He linked the relatively slow response of females to a culturally conditioned caution regarding sexual matters which is sex-specific. Society places no such inhibition of males' responses to erotic stimulation, and consequently the male responds much more rapidly. Males and females also show distinctions in terms of their attitudes toward sex. Athanasiou (1973) reported females have more conservative sexual attitudes. A significantly larger percentage of the females in his sample felt that affection was a necessary part of the sexual experience than did the males. Also, more females regretted premarital sexual experiences, while few, if any, males indicated this attitude.

Udry (1968) has discussed some of the hazards inherent in the middle and upper class "egalitarian" position regarding male and female sexuality. He argued that equality of sexual rights has been erroneously translated into similarity of sexual needs, and that this distorted criterion then leads to an expectancy of equivalence in the degree and pattern of sexual gratification. The egalitarian position has also drawn fire from May (1969) who wrote, "Egalitarianism is clung to at the price of denying not only biological differences—which are basic, to say the least—between men and women, but emotional differences from which come much of the delight of the sexual act" (p. 54). There are numerous sources that contradict this aberrant posture, and it is worth reviewing several here. First, the contexts within which sexuality develops are different for the two sexes: masculine sexuality develops in a twin context of hedonistic pleasure and masculine status; feminine sexuality evolves from a belief system that associates sex first with procreation and then as a means of expressing love. Second, sexual roles are quite distinct: the male tends to be the initiator of sexual encounters, while the female's role is reactive in nature, responding in a receptive or nonreceptive fashion to the male's overtures. Finally, few females seriously consider sexual encounters without some degree of emotional commitment to their partners; emotional investment is clearly not a prerequisite for satisfactory sexual performance in the male, and it is often seen as "getting in the way" of satisfying sexual involvements.

This brief discussion is intended to convey the idea that there are significant gender differences with regard to the experience of sexuality. Its function, expression, importance, and phenomenal experience are distinct for males and females. The clinician can do an adequate job of assessment and treatment of sexual dysfunctions only if he bears this fundamental difference in mind. He cannot allow the distortions of the egalitarian posture to obscure the basic fact that men and women are not sexual equals. They merely have equal rights to enjoy sexuality.

Age as a Mediating Variable

The incidence, prevalence, and character of most psychological disorders are strongly mediated by age (Goldfarb, 1967), and the disorders of sexual functioning are no exception. As both male and females become older, there are changes in erotic drive levels and the ability to achieve sexual satisfaction. In general, the ability to achieve gratifying sexual performance decreases with age. In a given individual, however, the nature of this decline is not necessarily gradual and continuous, since there is a great deal of individual variation in sexual responsiveness through the middle and later years.

Kaplan (1974) described an intense peak for sexual responsiveness in males as occurring in late adolescence. Subsequently, a gradual decrease in responsiveness, interest, and capacity characterizes the 3rd, 4th, and 5th decades, followed by a more rapid diminution in activity beyond age 60. She describes sexual responsiveness in females as reaching its peak in the later 3rd and early 4th decades, with a more gradual rate of decline beyond that period. Kinsey (1953) was in essential agreement with this description, Katchadorian and Lunde (1973) depicted similar response curves for both sexes, but they did not emphasize female responsiveness during the middle years to the same degree. Their observations tend to be more directly focused on the limitations imposed by age-related physical changes; while Kaplan considered responsiveness in a broader psychoemotional context, with particular emphasis on the role of the learning process. Similar findings, including some very interesting detailed relationships, have also been advanced by Pfeiffer, Verwoedt, and Wang (1968) in their longitudinal study.

Regardless of the precise nature of the sexual response curve, it is clear that the aging process does play a mediating role in the nature of sexual experience. Behavior probably indicative of pathology in a 20-year-old male may simply reflect normal age-related changes in a man in his fifties. Clinical evaluations should be made with appropriate age norms in mind, if they are going to have predictive validity. Although there is notable variation in sexual capacity at all age levels, it does not preclude incorporating age data into the assessment. The presence of variation does not invalidate the norm; it merely counsels caution in its use.

Health Status and Sexual Disabilities

Owing to the broad spectrum of physical disorders and diseases that have an inhibitory effect on sexual desire and performance, it is impossible to assess adequately the psychological aspects of sexual disabilities without first establishing the health status of the patient. Numerous systemic diseases involving the liver, heart, kidneys and lungs tend to suppress sexual behavior through general debilitative effects. Endocrine disorders, such as those involving hyposecretion from the pituitary, adrenals, or thyroid, are also responsible for reduction in sexual functioning owing to lowered androgen levels. And one of the frequent incipient signs of diabetes involves disturbances in erectile responses.

Surgical intervention in various disorders can also result in erectile, ejaculatory, and orgasmic dysfunctions through inadvertant damage to genital nerve networks. In addition, surgical procedures involving the sexual organs directly always introduce the risk of disturbance in some aspect of sexual functioning. Beyond these conditions, there are a number of central nervous system (CNS) disorders (*e.g.*, multiple sclerosis) that, although infrequent, do involve interference with normal sexual functioning through damage to the spinal cord and peripheral innervation. Traumatic injury to the lower cord and/or associated autonomic centers can also result in dysfunction.

Owing to the central role the local vascular system plays in the normal functioning of the sexual apparatus, disorders and diseases involving the interruption of normal blood supply in this area can also cause disturbances in function, particularly noticeable in males. A large number of local genital disorders may also inhibit normal sexual functioning because of physical irritation and discomfort. A representative list and review of these conditions were given by Kaplan (1974).

It is obvious from this brief outline that, before the clinician can conclude that sexual dysfunction is primarily of psychogenic origin, he must first rule out the probability that it is the result of a physical condition or disorder. This may be accomplished to various degrees of certainty and in some cases may involve several series of laboratory tests; in no case should the procedure involve less than a thorough physical examination, with particular attention to the sexual organs.

Medication and Other Drugs

Considered in light of notable increases in prescription rates recently, particularly for the psychoactive classes of drugs (Balter and Levine, 1971), it is important to have some appreciation of the effects that medicines and other drugs (particularly those with abuse potential) may have on sexual performance.

Many drugs have a diminishing effect on sexual functioning, thereby making it imperative that the clinician obtain a thorough version of the patient's medication history and his extramedical use of drugs.

There are several routes of action that various pharmacological agents take in effecting diminished sexual functioning: one is *central*, and presumably alters the function of higher level motivational centers, while the other is *peripheral*, involving interference with the normal functioning of the sex organs *per se*. A wide variety of pharmacological agents have clinical affects on sexual performance, and it is worth briefly noting some of them.

Probably the most frequently used drug to have a detrimental effect on sexual ability is alcohol (Lemere and Smith, 1973). Although promoted through literature as a libido-enhancing substance, alcohol actually serves to interfere with successful sexual activity by virtue of its being a general CNS depressant. In moderate doses it may aid in creating a more conducive atmosphere for sex through the inhibition of normal anxiety responses, but sufficient ingestion of the drug will ultimately produce depression of voluntary activity, including sexual behavior. For this reason, it is valuable to have a detailed account of the patient's drinking habits so that alcohol-related disabilities can be detected.

As is the case with a large number of other common effects, the sedatives tend to have an influence similar to alcohol on sexual performance. This comes about by the mechanisms shared in common with other general CNS depressants, and contributes to the frequent stance which treats sedative-hypnotics as "alcohol in capsule form." Narcotics also tend to have a depressing affect on sexual functions through both central and peripheral routes; however, it is often difficult to gain accurate information on their use.

Two drugs of particular interest in this regard: *methadone* and *antabuse*. Both compounds are utilized therapeutically in the treatment of addictive conditions, and both have the potential to produce impotence in males. The former is a narcotic antagonist which has come into frequent use recently as an alternative to heroine addiction; the latter is a drug which blocks the catabolism of alcohol and has been used with some success in the treatment of chronic alcoholism. Available data indicate a fairly wide range of individual sensitivity to these side effects, suggesting that the clinician remain alert to this potential source of dysfunction.

Still within the category of compounds termed medicines, two rather broad classes of drugs have been found to be consistently related to disturbances in sexual functioning: the *anticholinergics* (*e.g.*, probanthine) often used as antispasmodics in the treatment of hypermotility disorders, and the *antiadrenergics* (*e.g.*, reserpine), used frequently in hypertensive conditions. Both these classes of drugs have their inhibitory influence by interfering with the normal functioning of the autonomic nervous system. The former class block functioning of the parasympathetic nerves resulting in impotence, while the latter disturb certain segments of the sympathetic system causing ejaculatory disorders.

Two classes of psychotropic drugs account for the greatest frequency of drug-related sexual dysfunction in patients under treatment for psychological disorders: the antipsychotics, used primarily with schizophrenia, and the antidepressants, prescribed for clinical depressions of moderate to extreme severity. The most thoroughly documented antipsychotic to show these effects is thioridazine (Carlson and Sadoff, 1971; Freyhan, 1971), a phenothiazine class neuroleptic which produces inhibition of ejaculation. Other phenothiazines have also been indicated as being problematic in this area because of their tendency to cause a reduction in sexual desire. The butyrophenones (*e.g.*, haloperidol), another class of antipsychotics, have also been observed to produce centrally mediated loss of libido and disorders of erection and ejaculation (Serafetinides, 1972; Honigfeld and Howard, 1973).

In evaluating the antidepressant medications there is some added difficulty because of the fact that a frequent symptom of depression involves a loss of interest in sexual activities. Nonetheless, there is substantial evidence that both the tricyclic and monoaminooxidate (MAO) inhibitor classes of antidepressants can produce diminished libido, and that the MAO drugs also interfere with ejaculation in males (Klein and Davis, 1969; Serafetinides, 1972).

Social Class Influences

Although the biology and physiology of sexual functioning are fundamentally determined, a large segment of the more stylistic aspects of sexual behavior are learned reflections of cultural standards. Socioeconomic status is one facet of the culture that has been shown to be clearly related to different patterns of sexual behavior. The style, extent, function, and importance of sex, particularly as reflected in marriage, shifts markedly as one progresses up the socioeconomic scale.

Rainwater (1965) depicted heterosexual relationships in the

lower classes as often being male-dominated, rigid, unimaginative rituals which frequently are "endured" by the female owing to a sense of obligation to fulfill her sex role expectancies. As length of marriage increases, there is a tendency for both parties to experience reduced interest in, and gratification from, sexual intercourse, with a concomitant reduction in frequency. He attributed this in large measure to the ". . . highly segregated conjugal role relationships" characteristic of this class. Both men and women tend to engage in much of their activity with like-sex subgroups rather than develop shared interests or activities. This segregation is often extended into the sexual relationship itself with the result that sexual gratification is inhibited by the basic alienation of the couple and their failure to achieve intimacy.

A distinctly different picture of sexual relationship, as well as the factors contributing to dysfunction, was provided by Cuber (1974, 1969) in his portrayal of upper middle class sexuality. In this segment of society, jointly organized tasks, socialization, and leisure activities are typical. Sexuality is explored on a much broader basis and tends to be shared at the intellectual and psychological-emotional levels as well as the physical. The dominating commitment in this group seems to be to "career." Particularly among males, there is great pressure to "succeed" as judged by one's peers. This form of achievement inevitably involves intense professional investment and effort and long hours away from home. These demands, coupled with fatigue-induced disinterest in sexual involvement, help lay the groundwork for somewhat of a class-specific dysfunction syndrome. Feelings of alienation, rejection, and resentment on the part of the female are countered by guilt, irritability, and the perception of unrealistic demands on the part of the male. Since many work situations in this class involve small bisexual teams of the "doctor-nurse" type, extramarital liasons with colleagues or coworkers are the stereotypic "tale" of the upper-middle class.

The rationale behind presenting these two brief vignettes of contrasting sexual orientations has been to highlight the scope of the influence that social status factors can have in shaping sexual behavior. Kinsey's work (1948, 1953) was perhaps the first systematic research to show how pervasive this influence can be. Aspects of sexuality as diverse as age of sexual initiation, incidence of masturbation, and the tendency to experience erotic imagery, have all been shown to be differentially related to social status.

Through an intricate network of ethnic, religious, educational, and other influences, a belief system concerning sexual behavior is evolved by each status group and communicated to those who emerge from it. Regardless of subsequent mobility, the status group of origin will still exert a strong influence on an individual's expectancies, concerning both himself and his partner regarding desirable patterns of sexual interaction.

The dominant status orientation can be such as to carry with it a high risk of sexual disability: Cuber estimated that less than 20% of upper-middle class couples "maintain a vigorous, meaningful, and fulfilling sex life." Another class-based problem revolves around what Ferriss (1974) termed "status inconsistency." This refers to couples whose status backgrounds do not match and therefore bring incompatible belief systems into their relationships. The lack of congruence in expectancies, attitudes, and values about sexual relationship render these individuals at high risk for sexual disabilities.

It is obviously important that the clinician be aware of the strong influence that social status plays in shaping the individual's sexual orientation, and that information concerning this influence be integrated in his assessment of the nature of sexual disability. Behavior perceived as exemplary sexual technique by one reference group may be considered disgusting, or even immoral, by another. The assessor should be aware of the nature of the patient's primary sexual orientation and how compatible it is with that of his present partner.

SUMMARY

In his superb treatise on clinical judgement Feinstein (1967), distinguishes three fundamental classes of information relevant to clinical disorders: data on the *disease*, information concerning the *host*, and knowledge concerning the *illness*. The first class describes the underlying "process" of the disorder, often in reductionistic detail. The second category provides data on the "individual" in whom the process is taking place. The final class of information describes the "interaction" between the underlying process and the individual who is the host; it is the phenomenal experience—the signs and symptoms—of the clinical disorder.

He further describes a second dimension of clinical judgement—clinical reasoning—which he divides into two distinct, but related, classes: the first set of rational procedures is involved with what he terms *therapeutics*, while the second set revolves around decisions concerning the *environment* in which therapeutics are prescribed.

Feinstein believes that clinicians have declined to accept fully the mantle of scientific method, in large measure because they refuse to adopt the explicit definitions that are one of the hallmarks of modern science. The arguments that clinical judgements are by nature "intuitive," or that clinical practice is inherently an "art," are rejected as specious. He insists, "... clinical judgement has a distinctive methodology for dealing with the tangible data of human illness; and clinical judgement ... has both the obligation and opportunity to be accomplished with scientific taste, discretion, and quality." (p. 28).

In focusing on the clinical assessment of the sexual disabilities, it seems to me that we are involved in an area that, at once, demands the articulate application of rigorous clinical judgement and at the same time is restrained somewhat by a traditional body of "clinical lore." Particularly in the assessment of psychological processes, it is incumbent upon us to utilize fully the techniques and rationale of clinical science.

To borrow Feinstein's algorithm for a moment, disturbed psychological functions may be treated as the "process" of the disorder and evaluated as suggested above. Salient characteristics of the "host" may be derived from the "mediating variables" reviewed above. Information about the clinical "illness" should be obtained via thorough clinical techniques, supported by psychological instruments designed with relevant clinical criteria in mind. "Therapeutic" decisions should be carefully considered and reviewed, and they should be made only in the context of accurate information concerning the "environment." The latter is precisely the knowledge that clinical assessment is designed to provide.

Clinical psychological assessment of the sexual disabilities has traditionally been viewed as a "soft" enterprise, abounding with unverifiable dynamic hypotheses and intangibles and lacking even the minimal structure usually provided by psychiatric nosology. One of the major goals of the present report was to discount this notion, to suggest a conceptual structure, and an incipient direction, which will serve to anchor the basic procedures of clinical assessment in this area squarely in the operations of "clinical science."

REFERENCES

Abraham, K. 1949. Ejaculatio Praecox. In Jones, E., ed., *Selected Papers on Psychoanalysis*, Hogarth, London.

Ambrosino, S. V. 1973. Phobic anxiety—depersonalization syndrome. N.Y. State J. Med. 73: 419.

Arieti, S. 1959. Manic-depressive psychosis. In *American Handbook of Psychiatry*, Vol. 1. Basic Books Inc., New York.

Arnold, M. B. 1960. *Emotion and Personality*. Vol. 1: *Psychological Aspects*. Columbia Univ. Press, New York.

Athanasiou, R. 1973. A review of public attitudes on sexual issues. In Zubin J., and Money J., eds., *Contemporary Sexual Behavior: Critical Issues in the 1970's*. Johns Hopkins Univ. Press, Baltimore.

Athanasiou, R., and Sarkin, R. 1974. Premarital sexual behavior and postmarital adjustment. Arch. Sex. Behavior, 3: 207.

Athanasiou, R., and Shaver, P. 1971. Correlates of heterosexuals' reactions to pornography. J. Sex Res., 7: 298.

Balter, M., and Levine, J. 1971. Character and extent of psychotherapeutic drug usage in the United States. Paper presented at the Fifth World Congress on Psychiatry, Mexico City, 1971.

Bentler, P. M. 1968a. Heterosexual behavioral assment—I, males. Behav. Res. Ther., 6: 21.

Bentler, P. M. 1968b. Heterosexual behavioral assessment—II, females. Behav. Res. Ther., 6: 27.

Brady, J. P., and Levitt, E. E. 1965. The scalability of sexual experiences. Psycho. Record, 15: 275.

Carlson, B. E., and Sadoff, R. L. 1971. Thioridazine in schizophrenia. J. A. M. A. 212: 1,705.

Cattell, R. B. 1970. An integration of functional and psychometric requirements in a quantitative and computerized diagnostic system. In Maher, A. R. ed. *New Approaches to Personality Classification*. Columbia Univ. Press, New York.

Cooper, A. J. 1968a. Neurosis and disorders of sexual potency in the male. J. Pyschosom. Res. 12: 141.

Cooper, A. J. 1968b. Hostility and disorders of sexual potency. Compr. Psychiatry, 9: 621.

Cooper, A. J. 1969. Factors in male sexual inadequacy: a review. J. Nerv. Ment. Dis., 149: 337.

Cuber, J. F. 1969. The sexless marriage. Med. Aspects Hum. Sexuality, 3: 19.

Cuber, J. F. 1974. Sex in the upper middle class. Med. Aspects Hum. Sexuality, 8: 8.

DeMartino, M. F. 1969. *The New Female Sexuality*, Julian, New York.

Derogatis, L. R., Klerman, G. L., and Lipman, R. S. 1972. Anxiety states and depressive neuroses: issues in nosological classification. J. Nerv. Ment. Dis. 155: 392.

Derogatis, L. R., Lipman, R. S., and Covi, L. 1973. SCL-90: an outpatient psychiatric rating scale. Psychopharmacol. Bull., 9: 13.

Derogatis, L. R., Lipman, R. S., Rickels, K., Uhlenhuth, E. H., and Covi, L. 1974. The Hopkins Symptom Checklist (HSCL): a self-report symptom inventory. Behav. Sci. 19: 1.

Derogatis, L. R., Yevzeroff, H., and Wittelsberger, B. 1975. Social class psychological disorder, and the nature of the psychopathologic indicator. J. Consult. Clin Psychol, 43: 183.

Eysenck, H. J. 1970. A dimensional system of psychodiagnosis. In Maher A. R., ed., *New Approaches to Personality Classification*. Columbia Univ. Press, New York.

Faulk, M. 1973. "Frigidity": a critical review. Arch. Sex. Behavior, 2: No. 3, 257.

Feighner, J. P., Robins, E., Guze. S. B., Woodruff, R. A., Winokur, G., and Munoz, R. 1972. Diagnostic criteria for use in research. Arch. Gen. Psychiatr., 26: 57.

Feinstein, A. R. 1967. *Clinical Judgement*. Robert E. Krieger, Huntington, N.Y.

Fenichel, O. 1946. *Psychoanalytic Theory of the Neuroses*. Routledge and Kegan Paul, London.

Ferenczi, S. 1950. *Sex in Psychoanalysis*. Basic Books Inc., New York.

Ferriss, A. L. 1974. Commentary on Cuber's "Sex in the Upper Middle Class." Med. Aspects Hum. Sexuality, 8: 32.

Fisher, S. 1973. *The Female Orgasm*. Basic Books Inc., New York.

Fisher, S., and Osofsky, H. 1967. Sexual responsiveness in women: psychological correlates. Arch. Gen. Psychiatr., 17: 214.

Freud, S. 1953. The dynamics of transference (1912). In Strachey, J., ed., *Standard Edition of the Complete Psychological Works of Sigmund Freud*, Vol. 12, Hogarth, London.

Freud, S. 1913. *The Interpretation of Dreams*. Translated by A. A. Brill. MacMillan and C., New York.

Freyhan, F. A. 1961. Loss of ejaculation during mellaril treatment. Am. J. Psychiatry, 118: 171.

Gebhard, P. H. 1965. Situational factors affecting human sexual behavior. In Beach, F.A., *Sex and Behavior*, John Wiley, New York.

Gebhard, P. H. 1973. Sex differences in sexual response: Editorial comment. Arch. Sex. Behavior, 2: 201.

Ginsberg, G., Frosch, W., and Shapiro, T. 1972. The new impotence. Arch. Gen. Psychiatr., 26: 218.

Goldfarb, A. I. 1967. Geriatric psychiatry. In Freedman, A. M., Kaplan, H. I., and Kaplan, H. S. eds., *Comprehensive Textbook of Psychiatry*. Williams & Wilkins Co., Baltimore.

Green, B. L. 1970. Sexual dissatisfaction. In *Clinical Approach to Marital Problems*. Charles C Thomas, Springfield, Ill.

Gutheil, E. A. 1959a. Sexual dysfunctions in men. In Arieti, S. ed., *American Handbook of Psychiatry*, Vol. 1. Basic Books Inc., New York.

Gutheil, E. A. 1959b. Reactive depressions. In Arieti, S. ed., *American Handbook of Psychiatry*, Vol. 1, Basic Books Inc., New York.

Guttman, L. 1950. The basis for scalogram analysis. In Stouffer, S. A., ed., *Measurement and Prediction*. Princeton Univ. Press, Princeton.

Hamburger, W. W. 1958. The occurrence and meaning of dreams of food and eating. Psychosom. Med., 20: 1.

Hansen, D. 1967. Physical symptoms that may reveal sexual conflict. In Wahl, C. W., ed., *Sexual Problems: Diagnosis & Treatment in Medical Practice*, The Free Press, New York.

Hariton, E. B., and Singer, J. L. 1974. Womens' fantasies during sexual intercourse. J. Consult. Clin. Psychol. 42: 313.

Harrow, M., and Amdur, M. J. 1971. Guilt and depressive disorders. Arch. Gen. Psychiatry, 25: 240.

Hastings, D. W. 1963. *Impotence and Frigidity*. Churchill, London.

Hochschild, A. R. 1974. A review of sex role research. Am. J. Sociol., 58: 1,011.

Hoenig, J., and Kenna, J. C. 1974. The nosological position of transsexualism. Arch. Sex. Behavior, 3: 273.

Hongifeld, G., Howard, A., 1973. *Psychiatric Drugs: A Desk Reference*. Academic Press, New York.

Jones, E. 1966. The early development of female sexuality. In Ruitenbeek, H. M., ed., *Psychoanalysis and Female Sexuality*. Connecticut Univ. Press, New Haven.

Kaplan, H. S. 1974. *The New Sex Therapy*. Brunner/Mazel, New York.

Katchadourian, H. A., and Lunde, D. T. 1972. *Fundamentals of Human Sexuality*. Holt, Rinehart & Winston, Inc., New York.

Katz, D. 1960. The functional approach to the study of attitudes. Public Opin. Q. 163.

Kaufman, J. J. 1967. Organic and psychological factors in the genesis of impotence and premature ejaculation. In Wahl, C. W., ed., *Sexual Problems: Diagnosis and Treatment in Medical Practice*. Free Press, New York.

Kendell, R. E. 1974. The stability of psychiatric diagnoses. Br. J. Psychiatry, 124: 352.

Kinsey, A. C., Pomeroy, W. B., and Martin, C. E. 1948. *Sexual Behavior in the Human Male*. W. B. Saunders Co., Philadelphia.

Kinsey, A. C., Pomeroy, W. B., Martin, C. E., and Gebhard, P. H. 1953. *Sexual Behavior in the Human Female*. W. B. Saunders Co., Philadelphia.

Klein, D. F. 1973. Endogenomorphic depression. Paper presented at International Symposium on Depression, Erbach, Germany.

Klein, D. F., and Davis, J. M. 1969. *Diagnosis and Drug Treatment of Psychiatric Disorders*. Williams & Wilkins, Baltimore.

Klerman, G. L., and Barrett, J. E. 1974. The affective disorders: Clinical and epidemiologic aspects. In Gershon, S., and Shopsin, B., eds., *Lithium: Its Role in Psychiatric Research and Treatment*. Plenum, New York.

Lazarus, A. A. 1969. Modes of treatment for sexual inadequacies. Med. Aspects Human Sexuality, 3: 53.

Lazarus, A. A. 1972. Psychological causes of impotence. Sex. Behavior, 2: 39.

Leary, T. 1957. *Interpersonal Diagnosis of Personality*. Ronald Press, New York.

Lemere, F., and Smith, J. W. 1973. Alcohol induced sexual impotence. Am. J. Psychiatry, 130: 212.

Lewis, J. M. 1969. Impotence as a reflection of marital conflict. Med. Aspects Hum. Sexuality, 3: 73.

Ley, P. 1972. The reliability of psychiatric diagnosis: some new thoughts. Br. J. Psychiatry, 121: 41.

Lidberg, L. 1972. Social and psychiatric aspects of impotence and premature ejaculation. Arch. Sex. Behavior, 2: 135.

Lorand, S. 1939. Contributions to the problem of vaginal orgasm. International J. Psychoanal., 20: 432.

Lorr, M. 1969. Syndromes of deviation. In Borgatta, E. F., and Lambert W. W., eds., *Handbook of Personality Research*. Rand McNally & Co., Chicago.

Lorr, M. 1970. A typological conception of the behavior disorders. In Maher, A. R., ed., *New Approaches to Personality Classification*, Columbia Univ. Press, New York.

Lorr, M., Klett, C. J., and NcNair, D. 1963. *Syndromes of Psychosis*. Pergamon Press, London.

Martin, B. 1971. *Anxiety and Neurotic Disorders*. John Wiley, New York.

Masters, W., and Johnson, V. 1970. *Human Sexual Inadequacy*. Churchill, London.

Masters, W., and Johnson, V. 1973. Current status of the research programs. In Zubin, J., and Money, J., eds., *Contemporary Sexual Behavior: Critical Issues in the 1970's*. Johns Hopkins Univ. Press, Baltimore.

May, R. 1969. *Love and Will*. W. W. Norton & Co., New York.

Mellan, J. 1971. Interpersonal relationships of female patients with sexual disorders as assessed by Leary's test. Arch. Sex. Behavior, 1: 263.

Meyer, J. K. 1975. Individual psychotherapy of sexual disabilities. In Freedman, A. M., Kaplan, H. I., and Sadock, B. J., eds. *Comprehensive Textbook of Psychiatry*. ed. 2. Williams & Wilkins, Baltimore.

Moore, B. 1964. Frigidity: A review of the psychoanalytic literature. Psychoanal. Q., 33: 323.

Mosher, D. L., and Greenberg, I. 1969. Females affective responses to reading erotic literature. J. Consult. Clin. Psychol., 33: 472.

Panzetta, A. F., 1974. Toward a scientific psychiatric nosology: conceptual and pragmatic issues. Arch. Gen. Psychiatr., 30: 154.

Pfeiffer, E., Verwoerdt, A., and Wang, H. S. 1968. Sexual behavior in aged men and women. Arch. Gen. Psychiatr., 19: 753.

Podel, L., and Perkins, J. C. 1957. A Guttman scale for sexual experience—a methodological note. J. Abnorm. Soc. Psychol., 54: 420.

Rainwater, L. 1965. Some aspects of lower class sexual behavior. J. Soc. Issues, 22: 96.

Salzman, L. 1967. Recently exploded sexual myths. Med. Aspects Hum. Sexuality, 1: 6.

Serafetinides, E. A. 1972. Assessing the sexual side effects of psychotropic drugs. Hosp. Physician, 8: 58.

Shainess, N., and Greenwald, H. 1971. Debate: Are fantasies during sexual relations a sign of difficulty. Sex. Behavior, 1: 38.

Shope, D. F., and Broderick, C. B. 1967. Level of sexual experience and predicted adjustment in marriage. J. Marriage Family, 29: 424.

Singer, J. L., and Antrobus, J. S. 1972. Daydreaming, imaginal processes, and personality. A normative study. In Sheehan, P., ed., *The Function and Nature of Imagery*, Academic Press, New York.

Steinmann, A. G. 1971. *Bibliography of Male-Female Role Research*. Mafer Foundation, Inc., New York.

Steinmann, A. G. 1972. Studies in male-female role identification. Paper presented at the Third Annual Society for Psychotherapy Research Meeting, Nashville, Tenn.

Tomkins, S. S. 1963. *Affect, Imagery, Consciousness*. Springer, New York.

Torgerson, W. S. 1968. Multidimensional representation of similarity structures. In Katz, M. M., Cole, J. O., and Barton, W. E. eds., *The Role and Methodology of Classification in Psychiatry and Psychopathology*. Public Health Publication No. 1584, Washington, D. C.

Udry, J. R. 1968. Sex and family life. Med. Aspects Hum. Sexuality, 2: 66.

Ullman, L. P., and Krasner, L. 1969. *A Psychological Approach to Abnormal Behavior*. Prentice-Hall, Inc., Englewood Cliffs, N.J.

Wallace, C., Wehmer, G., and Podany, E. 1974. Contemporary community standards of visual erotica. In *Technical Report of C.O.P.*, Vol. 9. U.S. Government Printing Office, Washington, D.C.

Weissman, M. M., Klerman, G. L., and Payke, E. S. 1971. Clinical evaluation of hostility in depression. Am. J. Psychiatry, 128: 261.

Wolpe, J., and Lazarus, A. A., 1966. *Behavior Therapy Techniques: A Guide to the Treatment of Neuroses*. Pergamon Press, New York.

Zuckerman, M. 1973. Scales for sex experience for males and females. J. Consult. Clin. Psychol. 41: 27.

FOUR

Sexual Problems, Therapy, and Prognostic Factors

JOHN F. O'CONNOR, M.D.

The extent of psychogenic sexual disorders existing within the general patient population has been recognized increasingly in recent years. One study (Burnap and Golden, 1967) of 92 physicians with differing backgrounds and specialties showed that, within their respective patient populations, patients with some type of sexual dysfunction comprised 15% of general practice, 6% of internal medicine, 14% of obstetrics and gynecology, and 77% of psychiatric practice. It is estimated that 50% of all married couples experience some degree of sexual maladjustment, and that sexual discordance may be a factor in as many as 90% of this country's divorces.

Despite the prevalence of symptoms of sexual dysfunction and the use of various forms of treatment—psychoanalysis, psychotherapy, group therapy, behavioral therapy, and hypnosis, to name the most common—there are very few systematic reports of the relationships between initial symptoms and the methods used to treat them in significantly sizeable populations (Lesnenko, 1967; Masters and Johnson, 1970; O'Connor and Stern, 1972).

HUMAN SEXUAL DYSFUNCTIONS

The purpose of this chapter is to describe typical sexual dysfunctions, the patients in whom they are present, and the prognosis for improvement. In addition, the methods and goals of various types of treatment programs, as well as the results obtained, will be reviewed.

The terminology of sex therapy has yet to reach a uniformly acceptable form. Definitions tend to vary from one investigator to another. Thus the concept of female orgasm is taken by some to refer only to a total bodily response that includes uterine and vaginal contractions, increased blood pressure and pulse rate, general body muscular contraction and carpopedal spasm, while another investigator will define female orgasm as a general sense of pleasure and well-being during intercourse. Table 4.1 presents an outline of the definitions of human sexual dysfunctions that has been adopted by the present investigators at the Columbia Presbyterian Medical Center. As with all other definitions, they leave much to be desired, but they do give a basis for validation of results.

Definitions

Impotence is a condition in which a male is unable to maintain an erection or experience orgasm resulting from coitus. A *totally* impotent male has never been able to experience coitus with orgasm even though he can masturbate with erection and normal heterosexual fantasies. Included under the category of *partial* impotence are (1) males who, with the same partner, are able to complete intercourse at times, but not consistently, or who have been potent in the past; (2) males who consistently maintain only a partial erection; (3) males who are able to have sexual intercourse only with certain types of women—usually women who are social or intellectual inferiors or who are from a different ethnic group (selective impotence); and (4) males who usually

TABLE 4.1

Psychological Disorders of Sexual Function

Male	
I. Impotence	III. Dyspareunia
A. Total	IV. Low libido
B. Partial	A. Chronic
1. Intermittent success	B. Acute
2. Partial erection	V. Penile anaesthesia
3. Selective	
4. Situational	
II. Ejaculation	
A. Premature	
B. Retarded	

Female	
I. Anorgasmia	III. Dyspareunia
A. Total	IV. Low Libido
B. Partial	A. Chronic
1. Intermittent success	B. Acute
2. Selective	V. Vaginal anaesthesia
3. Situational	
II. Vaginismus	

perform satisfactorily with a given female, but who may not on occasion because of certain anxiety-provoking situations such as the commitment to marriage or the birth of a male child (situational impotence).

Masters and Johnson (1970) included all types of partial impotence in their category "secondary impotence" without differentiating one from the other. The subdivisions of this category are extremely useful since the prognoses for the subcategories differ markedly. For example, the prognosis for a male in the "situational impotence" category is considerably more favorable than that for a male who achieves only a "partial erection."

Premature ejaculation is defined either by the length of time it takes the male to achieve orgasm after penetration or by the number of thrusts necessary to achieve orgasm. Usually ejaculation that occurs before penetration, in less than 2 min after penetration, or upon fewer than 10 thrusts is considered premature. Kaplan (1974) emphasized the lack of voluntary control in these males.

Masters and Johnson (1970) defined this condition in terms of an inability to satisfy the female partner at least 50% of the time. This definition adds an unnecessary complication to the issue, since a female who is consistently slow to respond may not be satisfied even by a male for whom the time between penetration and ejaculation is satisfactory for other women, *i.e.*, a male who remains intravaginal for 10 or more min could be considered a premature ejaculator.

Retarded ejaculation is the inability of a male to achieve orgasm and ejaculation or who may take hours to ejaculate. Though this condition is thought of as relatively rare, actually, this is not the case. In a 2-month period the wives of six retarded ejaculators requested to come into the Columbia program for treatment; in all cases the husband refused. So to restate it, the condition is *relatively rarely treated.*

Dyspareunia is pain during intercourse and may be either physiological or psychological in origin. Physiologically caused dyspareunia must be diagnosed and treated medically before any possible underlying psychological symptoms can be treated (Fullerton, 1971; Zelle, 1971). Psychogenic dyspareunia in the male usually indicates severe psychopathology and is extremely difficult to treat. Female dyspareunia is analogous to male dyspareunia and, except when there is a physiological cause, it is an hysteric disorder which generally can be traced to childhood trauma and is not as psychopathological as in the male.

Low libido is a lack of desire to engage in sexual activity, for both males and females. There has been very little success in treating chronic, or long standing, low libido; however, acute low libido, which usually results from an immediate situational problem, is fairly easy to treat.

Penile anaesthesia or *vaginal anaesthesia* is a lack of sensation which is a manifestation of conversion hysteria. They are very rare conditions.

Anorgasmia is a condition in which a female is unable to achieve orgasm through coitus. A female who has never experienced orgasm during coitus is considered totally anorgasmic, even if she is able to achieve orgasm with masturbation. The female conditions of intermittent, selective, and situational anorgasmia are defined analogously to the male conditions which are also divided into intermittent, selective, and situational impotence.

Vaginismus is a spasm of the vaginal and pelvic musculature inhibiting penetration with a resulting lack of sexual excitement. In some rare cases penetration can occasionally be accomplished in the presence of vaginismus. The symptom can be caused by certain organic lesions (Finkle and Thompson, 1972), but more often its causes are psychological. It can be associated with dyspareunia, but both can exist independently. Both conditions are unrelated to a female's ability to experience orgasm.

Psychological Aspects of Sexual Dysfunction

Defining the physical symptoms is insufficient to a full understanding of the sexual disorder. The presenting physical symptom cannot be isolated from its psychological components, which are equally related to their developmental roots. For example, in 85% of the frigid women that were studied by Kleegman (1971) there was evidence of neurosis; only 15% manifested frigidity as the single symptom. On the other hand, Meyer (1974) and O'Connor (1974) found fewer patients who could be diagnosed as being neurotic in the patient population at their centers. As with most overt behavioral symptoms, sexual dysfunction is generally the result of a complex interaction between less accessible historic problems and certain maladaptive personality variables. An explication of both components will lead to a more complete understanding of the sexual disorder.

In 1968 an extensive review (O'Connor and Stern, 1972) of the backgrounds of 96 patients, whose primary complaint was a sexual disorder, was undertaken by a group of researchers at the Columbia Psychoanalytic Clinic. The patients ranged in age from 18 to over 50 years, the majority being in their middle twenties and thirties. Sixty-one percent had been married. Their educational level was beyond high school. Most were white collar workers; a few were professional workers. More than 50% were Jewish; the remainder was evenly divided between Catholic and Protestant. The backgrounds of this patient group reflect quite accurately the backgrounds of other patient groups in the Psychoanalytic Clinic. However, the family histories of these patients were more chaotic than those of other patient groups seen at the psychoanalytic clinic and more disturbed than those seen in the short term treatment program.* Interestingly enough, though the short term group had less psychological trauma, the same pattern of trauma was observed *i.e.*, separation, death, parental coldness, etc. was present. Fifty-seven percent of the patients in the original study had at least one parent who evidenced problems such as alcoholism, abnormal sexual behavior, incestual activities, exhibitionism, psychosis, or excessive brutality. Almost one-third of the patients were partners to some form of bizarre sexual activity within the family structure. An equal number were reared in an atmosphere of excessive prohibition in which direct threats instilled fears of pregnancy in females or predicted severe disease from masturbation or intercourse in males.

Other important findings were the high incidence of death within the immediate family and prolonged separation from either the mother or father before the patient reached age 16. Traumatic separation included divorce, desertion, war, illness, and extended business trips, *i.e.*, traveling salesman, career serviceman, etc. These separations were generally accompanied by considerable anger and frustration on the part of the other parent. Parental loss is an influential factor relating to the individual's ability to enjoy a warm, intimate relationship in later life. The death or separation was usually so traumatic that future relationships were limited in depth because of an unconscious reluctance to rely on others, with a limited ability to make an emotional investment or commitment to a future partner.

It was our impression that those children who were deprived of an atmosphere of warmth and care within the family unit gravitated toward friends, school teachers, and parental substitutes, where at least some of their needs could be fulfilled. The males were rarely leaders; they tended to be followers who relied on the strength of another male or the care of a female. There was no discernible pattern in the female population. O'Connor (1975)

* The short term treatment program at Columbia is the 2- to 3-week program used at the Reproductive Biology Foundation in St. Louis, Mo. with no modification. The groups described in detail are those from the Columbia Psychoanalytic Clinic, and unless otherwise noted, they were treated by psychoanalysis and psychotherapy. Psychotherapy includes classical psychoanalysis, a minimum of 4 visits a week for 2 years, and interpretive therapy twice a week for a minimum of 1 year.

reported that the female patients with sexual disorders maintained a better peer group relationship through adolescence than the males. The males with premature ejaculation had a particularly bad peer-group relationship. A large number of patients had been subjected to a severely traumatic initial sexual experience. Over 25% of the patients reported that their spouse also had an overt sexual disorder.

Exclusive of sexual pathology, the current, general life adjustment of many of the patients appeared to be adequate. Diagnostically, 65% of the patients seen in psycholanalysis and psychotherapy were classified as having personality disorders, 33% as psychoneurotic, and only 2% as schizophrenic, considerably different from Kleegman's sample. The majority evidenced a marked obsessional character structure with varying degrees of anxiety. Depresssion was common, more noticeable in the female than in the male population. The males tended to be affable, although not particularly outgoing, and as a rule they were friendly and related well to others on a superficial level. The females, on the other hand, presented a rather obsessive controlling pattern, adhering strictly to rules and standards, and frequently exhibiting mild phobic symptoms.

The three predominant personality factors seen in patients with psychosexual dysfunction were phobias, passive and passive-aggressive dependence, and fear of loss of control by onself or one's partner during sexual activity. Phobias were present in males and females and were primarily seen in three forms: direct, symbolic, and counterphobias.

In the direct phobia, the individual straightforwardly expresses a fear of sexual intercourse and intimacy. This can occur at the time of discussing sex, entering the sexual situation, or just prior to orgasm. Typically, the female expresses a fear of being crushed or suffocated, saying that "he is too heavy." The male will state, "she loses control of herself, acts like a wild person." A frequent physical manifestation of a direct phobic condition in females is vaginismus and in males, premature ejaculation, although success phobia has been associated with retarded ejaculation (Friedman, 1972).

The individual with a symbolic phobia establishes a "situation" as a prerequisite for sexual satisfaction. He may require the door or window to be open, or to lie away from the wall, because on previous occasions it has been associated with marked anxiety. Later, he may insist on the condition and be sufficiently relieved to enjoy sexual intercourse.

The counterphobic reaction is also generated by fear of the sexual situation, but it is disguised by behavior which is opposite to the fear. Females can become extremely seductive and appear very open in sexual matters to dispel and deny any notion that they are afraid of sex. The male will assume an aggressive masculine role to counter his anxiety about his own sexual adequacy. The counterphobic female reduces the feelings of aggression and responsibility of the male, while the directly phobic female makes the male feel brutal and destructive, causing guilt and limited sexual activity and increasing the possibility of sexual dysfunction in the male.

The counterphobic presents a more difficult treatment situation. The counterphobic adaptation, if successful, becomes so ingrained and necessary that any attempt to touch it is met with rage and rejection. The classical examples of the counterphobic personality is in the males in many of the private detective and cowboy heroes of the movies and television. In all cases, however, it is important to determine to what extent the partner is supporting the phobia or counterphobia by anxiety- or fear-producing behavior. Partner support of the sexual problem is frequently seen in couples with sexual disorders.

A crucial personality factor in the marital situation is the ability to be realistically dependent upon the spouse and to accept his dependence in return. Both male and female children are dependent upon their mothers for the first 6 years of life and that dependency is not ever completely eliminated in adult life. The female later resolves her dependency needs by becoming a mother, because until lately in our society it was acceptable for females to be completely dependent upon males and to be the object of dependency by children. The male, however, is forced by social values to become independent, to be the aggressor and provider, but frequently this independence becomes a pseudoindependence. The male has real needs to show some dependence, but threats to his masculine identity prevent him from expressing them. These difficulties arise in the short term treatment situation where the male begins to retaliate on a sexual level. For these problems to be eliminated, both partners must come to grips with their realistic dependency needs in order to become truly independent and interdependent.

Another category included in personality factors is a fear of loss of control. One who cannot allow himself the freedom to engage uninhibitedly in sexual relations fears a loss of his own control. The same prohibition is exercised by the individual who cannot accept seeing the partner "out of control" and withdraws from sexual participation in anticipation of such loss of control or will force upon the partner a sufficient feeling of self-consciousness to prevent successful completion of sexual intercourse. This is seen more frequently in the obsessive personality.

While neither personality factors nor poor role identification necessarily leads to a sexual problem, they can be contributory.

PROGNOSIS

Identification and Ego Strength

In this section the factors that influence prognosis will be reviewed. These include diagnosis, life factors, duration of symptoms, the sexual partner, and the sex of the patient (Kinsey and associates, 1948, 1953; O'Connor and Stern, 1972). Basic role identification appears to be an important factor in choosing the type of treatment, and it possibly influences prognosis.

Many studies have been concerned with the dynamics of female sexuality, and fewer with the dynamics of the male. Blair and Pasmore (1964), reporting on successful psychotherapy in 58 females suffering from anorgasmia, divided the sample into 4 groups based on each patient's own image as a female. Group I consisted of women who were having transitional problems in a new marriage, group II included women who were uncertain as to their own femininity, group III comprised those women who were overtly angry at being female, and in group IV were women whose anxiety about their role was so overwhelming that they denied any sexual feeling. Prognosis was excellent for group I, good for groups II and III, and poor for group IV.

Another factor is the individual's ego strength, whether or not one enjoys and identifies with one's own sex. A strong ego with good respective masculine and feminine identification are positive prognostic factors. Although, as a general rule, the aforementioned statement may be true, bisexual males who have made good heterosexual adjustments function well, but in all cases it appeared to be more dependent on the attitude and receptivity of their female partner than was the case of the heterosexual male.

Diagnosis

As mentioned previously in patients with sexual dysfunction, it was very difficult to make a definite psychiatric diagnosis. They are at times "too normal" in their behavioral pattern, their personalities tended to be stereotyped and based on what they perceived as "normal" for society's standards. In general, those who exhibited gross symptoms such as phobias, anxiety, and compulsions had a poorer prognosis than those patients with milder psychopathological conditions. A major determinant for improvement was the original psychiatric diagnosis.

The fact that the more neurotic patients did not improve as much as those with less psychopathology was not surprising. The basic psychiatric diagnosis is certainly a very important prognostic factor in all forms of psychological treatment.

Table 4.2 presents the number of improved patients in each classification from mild to severe psychopathology. The figures are compiled from three separate studies (Cooper, 1969; Faulk, 1971; O'Connor and Stern, 1972). Obviously compiled data from different investigators leave much to be desired. It was difficult to correlate symptom, patient type, and response. Any questionable patient, symptom, or response was dropped from the compilation.

Interviews, psychiatric diagnoses, psychological testing, neuroticism and hostility scales, and attitudinal and personality scales were used to classify the extent of psychopathology. In reviewing all three of the studies, "A" patients seemed moderately well adjusted with the exception of the sexual problem; "B" patients had the sexual problem with other areas of obvious psychological maladjustment; and "C" patients combined sexual problem with severe maladjustment on either an intrapsychic or behavioral level. Grossly, it would be like dealing with a personality or characterological disorder (A), psychoneurotic disorder (B), and borderline schizophrenia (C). None of the patients described in the three studies was grossly schizophrenic.

Life Factors

These can be divided into three subcategories—past history, current emotional status, and current functional status. Some personality aspects included here have been discussed earlier in terms of symptoms; now, they will be related specifically to prognosis. They have been found to be of significant prognostic value as have other life factors indices. These results are summarized in Table 4.3.

Perhaps the most important attribute, and certainly the basic one for successful therapy, is the capacity to establish a good

TABLE 4.2

Improvement Rate as Related to Degree of Psychopathology: A Summary of Various Treatment Methods—204 Patients

Patients	Number	Improved	Unimproved
		%	%
A	110	60	40
B	61	51	49
C	33	19	81

one-to-one relationship with the opposite sex. This must be differentiated from popularity, good peer relationships, or even a successful affair which is markedly different from the sexual and social commitments of marriage.

It has been suggested that premarital sexual experience leads to a better marital adjustment (Shope and Broderick, 1967). However, the investigators did not evaluate the quality of such experience, which is probably the ultimate determining factor. Kinsey's and associates' (1953) studies indicated that the older a woman is before marriage, the less problem she has in adjusting to a sexual life, which is a radically different concept than one would expect.

Age appears to have negative value for males over 40 years particularly in a second marriage. They had more difficulty in

TABLE 4.3

Life Factors Important in Prognosis

	Prognosis
Past history	
1. Ability to form good one-to-one relationship with the opposite sex	+
2. Ability to get along well with peers	
Male	+
Female	Undetermined
3. Previous good sexual responsivity	+
4. Previous poor sexual responsivity	–
5. Traumatic loss of previous partner (males over 40)	–
6. Symptoms present over 10 years in marriage	
Female	–
Male	Undetermined
Current emotional status	
1. Excessive generalized anxiety	+
2. Excessive sexual guilt	–
3. Excessive partner anger	–
4. Fear of injury resulting from sexuality (fantasies, dreams, etc.)	–
5. Severe psychopathology	–
Current functional status	
1. unmarried	–
2. Partner resistance to treatment or cure	–
3. Good marriage exclusive of sexual symptom	+
4. Chaotic marriage	–
5. Extramarital affair	–
6. Individual feels sexually attractive	+
7. Poor role identification	–
8. New marriage (except in males over 40)	+
9. Age of patient	Undetermined
10. Bisexuality	Undetermined

relating to a new partner than did the females in our group. The over-40 male manifested considerable guilt about his dead or divorced wife. This was not true with females or the under-40 male. Older couples who had remained together did well in our short term therapy group.

Duration of Symptoms

Most studies emphasize that the existence of symptoms over a long period of time is indicative of a poorer prognosis. Cooper (1969) stressed that this is particularly true of female patients, and our findings corroborated his observations. Fifty-seven percent of our female patients with symptoms for 10 or more years improved significantly less than the males, and 11% less than females who had symptoms for less than 10 years.

It is a generally accepted fact that 30% of the average female population do not achieve orgasm during their first experience of intercourse (Kinsey and associates, 1953). After a period of 10 years or more, this percentage is reduced to 10% and remains static thereafter if they receive no therapy. In our group the improvement rate for females who had been anorgastic for more than 10 years was 30% as compared with 66% of the females who had been anorgastic for shorter periods of time. In the male, sexual symptoms usually persist if untreated. However, the length of time the symptom existed did not appear to be a prognostic factor; 8 of the 10 males who were impotent for more than 10 years improved.

The Partner

Aside from those factors listed in Table 4.3, it is extremely difficult to prognosticate in terms of previous history of the patient. Early life situations contribute significantly to the development of the sexual disorder but have no demonstrable relationship to the patient's response to treatment. Poor parental attitude, extremely religious background, sexual trauma, and life all give way to the state of the current relationship of the couple.

The married patients with minimal problems outside of their sexual life seem to have a better prognosis than similar unmarried patients. The couple has a much greater motivation in keeping what is an already good situation intact. However, we do see married couples for whom the prognosis is poor. For example, the couple who show marked disturbance in all areas of the marriage or where one partner is motivated consciously or unconsciously toward breaking up the marriage.

Probably it is impossible to effect treatment in a situation where one partner is currently having an affair. If the relationship in the marriage is based on the maintenance of the symptom, through a fear of the symptomatic partner recovering, he or she will be unable to cope with his "newly sexual" partner. This is dealt with in the pretreatment phase. If the symptom is acute and secondary to the marriage—such as a stress event, for one partner or the other, *i.e.* business failure, birth of a child, etc., the prognosis is favorable.

Anxiety

Other investigators have indicated that "sex-specific anxiety," *i.e.*, fear of physical injury, has a poorer prognosis than a more generalized anxiety (Faulk, 1971) and our observations concur with their findings. Partner anger is also a major problem. All of these patients have been referred for counseling before taking them into the rapid treatment program. This is necessary because when treating a patient with a sexual disorder using the intensive 2-week Masters and Johnson treatment program, one has to be extremely careful to avoid a situation where a break in the relationship could occur. This treatment method very quickly surfaces basic conflicts and problems; many times preoedipal situations emerge during the 1st week of treatment. To cope with such a situation requires a certain degree of ego strength on the part of the patient and deftness on the part of the therapist. Although we have not had overt breaks in our patient groups, we have seen episodes of depersonalization, conversion reactions, and almost autistic behavior. In such cases, a psychiatrist who has seen the patient before can be extremely helpful in overcoming such a crisis in the midst of treatment.

The Sex of the Patient

This was the most important prognostic factor aside from the psychiatric diagnosis. One might expect, in terms of anatomic and physiological structure, that it would be easier for the woman to improve partially even though she may not achieve complete improvement. Improvement, for the female, included more pleasure in the sexual act, positive attitudinal changes, and orgasm during foreplay without orgasm during intercourse itself. With the male, however, the potential for partial improvement is lessened; he is more likely to be completely improved or remain unimproved, since improvement is dependent chiefly on performance, that is the ability to achieve and sustain an erection and ejaculate intravaginally.

As show in Figure 4.1, the male has a more favorable prognosis using the treatments of psychoanalysis, psychotherapy, and the Masters and Johnson method. In the studies of behaviorial and hypnotic treatment, the female tends to have a better prognosis. As of now, we cannot really state why this is so, but it may be that the female has been so suppressed sexually by familial and societal prohibitions that these treatment techniques give her a greater degree of permissivity to enjoy herself. On the other hand, the female in most sexual disorders is dealing with a conversion reaction, whereas the male is dealing with a psychophysiological disorder. It is obvious to any practicing physician that conversion reactions respond to suggestive therapy, and physiological disorder. It is obvious to any psychologically trained physician that conversion reactions respond to suggestive therapy, and psychophysiological disorders respond more to interpretive therapy. The reason is undetermined, but one can guess that the motivation is much stronger for the male, as the female can have intercourse despite the fact that she has a problem, while the male is unable to have satisfactory sexual relations while his problem is existent.

An exception, the classic counterphobic male, is the retarded ejaculator. He is open, outgoing, and aggressive but will generally not enter treatment. He is angry at the female and unconsciously views his symptoms as a weapon to be used against her, equating the loss of the symptom with his loss of power and control. As a result, he has a countermotivation for improvement in treatment. In our original Masters and Johnson treatment program, only 2 of the 11 males suffering from retarded ejaculation who came for consultation entered the treatment program. It is our impression and that of others (Murphy and O'Connor, in press) that prognosis is not good for this group.

Symptoms

Table 4.4 divides the symptoms into 4 groups, in terms of response to treatment and the sex of the patient. The symptoms fall into one of 2 categories, physiological or psychogenic, and 1 of the 2 severities so that there is psychogenic simple, physiological simple, psychogenic complicated, and physiological complicated.

Psychogenic Simple. Masters and Johnson (1970) and other investigators have found that dyspareunia in females, premature ejaculation, and vaginismus are generally the most easily treated sexual problems. Our experience at Columbia has confirmed these findings. Physicians for hundreds of years have been

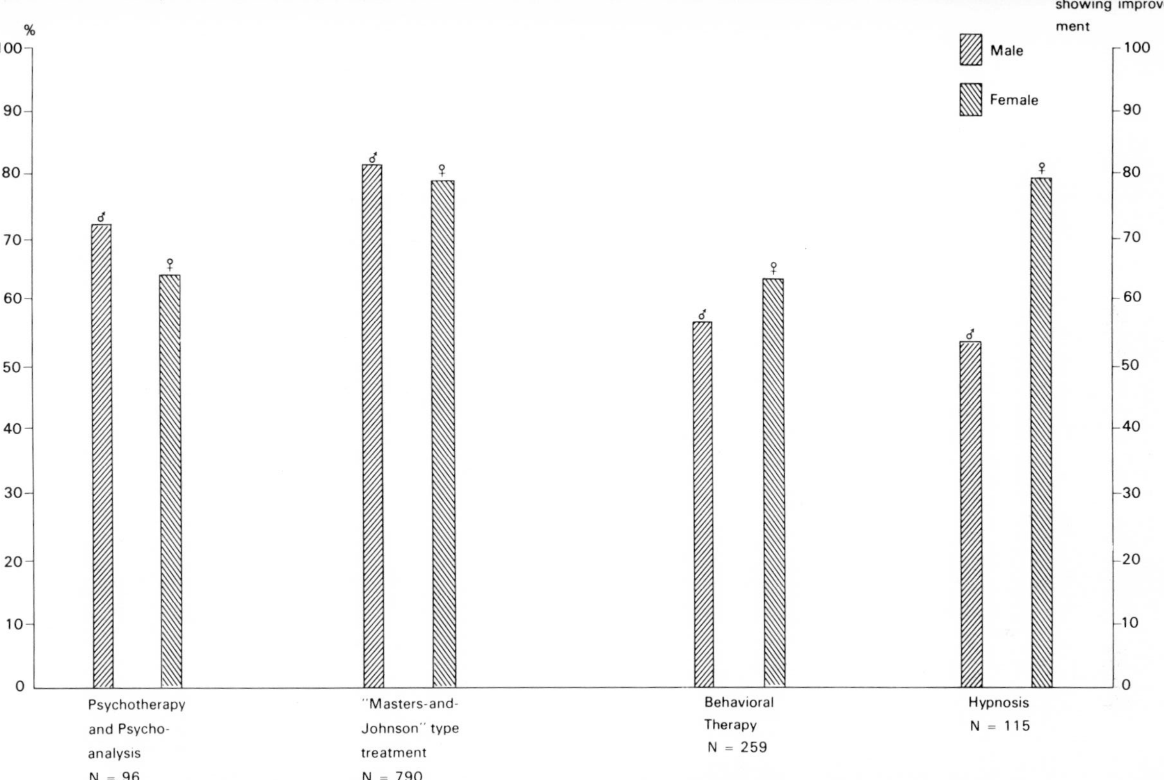

Fig. 4.1 Improvement rates with various treatment modalities in sexual dysfunction.

TABLE 4.4

Symptoms Relative to Prognosis and Origin

Psychogenic simple[a]	
Male	Premature ejaculation
	Secondary retarded ejaculation
	Total impotence
	Partial impotence: intermittent, situational
Female	Vaginismus
	Dyspareunia
	Total anorgasmia
Both	Sexual symptoms acutely developing
	Low libido, acute
Physiological simple	
Male	Correctable urological disorders
Female	Correctable gynecological disorders
Both	Myocardial infarction
	Stroke
	Iatrogenic: tranquilizers, antihypertensive drugs
Psychogenic complicated[a]	
Male	Partial impotence: partial erection, selective
	Penile anaesthesia
	Dyspareunia
	Retarded ejaculation
Female	Partial anorgasmia
	Vaginal anaesthesia
Both	Low libido, chronic
Physiological complicated	
Male	Perineal prostatectomy
	Colostomy for carcinoma
Both	Diabetes (long standing)
	Hormonal disorders

[a] Simple and complicated do not refer to the physical manifestation of the symptom but rather to the response to treatment. Therefore, simple means a good expected response and generally an easier therapeutic process; complicated, the opposite. This is based on our experience at Columbia.

successfully treating sexual symptoms; the first reported case was in 1,500 B.C. (Papageorgiou, 1969). What is needed is explanation, support, and encouragement to begin or to resume sexual activity in an atmosphere that is free from ignorance, embarassment, and anxiety (Finkle and Thompson, 1972; O'Connor, 1975; Seid, 1970). This is also true of males or females who suddenly lose their sexual drive (acute low libido).

Physiological Simple. This category includes iatrogenic symptoms which result from use of tranquilizers, antihypertensive medication, and the like which can readily be handled by changing the medication, reducing the dosage, and reassuring the patient. Postsurgical symptoms, assuming a lack of damage to the sacral nerve plexus, also fall into this category, as do cardiovascular and pulmonary illness. All of the aforementioned symptoms seem to respond to supportive educative psychotherapy from either the surgeon, the internist, or the psychiatrist (O'Connor, 1973).

When we are dealing with postmyocardial infarctions, emphysema, or other such medical problems, the cause of the sexual disorder is most likely psychological. These patients as a rule become overprotective of themselves, fearing that physical activity could lead to death. The astute physician recognizes this and can, with reassurance, encourage more physical activity with an eventual return to normal sexual activity. In resistant cases, couples can be referred for psychotherapy. The partner is very involved in the recovery process, and it is necessary to reassure him also. Many times the wife of a postmyocardial infarction patient will see herself as contributing to the original infarction and refrain from sexual activity because of her fear of precipitating another attack. Direct intervention and explanation of the physical and psychological factors can do a great deal to reestablish the couple's normal sexual life. The prognosis in this group is generally excellent, but one has to reassure them that they are not as vulnerable as they currently feel, and with the passage of time there is no reason that normal activity cannot be reestablished. The physician has to assume the patient will recover and dispel the equation sex = death. He should not be overly sympathetic or identify with the patient, as this will lead to decreased expectations on the part of the patient and eventual sexual failure. Instead, he must constantly balance the realistic physical impairment with the fantasied fears.

Psychogenic Complicated. The most difficult of the psychogenic problems to treat in the male is partial impotence, and in the female, partial anorgasmia. For males over 50, this disorder is further complicated by its relationship to the aging process. For both males and females in the partial cases, much may be related to the existing partner, but it is not feasible to expect a bond that has existed for many years to dissolve because of sexual problems. Treatment is obviously indicated, but the results are not as good as in the first 2 categories, *i.e.*, psychogenic and physiological simple. Therefore, one has to take into account that long term treatment may be indicated for this group of patients. Although one would expect them to be more difficult to treat, total lack of orgasm in the female or total impotence in the male can respond better than most of the partial problems.

There are not enough data available on penile or vaginal anaesthesia for any meaningful account of prognosis. These are symptoms of a conversion hysteria which would indicate a generally good prognosis. However, as they are accompanied at times by impotence in the male and, in the female, always with anorgasmia, the symptom is compounded and more difficult to treat. Therefore, a poorer prognosis is expected. Two patients seen in psychotherapy, one male and one female, continued to have intercourse to orgasm with no functional problem, but neither of them experienced pleasure and both dealt with sex as a necessary duty. The female no longer suffered from vaginal anaesthesia but though she had all of the physiological components of orgasm and was cerebrally conscious of "the phenomena," to date she does not allow herself enjoyment. The male terminated treatment, at the point of emergence of anxiety-provoking homosexual fantasies. He was still functional sexually, but the penile anaesthesia remained.

Chronic low libido, in the few males seen has been very difficult to treat. It is generally a life long problem originally manifesting itself in adolescence and even preadolescence. These patients do not masturbate, or they masturbate infrequently. They date but unconsciously avoid sexual contact. They offer a variety of excuses, such as religion, to explain the absence of sexual activity, but none of these stand up to critical scrutiny. If after marriage the sexual avoidance continues, this can lead to the dissolution of the marriage. There has not been enough experience in treating psychogenic dyspareunia in the male to even attempt to prognosticate.

Physiological Complicated. If damage to the sacral nerve plexus has been determined, the goal of treatment is different. One changes from achieving a cure to using other techniques and ways of obtaining sexual satisfaction. Some diabetics seem to fall into a psychophysiological threshold phenomenon in which reversal is possible, if the nerve damage is not too extensive, and the accompanying psychological problems are not too severe.

TYPE OF TREATMENT AS RELATED TO PROGNOSIS

Masters and Johnson Treatment

In 1959 a clinical program for the treatment of sexual dysfunction was initiated by Masters and Johnson at the Washington University School of Medicine, St. Louis. In 1964 this program was enlarged and transferred to the Reproductive Biology Research Foundation (RBRF). The behaviorally oriented therapeutic technique developed there resulted in the effective treatment of more than 80% of patients with sexual inadequacy (Masters and Johnson, 1970). The basic premise underlying this therapeutic technique is that both partners must be involved when there is sexual dysfunction. Therefore, the marital unit *per se* is treated, even if only one spouse appears to be sexually dysfunctional. There are 4 major features of the treatment program: (1) it is specifically oriented towards sexual dysfunction; (2) it uses both a male and female therapist; (3) both partners are involved in treatment; and (4) the marital unit is usually on "vacation."

The rapid treatment technique developed by Masters and Johnson lasts for 2 to 3 weeks, for 12 to 20 sessions. It is primarily an intensive behavioral and interpretive form of treatment oriented toward the alleviation of sexual symptoms in couples. In various facilities throughout the country, modifications of this technique are now being used, but we will have to wait for careful studies and follow-ups to evaluate them.

Hypnosis

Hypnosis is one of the oldest treatments for sexual disorders (Schrenck-Notzing, 1888; Bernheim and associates, 1892; Bertschinger and associates, 1899). However, it also is currently being reevaluated (Beigel, 1971; Levitt, 1971; Mirowitz, 1966; Schneck, 1970).

There are two types: a deep trance where the conscious mind does not function but the subject obeys commands; and a superficial, where the conscious mind continues to function but is suggestible to the commands of the hypnotherapist.

Hypnosis has limitations because a large segment of the population cannot be hypnotized. Further, one has to be extremely careful in evaluating the past and current history. Patients with a past history of schizophrenia or severe depressive illnesses are automatically eliminated as are patients with suicidal ideation and borderline schizophrenics. Although the expected success and failure rates have been seen, in our early program there have been some totally unexpected results.

Mrs. A., a primarily anorgastic female, was hypnotized and taught to put herself into a trance while remaining conscious, eliminating all sexual anxiety. After hypnosis, she returned home to an eager husband. That evening she prepared herself for bed, induced the trance, and fell asleep without having had intercourse. However, she had six sexual dreams that night accompanied by orgasm.

Mr. B., suffering from premature ejaculation, went through the same treatment. A week later his premature ejaculation had become less severe, but he had also given up smoking. Smoking was not mentioned during his session with the hypnotist. In essence, hypnosis can probably be used, but it has many limitations. It is probably most effective in the hysterical conversion symptoms, *i.e.*, vaginismus and dyspareunia, and it is less effective in those patients whose sexual problem is more psychophysiological and involves the autonomic nervous system.

Leckie, a gynecologist using hypnosis to treat sexual dysfunction, reported a complete improvement of roughly 80% of 82 females. However, more than 18% (2 vaginismus and 6 anorgasmia) of these patients required additional "deeper therapy or special techniques." This brings the cure rate through the use of hypnosis alone down to 62% rather than the reported 80%.

We have experimented with hypnosis. The population studied has been so small that it does not allow us to present any real statistics, but there are some observations worth making. Some of the hypnotic subjects were definitely cured, others partially so, and in others, the symptoms remained. However, the patients universally reported a decrease in anxiety not only about their sexual activity but in all areas of their lives. Our initial experience, though not particularly impressive, may produce future results if the hypnotic treatment is combined with a more sexually educative program. Hypnosis has adherents who see it as *the* treatment for sexual disorders; others discard it entirely. However, it probably will establish itself as one of the forms of sexual treatment.

Behavioral Therapy

In recent years, behavioral therapy or modification has become a major influence in psychiatry in this country and the United Kingdom (Benkert, Crombach, and Kockott, 1972; Beumont, Bancroft, Bearwood, and Russell, 1972; Ince, 1973; Cooper, 1969, 1970; Jain, 1969; Friedman, 1972). It does not delve into childhood traumas or the unconscious. Primarily, it focuses directly on the presenting symptom. The reports in the literature on treating sexual problems present a method called systematic desensitization rather than aversion therapy. Densensitization replaces the complex determined symptom with more adaptive resources and behavior patterns. Aversion therapy, on the other hand, sets up punishment patterns for what is considered pathological behavior and has not been used in the treatment of heterosexual dysfunction.

Behavioral therapy has many advantages. It is inexpensive and of short duration; it does not involve much of the therapist's time, therefore allowing the behavioral therapist to see larger numbers of people. By contrast, the other therapies, except for hypnosis, involve extensive time on the part of the therapist and a relatively large expense to the patient. Generally, patients with partners who refuse short term therapy are referred for behavioral therapy. In behavioral therapy, diagnosis is less important than in the other treatment methods. Since it is the philosophy of sexual therapy that in one way or another both partners are involved, it is wise to pay attention to the nonsymptomatic partner. This is the major disadvantage of behavioral therapy, because the nonsymptomatic partner can readily sabotage the gains established in treatment. In behavioral therapy as reported in the literature, this is rarely dealt with, and therefore, it is a formidable problem that may result in recurrence of the symptom if left untouched.

Jones and Park (1972) saw 81 couples who complained of single partner sexual dysfunction. They were treated by systematic desensitization until the symptoms were removed or for at least 20 half-hour therapy sessions. Seventy-seven couples remained in treatment. Forty-five of 55 female patients previously partially or totally anorgastic were relieved of symptoms. Six females were partially improved. Six of 7 partially impotent males were restored to coital competence.

Cooper (1970) reported on the outpatient treatment of 44 males with a primary psychogenic complaint of impotence. Therapy was limited but included, when possible, active participation by the partner as well as the patient. Treatment criterion was a minimum of 20 sessions in 1 year. Therapeutic results were discouraging; only 43% improved, and 57% remained unchanged or became worse. However, others report a much higher improvement rate.

Of all the new therapies, it is our experience that behavioral therapy combined with some of the techniques developed by Masters and Johnson is the most promising for the future. Although the results fall somewhat short of those already established by Masters and Johnson, there is the possibility that the various aspects of this form of therapy can be incorporated into the currently existing form of Masters and Johnson treatment. Actually, our success rate with behavioral therapy with a small sample of 40 patients is far ahead of the other forms of treatment used at our institution (Albert, 1974). The problem with behavioral therapy as we see it is that there are too many different techniques and none specifically oriented toward the treatment of sexual disorders. Our hope is to develop a program that is specifically oriented toward both the sexual symptom of the patient and the partner.

Group Therapy

There are very few reports in this literature on group therapy although many group therapists report cures of individual patients (Reckless, Hawkins and Fauntlerd, 1973). Lesnenko

(1967) treating three groups of "impotent and frigid" patients classified them as (1) personality disorder associated with anxiety, "fear of intercourse and masturbation;" (2) having a history of traumatic experience; and (3) neurasthenics. He found a group therapeutic approach to be most successful for decreasing anxiety and increasing "strength of character." He also emphasized the need for rest, relaxation, and vacation. The "neurasthenic" group was most difficult to treat and required drug therapy. His results were as follows: of 300 patients treated in group therapy, 76% were reported as cured, and 10% improved, and 14% were unimproved. He concluded that symptomatology tends to disappear more quickly in group therapy and also leads to more frequent recovery. His basic therapeutic premise presupposed that reassurance and removal of fears would result in cure. The conclusions of this study and the high success rate are quite remarkable and somewhat unusual when compared to other studies. However, his data collection and presentation left much to be desired.

An innovation by Barbach (1975) is the treatment of female groups by a female therapist. Her initial results are encourageing, 93% cure in an average of 10 sessions. The New York Medical College is currently repeating this work and reports excellent results (O'Connor, 1975).

Psychoanalysis and Psychotherapy

Psychotherapy is done by a trained professional establishing a therapeutic relationship with a patient through which he is able to develop varying degrees of insight. The patient is generally seen 1 to 3 times per week. Psychotherapy is used to remove, modify, or change symptoms; to mediate disturbed patterns of behavior; and to promote positive personality growth and development.

Psychoanalysis and psychotherapy have been and still continue to be the major treatment for sexual disorders. The shorter methods are unavailable throughout most of the country, so that these problems are being dealt with by psychotherapy. The results of analysis are quite good, but it is long term, expensive, and not oriented toward specific symptoms but rather toward basic changes in the characterological structure of the individual.

Psychoanalysis is probably the most intensive form of psychotherapy. Seventy-seven percent were improved but less than 60% were totally cured. Both the Lesnenko study in Russia and our study at Columbia reported an improvement and rate of less than 46% and a cure rate of less than 50% in psychotherapy.

Our most impressive cure to date was a male who during 16 years of marriage was totally impotent being seen in intensive analysis and during this period also entered the short term treatment program. The personality change, change in dream material, and change in the marital relationship were striking. What appeared to be an extremely long analysis may now be terminated within the year. This was a striking result of the combination of two forms of treatment. During the course of sexual therapy, the patient did not see the analyst. At the termination of the rapid treatment, the patient was referred back to the original psychoanalyst.

Of the patients seen in our rapid treatment program the group which falls into the initial failure rate are referred to psychotherapy or behavioral therapy. In our experience, most of these patients have done rather well. We do not view any treatment techniques as mutually exclusive but rather all are adjunctive one to the other. This feeling is becoming increasingly accepted (Marmor, 1971). Figure 4.1 presents a summary of the results from various forms of treatment.

Generally surprising are the relatively poor outcomes produced by psychotheraphy and superficial therapy. However, the effects of the Masters and Johnson method, psychoanalysis, and group therapy are most impressive. Behavior therapy and hypnosis, within the limitations already discussed, also seem to be quite effective.

While there has been no well done statistical validation of any method of treatment of sexual dysfunction, empirically it can be seen from the aforementioned results that these treatments do seem to be effective initially. The long term results are not yet known. It is clear that progress is being made in the field of sexual therapy, but unless validation and long term follow-up studies are done, it will detract from the currently successful rate of improvement. At Columbia, for example, we have had great success at the end of the 2-week rapid treatment program. However, some of these apparent successes have reverted soon thereafter, while some of the apparent failures have, on follow-up, achieved sexual adequacy. As the permanency of the results in all forms of sexual therapy remains in doubt, additional studies of the various techniques will be required. Definition of symptoms and definitions of cure, improvement, etc. are needed, as is good repeatable statistical validation.

This chapter is primarily a review of psychological forms of treatment, but there has been so much material on hormonal and surgical treatment that some mention should be made. None of the hormonal studies really prove that any of these techniques do help to improve the sexual life of a couple. The results of silicone implantation (Arthaud, 1973; Morales and associates, 1973; Suarez and Delgado, 1973; Pearman, 1972) in the male penis remain to be evaluated with more sophisticated studies on larger series. The surgical treatment of vaginal or labial damage certainly is effective; these procedures can be enhanced by psychological counseling including partner participation.

The use of hormones, although extremely common, has not been shown to be effective (Benkert and associates, 1972; Beaumont and associates, 1972; Cooper, 1972; Meyer, 1974; Margolis and associates, 1971). It is known that testosterone administered to the female will increase her sexual drive and desire. In fact it can be a problem in the mastectomy patient (Prudden, 1974). Obviously testosterone could stimulate the low libido female but that includes the danger of permanent changes, *i.e.*, hirsutism and deepened voice.

The one area where hormones do appear to be effective is where there is a genetic or acquired hormonal deficiency (Nash, 1970; O'Connor, 1973). In such cases there is a rationale for their use. There is much work to be done in humans to further understand the neurohormonal sexual interaction.

REFERENCES

Albert, H. 1974. Personal communication.

Arthaud, J. B. 1973. Silicone-induced penile sclerosing lipogranuloma. J. Urol., 110: 210.

Bailey, B. R. 1973. Studies in depression: II. Treatment of the depressed, frigid woman. Med. J. Aust., I: 834.

Barbach, L. G. 1975. *For Yourself*. Doubleday, New York

Beigel, H. G. 1971. The hypnotherapeutic approach to male impotence. J. Sex Res., 7: 168.

Benkert, O., Crombach, G., and Kockott, C. 1972. Effect of L-Dopa on sexually impotent patients. Psychopharmacologia, 23: 91.

Bernheim *et al.* 1892, 1893. Zeitschrift Fur Hypnotismus-Suggestionsherapie, Suggestionslehre und verwandte psychologische Forschungen. Verlag von Hermann Brieger. I Jahrgang, Berlin.

Bertschinger, Z. *et al.* 1899. Zeitschrift Fur Hypnotismus-Psychophysiologische und Psychopathologische Forschungen Verland von Johann Ambrosius Barth, Leipzig.

Beaumont, P. J., Bancroft, J. H., Bearwood, C. J., and Russell, G. F. 1972. Behavioral changes after treatment with testosterone: case report. Psychol. Med. 2: 70.

Blair, M., and Pasmore, J. 1964. Frigid wives: a clinical classification. Proc. 6th Int. Congr. Psychother, 4: 1.

Burnap, D. W., and Golden, J. S. 1967. Sexual problems in medical practice. J. Med. Educ., 42: 673.

Cooper, A. J. 1972. Diagnosis and management of "Endocrine Impotence". Br. Med. J., 2: 34.

Cooper, A. J. 1970. Frigidity, treatment and short-term prognosis. J. Psychosom. Res., 14: 133.

Cooper, A. J. 1969. Guide to the practical management and prognosis of frigidity in general practice. Practitioner, 203: 677.

Cooper, A. J. 1970. Guide to treatment and short-term prognosis of male potency disorders in hospital and general practice. Br. Med. J., 1: 157.

Cooper, A. J. 1969. Outpatient treatment of impotence. J. Nerv. Ment. Dis., 149: 360.

Cooper, A. J., Ismail, A. A., Harding, T., and Love, D. N. 1972. The effects of clomiphene in impotence. A clinical and endocrine study. Br. J. Psychiatry, 120: 327.

Cooper, A. J., and Ismail, A. A. 1972. A pilot study of mesterolone in impotence. Psychopharmacologia, 26: 379.

Daly, M. J. 1972. The physician's role in human sexuality of the future. South. Med. J., 65: 1475.

Continuous Time-Limited Treatment of Standard Sexual Disorders

LEON ZUSSMAN, M.D. and SHIRLEY ZUSSMAN, Ed.D.

FIVE

Since 1970, when Masters and Johnson published their monumental contribution to the treatment of sexual dysfunction (Masters and Johnson, 1970), there has been an enormous increase in the demand for such treatment. In the attempt to meet this demand, many therapists and clinics have offered what is described as the Masters and Johnson technique to alleviate sexual distress. One of the major modifications of the rapid treatment method described by Masters and Johnson is in the direction of the distribution or spacing of appointments. Their method consisted of daily therapeutic sessions over a 2-week period, involving the couples living away from home and immersing themselves completely in the therapy experience.

In 1971, the Human Sexuality Center of Long Island Jewish-Hillside Medical Center opened the first community-based hospital program for the treatment of sexual problems. To meet the needs of the people living in the community who could not leave their families and employment, it was not required that couples seeking treatment live away from home. Although treatment remained on a time-limited basis (15 sessions plus 3 follow-up visits), weekly, rather than daily appointments were offered. In this way, it was felt a wider segment of the community could be reached and therapy could be integrated into the framework of the couple's everday lives.

At the same time, therapy on a continuous time basis was offered to serve the needs of those outside of the geographical area, to meet special needs as outlined below, and to offer an opportunity to compare the efficacy of the two methods of time distribution. In the following discussion, the emphasis is on the continuous time method although experience has indicated that the underlying principles of treatment do not differ significantly. The scope of the

paper is general, and its intention is to serve as a guide for office counseling and as an outline for those wishing to pursue further study in the field of sex therapy.

THE BASIC FORMAT

1. The treatment of the couple (conjoint therapy).
2. By a couple (dual sex team).
3. Based on a knowledge of normal sexual functioning.
4. In a continuous time-limited psychotherapy framework.
5. Including a conjoint physical examination.

While the first four techniques were made popular by Masters and Johnson (1970), the last technique is an addition which facilitates the affective learning, the communication, and the interpersonal relationship of the couple. The dynamics and rationale of all the five techniques will be discussed.

1. The Treatment of a Couple

Basic to the rapid treatment approach for sexual dysfunction developed by Masters and Johnson (1970) is the concept that sexual functioning develops within the context of a relationship and is influenced and largely determined by that relationship. Therefore, to treat a sexual dysfunction, both partners need to be involved in the treatment. Actually, it has been our experience that in 50% of all couples seen both at Long Island Jewish-Hillside Medical Center and in the private practice of the authors, both partners have a sexual dysfunction. In the other 50%, the partner is indirectly involved in the sexual dysfunction through lack of knowledge and understanding. Therefore, the mutual responsibility of both partners is emphasized as a factor in the perpetuation or solution of the sexual distress. The focus of therapy throughout is not on the sexual symptom but on the interaction between the two partners in their sexual behavior, and in other areas of their living and relating, and on what the possibilities are for change and growth. The very fact that so many couples apply with the expressed statement that "something must be done" acts as a positive force in many instances. "The crises of life, precipitated by temporarily insoluble problems, are way stations at each of which there is the opportunity for learning new problem solving skills" (Caplan, 1961).

From the very first telephone call, the expectation that both partners need to be involved opens up the channels of communication about their sexual lives, which may represent the first discussion the couple has ever had about this area of their lives. The mutual decision-making process that results in the joint application for treatment is a first step toward the couple's recognition of mutual involvement in the problem and their need to make a mutual investment in its solution. The groundwork for the conjoint therapeutic experience is laid therefore before the first appointment takes place.

Rationale for Conjoint Therapy. Unless both partners are involved in therapy, the part each one plays in the sexual distress often remains unknown both to the patient and to the therapists and, therefore, it cannot be treated. For example, a male with erectile difficulty, whose marriage has not been consummated, would have considerable difficulty in reversing his dysfunction if it were unknown that his wife had vaginismus and her condition remained unchanged. The ignorance, the inhibitions and restrictions, the hurts and fears of each partner, the barriers to communication both in and out of bed, are also unavailable to therapeutic intervention unless both partners are seen together. Seeing the couple together also serves to reduce the distortions that each person tends to present, both consciously and unconsciously.

At each session, specific suggestions are made to be carried out at home, which serve many purposes, such as enjoying new experiences, improving communication, both verbally and nonverbally, and exploring problem areas. These suggestions are carried out in the privacy of the couple's home or hotel and reported on in subsequent sessions. Unless both partners are present to understand their role in these specific tasks, the suggestions could be interpreted by the absent partner as a demand or imposition; this could thus create additional distress.

"Conjoint therapy also serves to use the marital relationship and the influence of each of the partners upon each other as a therapeutic agent. Whatever the problems each one brings and weak as the marriage may be, the relationship has strengths and assets of its own, apart from the assets of the individuals of which it is composed. The therapeutic couple can make use of the positive forces in order to search for and to eradicate the negative or destructive elements which are at the root of their difficulties" (Reding and Ennis, 1964). It is the use of these positive forces that contributes to the success of the rapid method of the treatment of sexual dysfunction.

2. The Treatment by a Couple (Dual Sex Team).

Four-way interviewing is the method of choice in the treatment of sexual dysfunction as it provides equal representation and interpretation for both sexes. The role of each therapist is to identify with and support, or challenge the marital partner of the same sex, for both members of the marital pair. The four-way interview also serves to give a more accurate picture of the interaction between two partners owing to the fact that each therapist's view is constantly compared with his (or her) colleague's.

Dual sex team therapy seems to reduce the need on the part of the partners to compete, overwhelm, seduce, or withdraw from the situation. This sometimes occurs when one therapist is seeing the couple, and each partner vies for the attention of the one available person. When transference reactions do appear, they usually can be handled in a nonverbal way, such as lessened activity on the part of the object of the transference reaction, or even withdrawal for 1 or 2 sessions. Transference reactions are not usually dealt with directly in sex therapy because the goal is to intensify the relationship between the patient couple, in contrast to individual therapy, where transference reactions between patient and therapist are used in the service of the treatment.

An important therapeutic function of the dual sex team is to serve as a model of identification for the patient couple in such a way that the therapy couple communicates with each other and works together as a unit. The male and female figures also serve as models in the degree to which they accept each other as equals and in the value they put on their own as well as their partner's sexuality. Where this has not been true in the parental background of each or both of the partners, this new model can often serve as a corrective emotional identification.

The attitudes and emotions, both conscious and unconscious, experienced by the therapists in working in the dual sex team mode cannot be ignored. If the therapist is active and directive as in sex therapy, the more likelihood there is that his own personality will affect the treatment process and countertransference feelings will interfere with the effectiveness of therapy. The observations of a cotherapist, following the sessions, are extremely helpful in pointing out countertransference feelings. The dual therapy method also serves as a learning process for both therapists, both during training and in ongoing treatment. The contributions of two therapists from different backgrounds can also serve to enrich the treatment considerably.

For some, working with another therapist is experienced as a threat because their therapeutic efforts are under constant appraisal. For others, competitive strivings tend to interfere on a professional basis, on a male-female dimension, and in relation to the way in which various disciplines are valued in society, *e.g.*, medicine versus nursing, social work versus psychology. To assume that two people can work together merely because they have the proper professional credentials is erroneous, and how a team is put together must be carefully evaluated. Because physiological factors plus frequent requests for information about bodily functioning play an important role in sex therapy, it is considered valuable that one member of the team be a physician and that the other be trained in the behavioral sciences. It can be counterproductive to the success of the treatment if there is not sufficient trust and comfort in the relationship between the therapists.

3. Treatment Is Based on a Knowledge of Normal Sexual Functioning

Prior to Masters and Johnson's physiological research, (1966), most therapy and indeed most theory was based on the study of individuals with sexual problems. The studies of Masters and Johnson, however, focused on the response patterns of sexually functional subjects. Some of the results of this research have exploded myths, corrected misconceptions, and established sexual functioning as a normal, natural physiological process, which is present in infancy and evolves throughout the lifetime of the individual as one aspect of his or her total existence, similar to other physiological functions, like breathing or digestion. The sexual function is unique, however, in that it can be deferred, denied, and is strongly influenced by culture and mores, and for its fullest enjoyment it involves another human being.

Thorough knowledge of the anatomy and physiology of normal sexual functioning needs to be part of the armamentarium of any therapist who deals with sexual problems. Knowledge of some of the more general findings about sexuality is essential in helping patients correct misconceptions and fallacies that interfere with natural sexual response.

For example, the Masters and Johnson research established that orgasms in men and women are physiologically similar and are a total body response for both sexes. The only variables other than the ejaculation of the male are the female's greater capacity for responsiveness because she has no refractory period, as compared to the male, leading to her capacity for multiple orgasm.

The refractory period is a period after ejaculation during which a male is unresponsive to further sexual stimuli. His ability to respond again varies with age and other factors unique to the individual. In the teenager it may be a few minutes, while 5 to 10 years later it may be 15 to 25 min or more. On the other hand, a female has no refractory period and can respond after cessation of stimuli at any point of the cycle or after the cycle ends, provided she is interested and has a willing and able partner. This information can be of considerable value to the couple who has not been aware of this difference.

Masters and Johnson's research also has established that there is no coital position in which the clitoris is directly stimulated by the penis, but it is continually stimulated during coitus by penile thrusting and traction on the labia minora, even though the erection and engorgement of the clitoris cause it to retract into the swollen clitoral hood. Ignorance of these facts often serve as a deterrent to enjoyable sexual interaction.

Another misconception is that the male is inherently active and the female is inherently passive. Actually, there are passive and active aspects in the sexual behavior of each sex, but cultural forces have encouraged the male to play an aggressive role and the female a submissive one. Anthropological evidence shows a wide variation in these cultural sterotypes.

The research of Masters and Johnson has also established that from a biological point of view, clitoral and vaginal orgasms are not separate, although subjectively they may be experienced in very different ways by different women or the same women at different times. The explosion of this myth encourages stimulation by hand, mouth or the partner's genitals, depending on the preferences of the particular couple (Saltzman, 1967).

4. Time-Limited Therapy

The choice of a 2-week period is based chiefly on the experience that most couples can be helped to reverse sexual dysfunction in that time, and some positive change in the marital relationship can be effected. For those outside the geographical area, a period longer than 2 weeks away from home and employment may be difficult. In our program, couples are not seen over the weekends affording an opportunity for both patients and therapists to acquire some emotional distance from the intense therapeutic experience.

In undertaking psychotherapy in which time is so limited, the therapist must begin with a sense of optimism about his ability to be of help in so short a time, as well as the patient's capacity to profit from it. Surely, optimism is a form of suggestion since it is communicated very quickly to the patient (Mann, 1973). In the particular case of sex therapy, such suggestion has also been strongly communicated by the media so that an expectation of magical results often needs to be dealt with.

The specificity of the duration of treatment seems to help the patients confront the reality of the work to be done and tends to reduce the magic wishes and expectations that somehow things will change without too much effort on their part. Although anxiety about the termination often develops around the 8th or 9th session, this often serves as a thrust towards resolution of the problem.

Indications for Continuous Method.

1. For couples who come from outside of the geographical area.
2. For couples who are under extraordinary pressure and must take time off from work, family, and social obligations in order for therapy to succeed.
3. For couples in which one or both partners seem to have a low level of libidinal interest and long intervals between sessions diminish sexual interest.
4. Where the marital relationship is in a state of crisis.

Advantages of Continuous Time-Limited Therapy. When the couple is seen on a daily basis, particularly if there is social isolation from family and work, there is the possibility of total immersion in the therapy process and in commitment to each other on an intensive basis.

If difficulties arise, they can be dealt with promptly, so that problems are not compounded and discouragement does not prevent the couple from moving ahead. There can be more active movement into behavioral changes.

The buildup of sexual tension can be used in the service of the treatment, a buildup which is sometimes dissipated when there are long intervals between sessions and many interfering elements in the life situation of the partners.

Disadvantages of Continuous Time-Limited Therapy. People learn at different rates, and behavioral changes may come about quickly to please the partner or the authoritative figures of the therapists, but the behavior may not be truly integrated into the total functioning of the person involved. Such changes are not stable. For patients whose tempo feels pressured by such an intensive program, a slower pace may be preferable. Others may fear that the pressure of a time limitation will intensify their fear of failure.

> *Case 1:* A 38-year-old male, with primary impotence, whose marriage had not been consummated, expressed fear of the 2-week continuous program, because he felt it put further pressure on him to perform. His wife, a virgin, with severe vaginismus, agreed with him. The couple were seen on a weekly basis and consummated the marriage at the end of 24 sessions.

Where couples are seen on the continuous basis, in social isolation, they often experience what can be termed a "re-entry phenomenon" when they return to their everyday lives. This manifests itself often in depression, concern about maintaining gains, and a feeling of loss and anxiety in relation to separation from the therapists. If geographically available, this can often be dealt with by a few additional sessions. Telephone communication can also be valuable if the couple cannot return to the area.

At Long Island Jewish-Hillside Medical Center, both continuous and intermittent time-limited therapy are available. The method chosen is based on the geographical residence, the needs of the particular couple, and the therapy time available. On the basis of initial clinical assessment, both methods seem to have the same degree of success and the number of sessions required to bring about change is almost identical, whether concentrated into a 2-week period or spread over a period of 3 months. Research is planned to devise more accurate methods of selecting the most effective method for a particular couple and to compare treatment results of the two methods. More important than whether treatment is done on a continuous or intermittent time basis seems to be the availability for further therapeutic intervention in the event that problems develop after treatment ends.

An analysis of 200 couples who completed treatment at the Human Sexuality Center between 1971 and 1973 shows that 77.7% demonstrated both reversal of sexual distress and improvement in their relationship. A 3-month follow-up indicated that 37% of the improved couples had regressed in varying degrees, to their previous state and needed additional therapy sessions. With additional sessions, some were able to move in a positive direction again, and 6-month and 1-year follow-up data so far indicate that the percentage of couples showing reversal of sexual distress and improvement in marital interaction stabilizes around 68% (Schumacher, 1974).

The Conjoint Physical Examination

An important part of our treatment of sexual dysfunction is described in detail in Session 4 below.

SELECTION OF PATIENTS

At the Long Island Jewish-Hillside Medical Center, an open-door policy has been followed in relation to patient selection. A majority of patients who were accepted for treatment in the first 2 years of the program were self-referred. The only contraindications were acute psychosis, severe depression, and either physical or psychological pathology severe enough to make adherence to the program impossible. In general, it has been our policy to accept all couples who have sufficient motivation to work jointly on the sexual problems disturbing to them. Included in our population have been patients with diabetic impotency, strokes. Peyronies disease, postmyocardial infarction, cancer, schizophrenia, mental retardation, and alcoholism.

Although a good marital relationship appears to be a contributing factor to successful treatment of sexual dysfunction, some couples with marriages in immediate or long time crisis have made significant progress, both in improvement in their relationship and in reversal of sexual dysfunction. Although a couple would not be rejected because of the deteriorated quality of their relationship, it is often necessary to work primarily with the marital relationship before sex therapy can be initiated.

THE TREATMENT AGREEMENT

Most requests for information about the sex therapy program originate with a telephone call. An attempt is made to answer questions raised, and it is often helpful to the inquirer if a brochure describing the program is sent. A short application form is also forwarded, requesting identifying data, some biographical material, and a short description of the problem from the point of view of each partner. About 1 in 7 couples who receive applications return them, indicating their wish to be scheduled for therapy.

If desired, a couple is offered an initial appointment, at which time they are interviewed together by a male and female therapy team for the 2-fold purpose of clarifying the dual nature of the distress and describing the therapy program.

Occasionally, one member of the marital pair is seen alone by a male and female therapy team to offer help in involving the other member of the pair. In a situation, for example, where the male complaint is secondary impotence, he may feel it is solely his problem, and he hesitates to involve his partner, since "it's not her fault." The presence of the female therapist, her understanding of the female's contribution to the problem, and her knowledge of what the female can do to help solve the problem may make it possible for the male to open up a channel of communication with his partner paving the way for her involvement in therapy, or even helping toward solution of the problem without further help.

When a couple decides to go ahead with treatment, an initial payment is required to confirm a schedule of appointments. Since the program of therapy is planned on a sequential basis, it is deemed advisable for the couple to pay a total fee rather than pay for individual appointments. This gives them an opportunity to commit themselves to the program as a total unit and avoids using the possibility of terminating therapy either in the service of resistance or as a threat between the couple. At any time, however, they can withdraw from the program without any obligation for the full fee.

The total fee includes all laboratory work, physical examinations, psychological testing, therapy sessions, and 3 follow-up sessions. If the couple lives in the community, the follow-up sessions are in person, at 3-month, 6-month and 1-year intervals. Those living outside the geographical area are encouraged to return for follow-up sessions. If this is not possible, telephone contact is maintained, as needed, on an individual basis.

BASIC GOALS OF SEX THERAPY

1. To reverse the specific sexual dysfunction for which the couple comes to therapy and to enhance and enrich the couple's sexual relationship within the framework of the basic therapy concepts.
2. To improve the marital relationship of the couple, chiefly in relation to improving their communication, so that they have a more effective way of understanding and relating to each other.
3. To improve each partner's individual functioning on an intrapsychic as well as an interpersonal basis.

SOME PRINCIPLES OF TREATMENT

The treatment of specific disorders differs in respect to the particular dysfunction and the particular couple being treated. However, certain principles underly the treatment of all dysfunctions and will be briefly described. The basic therapeutic task is to remove the impediments that interfere with the natural sexual functioning, rather than merely teach techniques. Since sexual activity is viewed as a form of communication or personal interaction, attention to the marital interaction is the primary focus. The individual requirements of each partner are honored and supported by the same-sex therapist but only within the context of the marital relationship. If these requirements are seen as needing additional attention or are too disruptive to the marital relationship, appropriate referrals are arranged.

Specific suggestions are made for improving communication, such as the encouragement of self-representation both at home and in the therapy sessions. It is repeatedly stressed that concepts of blame, withdrawal, and attack must be discarded, if therapeutic results are to be obtained.

Another concept underlying all treatment, regardless of the specific distress, is the view that sexuality represents a broad panorama of experience, including touching, stroking, kissing, looking, tasting, smelling, and feeling, with the possibility that all experiences can be equally pleasurable and meaningful in themselves. This viewpoint is in marked contrast to the culturally dominant view of sexual interaction as only important if it ends in orgasmic experience. The couple's integration of the concept of sexuality as a panorama reduces the demand each one has for himself and his partner for orgasmic expression and makes possible the enjoyment of each experience in and of itself. Such enjoyment reduces anxiety about performance and plays a major role in alleviating dysfunction. It is extremely important that the therapists share this view of sexuality; otherwise, their emphasis on the importance of goal-oriented release can seriously interfere with the resolution of difficulties. The importance of dual sex team therapy is seen as transmitting healthy attitudes about sexuality as well as correcting sex-biased attitudes about orgasmic expression for both the same sex and other sex partner. Since many therapists are male, the inclusion of a female on the team seems one effective way of helping females with healthy attitudes about their sexuality.

Some other basic concepts that are inherent in the therapeutic philosophy follow:

1. Each person is responsible for his or her own sexuality. Our culture has implanted the idea that the male is the sexual expert, the guide, the one with the knowledge and experience to instruct his partner in the art of love. He often feels this as a responsibility and blames himself for his wife's lack of response or failure to enjoy sexual play. The female tends to go along with this cultural directive and also tends to blame the male if she is unresponsive. Although it is generally accepted that a partner brings to a marriage a life history of personality development and experience, it is less generally accepted that a female as well as a male has a long history of psychosexual development and experience which she brings to the relationship.

2. Sex needs to be given a higher priority in the context of a relationship. Despite the fact that the society gives sex a high priority for commercial purposes and the media saturates the public with sexual stimuli, sexual activity between two marital partners is not honored as a planned activity, for which time is set aside at peaks of physiological functioning. Rather, it often takes place at periods of physical and emotional fatigue, when all other tasks have been completed.

PROTOCOL

Session 1

On the 1st day, the couple is seen together by the male-female team to explore the nature of the presenting distress, explain procedures, answer questions raised by the couple, and evaluate the suitability of the couple for treatment, although as described above, there are few instances where the couple would be rejected. This session serves to underline the concept that there is no such thing as an uninvolved partner in a sexual dysfunction and is usually the couple's first oportunity to experience the dual sex team approach. On this same day, each partner of the couple is given a battery of psychological tests, including the Minnesota Multiphasic Personality Inventory (MMPI), which is again given at the 3-month and 6-month follow-up visit, as one measure of therapy outcome.

Sessions 2 and 3

The 2nd and 3rd sessions are devoted to seeing the partners individually. The initial history-taking sessions begin with the male therapist seeing the male patient and the female therapist seeing the female patient to encourage rapport with the cotherapist of the same sex. The cross-sex history-taking of the 2nd individual session contributes to further understanding of the marital partner and also gives the cross-sex partner the opportunity to feel that the therapist who will be helping his or her partner understands him as well and may be trusted to help him meet his needs. Questions, such as "What do I need to know about you in order to help your wife?" or "How can I help her meet your needs?", further a feeling of trust and confidence.

The concept of taking a "sex history" reflects the cultural misconception that sex is a separate activity, unrelated to other aspects of a person's past or current experiences, rather than a dimension of one's total personality. The purpose of the two history-taking sessions is to create a climate within which the patient may discuss the life experiences and primary relationships which have shaped his sexual value systems. The individual history-taking sessions not only serve to secure information and to deepen the understanding of each individual, but they also lay the groundwork for a therapeutic alliance.

Session 4

The 4th day is devoted to laboratory tests and the physical examination described below. The laboratory tests include an SMA-12 evaluation, an estimation of 17-ketosteroids, and the 17-hydroxycorticosteroid hormones in the 24-hour urine sample. A 3-hour glucose tolerance test is administered to rule out diabetes in males. This is essential since it is estimated that 59% of the 2 million diabetic males in the U.S. are impotent (Ellenberg, 1972, 1973).

The Conjoint Physical Examination. The "conjoint physical examination" is customarily employed in our treatment of sexual dysfunction. "While the incidence of a physiological etiology of sexual inadequacy is low, there is never any excuse for treating a physiological dysfunction as a psychological inadequacy" (Masters and Johnson, 1970).

It is our contention that the physical examination, in addition to ruling out pathology, can in itself serve a therapeutic purpose, particularly when the conjoint physical examination is employed.

Method. Following the history-taking sessions, the couple is introduced to the concept of the conjoint physical examination. The therapeutic team explains that each member of the marital unit will have a complete physical examination. This will include not only head, heart, lungs, abdomen, and extremities, but also a gynecological examination of the woman. A Papanicolau test and a vaginal smear for estrogen influence are also performed. The examination of the man will include the genitals and prostate. We explain that this examination probably differs from any they have undergone before, since 4 persons will be present in the examination room: the couple and the 2 therapists. Before proceeding with the examination, each partner's reaction to the proposed examination is discussed, and each partner is encouraged to talk about the way he views his body and that of his partner. Sometimes, diagrams and models are used if questions arise, or if it is felt that use of these devices will better prepare the marital unit for the procedure.

When there is resistance, it is usually on the part of the females. Because of cultural conditioning, many females regard their genitals as "dirty" and "secret" and are reluctant, not only to view themselves in this area, but feel their husbands will be "turned off." They are often amazed at their husband's interest and positive reaction to the genital examination.

During the examination, the couple is encouraged to communicate their feelings to each other and to the therapists. The therapists, especially the one not conducting the examination, is alert to the interaction and helps to facilitate communication.

While the woman is being examined, she is given a hand mirror to help her see the anatomical parts being pointed out. If the nonmedical therapist is a female, she stands at the side of the examining table and encourages the patient to look and ask questions. She offers physical support, if necessary, so that the patient is in a comfortable position to view her pelvic anatomy. Very few couples have refused this opportunity, even if already familiar with their anatomy. The husband stands behind the examiner and is encouraged to assist by adjusting the light, handing the vaginal speculum, the gloves, and the cotton applicators to the examiner. The husband is instructed to insert his finger and feel the contraction of the pubococcygeus muscle. The Kegel perineometer is used to measure the strength of the contraction, and if necessary, the woman is given instructions in exercising the muscle to increase her awarness of it or to augment its strength.

Any significant gynecological pathology is discussed at the time. The emphasis of the examination, however, is focused on sex education and on explanation of sexual response, rather than insignificant or potential pathology. For example, we deliberately avoid instructions about self-examination of the breast (so important in another context) but prefer to focus on the pleasure and the changes of the breast in the 4 stages of sexual response. It is more important for the husband to be conscious of the exciting sexual changes while caressing his wife than concerned about finding a breast nodule.

When the man is examined, the woman stands next to the examiner and in a similar manner becomes acquainted with his anatomy.

The role of the nonexamining therapist is most important in encouraging communication and asking questions. As a result, we find that the couple discusses certain matters related to or provoked by the examination and the situation.

The more frequent topics brought up for discussion, in addition to questions about the anatomy of the partner, particularly that of the female, are: (1) feelings about body image; (2) reactions to the presence of the mate and the therapists during the examination; (3) human sexual response; (4) methods of contraception; (5) menopause and estrogen replacement therapy; and (6) the role of culture in shaping attitudes about genitals and sexual feelings.

The conjoint examination serves as an opportunity for each partner in a marital unit to increase knowledge of his own body and the body of his partner. The acquisition of this knowledge is aided by the presence of both partners and both therapists during the examination. This provides a permissive, as well as authoritative atmosphere in which learning can take place most effectively.

To counteract the prohibitions and restrictions in the past history of most patients, there is now the authority of the medical profession, the behavioral sciences, the prestige of the institutional setting (a major medical center), the male and female figures all saying it is all right to know, to learn, to ask, to see, and to touch.

A reaction to the examination is illustrated by the following

Case 2: A couple, in their early 30's, with two children, had been married for 14 years. The wife described herself as nonorgasmic. The marriage was threatened because she refused to have intercourse, except on rare occasions. She never undressed in front of her husband, wore heavy, long sleeved nightgowns to bed and recently had taken to falling alseep fully dressed. Her mother had described sex as bestial and ugly, something you have to do until a certain age, "then you won't have to."

When the physical examination was described to her, she commented, "You must be kidding, I'm not that sophisticated." On the day of the examination she was tense and confided that she had almost decided to call it off (in other words, avoid the dangerous area as she had been warned to do in her earlier life). During the physical, she was extremely interested, asked many questions about her own body and that of her husband, and questioned how she had grown up knowing so little about her own body. (She is a grade school teacher.) Her husband expressed admiration for and interest in her pelvic anatomy, and she kept repeating, "I can't believe this is happening." After the physical, she commented, "I feel easier now, less nervous. I learned about my own body. I never really understood it before. I haven't even been curious about my body. I have covered it up even to myself for many years."

In the next session, she reported that she had undressed in front of her husband for the first time in 14 years. The first time she felt uneasy. It had been easier during the examination. She thought everything had been swept away but it wasn't. She did undress, but she was frightened about the light being on. The next time that didn't bother her. She "undressed easier," and for the first time in their marriage she permitted her husband to touch her vagina.

In the case of certain psychophysiological or physical syndromes affecting sexual functioning, the presence of both partners seems of particular value. In the case of vaginismus, for example, a clinical examination is essential to establish the diagnosis. In treating this condition, Masters and Johnson (1970) pointed out that the initial and most important step is physical demonstration of the vaginal spasm to both partners. This involves careful anatomical explanation, using diagrams and models. Once demonstrated to the satisfaction of both partners, resolution of this form of sexual inadequacy is relatively easy.

The conjoint physical examination facilitates the understanding of other conditions, physical as well as psychological. For example: if dyspareunia is caused by endometriosis or other pathology, such demonstration will convince the couple that the difficulty is not imagined and will lay the ground work for the initiation of specific treatment.

An almost perfect indication for this examination is the unconsummated marriage. The program has had 28 such couples who have been married for years. Some have not seen each other nude. One couple never went to bed without clothes on. Following the physical examination, without exception, the therapeutic process was accelerated.

The physical examination also serves to facilitate the therapeutic alliance, the couple feeling that the therapists know them from a physical point of view, as well as by history.

Session 5—Evaluation Conference

After the history, the physical examination, and the laboratory findings are reviewed by the therapists, they are discussed with the couple in what is referred to as a "round table conference." The use of the words "round table," reflects the basic character of this meeting, *i.e.*, to involve all the participants in a joint discussion. The therapy team reflects back what they have learned from the initial interview, the history-taking sessions, and the physical examination, as well as the laboratory findings. This material is presented to explain its relationship to the present sexual distress. Other contributing factors from the therapists' point of view are discussed, such as myths and misconceptions, failures of communication or fears of failure. The couple is encouraged to add, correct, or modify the material as it is presented. If confidential material has been presented during the history-taking sessions, it is never disclosed without specific permission of the particular individual who has confided this information. Occasionally, a secret acts as a deterrent to therapy, and decision how to deal with this must be made on an individual basis.

To reinforce the alignment of female to female, and male to male, the material about the female is usually presented by the female therapist, the male material by the male. It is conveyed to each partner that the same sex therapist will be "their friend in court." That patients incorporate this is often demonstrated by their feeling of being deserted or abandoned if the same-sex therapist is absent from a session for some reason.

As round table discussion proceeds and each partner becomes aware of the myriad influences that have contributed to their current sexual and marital difficulties, there is a tendency for mutual empathy and understanding to replace anger and recrimination. Communication between the partners begins to develop during this session on a verbal basis, and the partners are encouraged to continue this communication after the session is over. Specific suggestions are made for self-representation, emphasizing the value of "I." "I need comfort; I feel sad or angry," rather than accusing the partner of never offering comfort, or making one angry.

It is recognized that making oneself open and vulnerable in this way entails risks, but it also offers the opportunity for greater intimacy and understanding of each other. During the therapy sessions, a good deal of emphasis is put on self-representation. Specific instructions are also begun in this session for communication on a nonverbal basis, as described below.

Sensate Focus—Exercise 1. The usual first set of instructions, regardless of specific distress, involves the couple in an exercise devised to increase their sensual, *not* sexual awareness. Taking individual differences into consideration, these initial instructions need to be specifically designed. For example, a couple who have not had any physical contact for several months or even years,who do not share the same bed, perhaps not the same room, would need considerable help before touching and caressing. The couple is always asked not to attempt intercourse or to indulge in any other form of sexual activity the day this exercise is suggested. It is explained to them that the intention is not to attempt to arouse the other person, or themselves, but rather to focus on their own sensual awareness as they touch, explore, caress, and look at the other person.

We might say to them:

> "You, Mary, begin this activity. We would like you to set aside some time before you come back tomorrow, when you are both completely undressed, in a lighted room, and feel relaxed and comfortable. Before dinner perhaps, or in the morning. You, John, lie on the bed and just enjoy the experience. Mary, you begin by stroking your partner on his back, then his shoulders, the back of his neck. See how his body feels to your touch, where he feels cool, where he's warm, where he's smooth, where he's hairy. See how these different temperatures feel to your fingers, the palm of your hands. Stroke him with different pressures, different rhythms. Explore his whole body, with the exception of his genitals. Approach him as if this were a totally new experience in learning to know his body. When you've finished, change places and you, John, return the favor, exploring Mary's body with the exception of her breasts and genitals."

The couple is encouraged to make this a nonverbal experience, using body signals for communication. If they like something, they can move into it with their bodies, if something is annoying, they can move away, but on the whole, the receiving partner is encouraged to allow the giving partner to touch and explore as he or she wishes. It is pointed out that this exercise is devised for the toucher, to learn that by giving pleasure, he experiences it in his fingers, his hands, his mouth, his senses, and his feelings.

The couple is encouraged to use a body lotion to enhance the tactile experience, as the moisture adds another dimension of sensuality. If they shower or bathe together, they can use soap lather in the same way, to touch, caress and explore each other all over. It is recommended that no intercourse be attempted during exercises 1 and 2.

Sensate Focus—Exercise 2. If the couple has a successful experience with these suggestions, they are extended the next day to include exploration and stimulation of the genitals. The couple is encouraged to teach each other what they like, what rhythm and pressure is preferable, again on a nonverbal basis. To accomplish this it is suggested that they take turns in guiding their partner's hand as each one touches and caresses the other, in a slow, exploratory fashion. In this way, a system of communication is established that is neither critical nor threatening, and it serves not only to increase knowledge and understanding between the partners, but a greater feeling of closeness as well. It is emphasized that the purpose is not sexual excitation, and that there is no other goal but to learn more about themselves and each other. They are advised that if they get aroused, fine; but the purpose of this exercise, again, is not sexual but educational, basic to eliciting sexual arousal. If the stimulation results in sexual arousal of either partner, that partner can be brought to orgasm, if he or she wishes, outside of the vagina, with the hand or mouth. The female is often encouraged to watch the male ejaculate, a phenomenon she may never have permitted herself to observe because of cultural taboos against looking, touching, tasting, or smelling sexual fluids. It might be suggested that the male view his wife's genitals during her sexual arousal, or observe the way the sex flush spreads over her body. Familiarity with each other's sexual responses is often a path to greater feelings of intimacy and openness with each other, as well as being highly erotic for some.

Those who are not familiar with their own bodies are unable to teach their partners what they like, they need, what feels good, or what intensifies their sexual responses. They are encouraged, therefore, to spend time learning about themselves, and specific instructions about masturbation are offered. If it seems appropriate for some, individual sessions are offered for this purpose.

TYPES OF DYSFUNCTION WITH PRINCIPLES OF TREATMENT

Subsequent suggestions for specific sexual activity are related to the individual problems presented by each couple and are individually modified by the quality of the relationship, the resistances manifested, and the particular medical or psychological difficulties inherent in the situation. Each therapy session deals with the reaction to the suggestions made and the experiences the couples have in private in carrying out or resisting these suggestions. For details of treatment, the reader is referred to Masters and Johnson (1970).

The following is a brief description of those dysfunctions most commonly seen and some general principles of treatment.

Dysfunctions in the Male

Erectile Difficulties

1. Primary impotence*: The primarily impotent male is arbitrarily defined as a man who has *never* been able to achieve or maintain an erection sufficient for penetration. Even if erections are adequate, fear or other influences interfere with successful intercourse. Some impotent males have never masturbated and treatment starts with exploring their early conditioning, dealing with inhibitions and restrictions, and giving them "permission" to do what was usually forbidden in early childhood. Basically, the treatment of primary impotence is similar to that of secondary impotence. The involvement of a female partner in treatment is essential.

2. Secondary impotence: A male suffers from secondary impotence when he has a history of successful intercourse, whether there have been one, or many such episodes, but, for various reasons he has reached a point where he cannot obtain an erection sufficient to enter the vagina or loses the erection shortly after penetration. This condition tends to perpetuate itself, since one episode of failure creates sufficient anxiety to set the stage for repeated failures.

The method of treating erectile difficulties is to emphasize to the patient that an erection (as well as all sexual response) is an automatic reflex phenomenon controlled by the autonomic nervous system. No man can will an erection. However, he can create an atmosphere in which he is a participant, not an observer or spectator, so that erections can occur as naturally and involuntarily as breathing. Treatment usually begins with encouraging verbal communication between the partners and dispelling myths and misconceptions that have interfered with their functioning prior to treatment. Often husband and wife have withdrawn from each other when there has been a problem of erectile difficulty, the male because he fears failure and the female because she, too, is fearful about his performance and, indeed, often interprets it as a rejection of her. Sensate focus

*The term, impotence, is avoided in treatment because of its pejorative implications.

without genital stimulation is then introduced as a way of reducing anxiety about performance on the part of both partners. Both are encouraged to focus on their own pleasurable sensations.

Sensate focus with genital stimulation is then encouraged, again without demand for penetration or ejaculation but chiefly to educate each other in what each one likes, since no one is born with the *a priori* knowledge of what another person wants. As the partners touch and stimulate and communicate nonverbally in this sensual way, an erection usually develops. Again, the male is encouraged to concentrate on the sensory stimuli that he is getting from touching and being touched, rather than on whether or not he is getting an erection. It is emphasized that his erection is his wife's concern. As an erection develops from manual or oral stimulation, she is advised to move to other parts of her partner's body and allow the erection to subside, returning again to penile stimulation. This "erect and subside" play is repeated several times and helps to convince the couple that the male can regain an erection, even if it subsides. The attitude that tomorrow is another day reduces anxiety and the humiliation of failure.

At the next session we advise the woman to take the "on top position." Her knees should be at the level of his nipple line, and lower if she is shorter. When an erection occurs, she is to bend forward, at a 45° angle, insert the penis into the vagina and slide down on the penis.

Some men, especially older men, find the "male on top" position more successful. In any case, the principle is the same: the male should concentrate on his pleasurable sensations with little concern about the state of the erection, and the female should regard his penis as her instrument for pleasure, and should insert it into her vagina when it is sufficiently erect and move slowly and undemandingly.

A problem seen with increasing frequency is illustrated by the following example:

> *Case 3:* A hard-driving, successful 60-year-old executive whose wife died 1 year before, after a long illness, came to be treated for secondary impotence. He was accompanied by his new fiancee, with whom he had had several episodes of erectile failure, and as a result he was now afraid to touch her. During the ensuing sessions he came to recognize and work through the inhibitions which developed during the long illness of his wife. During the sensate focus exercise 2, he had successful intercourse, and he was dismayed to hear the therapists were disappointed that he had disobeyed instructions not to attempt intercourse. When it was explained to him that his general pressure to perform was also part of the reason for his sexual dysfunction, he agreed to follow our suggestions more diligently.

The therapy progressed to a successful conclusion with reversal of the erectile difficulty. At the 3-month follow-up, he stated that the most meaningful part of the therapy was the removal of the pressure to perform whenever he approached or caressed his partner.

Ejaculation Difficulties

1. Premature ejaculation: Males contending with rapid ejaculatory response appear to fall within 2 groups. (a) Those whose response occurs so quickly that it precedes intromission on repeated occasions, is felt as seepage rather than expulsion, is sometimes felt as only partial ejaculation, and can be of such short duration that little if any pleasure is experienced. (b) The second group includes males who can effect intromission on most occasions but who are unable to identify a stage between onset of excitation and orgasm and are thus unable to delay final response for their own increased pleasure as well as their partner's satisfaction.

Those in the first group are relatively rare and do not respond well to present methods of treatment. It is chiefly those in the second group that we see clinically and with whom we have a high degree of success in reversing this dysfunction.

A definition of premature ejaculation is given by Masters and Johnson (1970) as the inability of the male to control his ejaculatory process for a sufficiently long time during intercourse to satisfy his partner at least 50% of the time. Where the female partner is nonorgasmic during intercourse for reasons other than the male's rapid ejaculation, this definition is not valid. In addition, it puts too much burden on the male to please his partner, rather than himself. We prefer to define the condition in terms of the male's ability to control his ejaculation for his own pleasure as well as for his partner's satisfaction.

A normal male feels rising sexual tension and reaches a point after erection which can be clearly identified as the point of ejaculatory inevitability. Several seconds after this point is reached, ejaculation will occur, and nothing can be done to inhibit the ejaculation. Treatment consists of helping the male to recognize the stage immediately preceding ejaculatory inevitability and signal his wife to apply pressure to his penis so that the urge to ejaculate disappears. For details of the "squeeze technique," readers are referred to Masters and Johnson (1970). Other therapists have used a "stop and start" method with apparently equal success in the treatment of premature ejaculation (Semans, 1956). The underlying principles of therapy are relatively similar. In both methods a cooperative partner is essential. As with impotence, premature ejaculation cannot be treated presently by the new sex therapy methods in a man without a partner. With a cooperative partner, couples can be assured at the beginning of treatment that the possibility of reversing this dysfunction is very good. Although not essential for the success of the treatment, it is recommended that sensate focus exercises be initiated at the start of therapy to reduce any demand for performance and to establish a feeling of closeness between the partners. The wife needs to be advised that initial focus will be on her husband, but that the resolution of his problem will contribute to her pleasure. In the event that she has a problem of nonorgasm or other dysfunction, the treatment focus will then turn to working on her problem. Both partners are helped to accept the principle that each partner is responsible for his or her own sexuality.

It is usually recommended in treating premature ejaculation that the male be on his back and that the female sit facing him with his legs straddling hers. She stimulates his penis to erection until he signals her that he feels ejaculation is imminent. With her thumb on his frenulum and her first and second fingers on the dorsal surface of his penis (above and below the coronal ridge), she squeezes for about 6 sec. She needs reassurance that the pressure will not hurt him. After the squeeze the male's urge to ejaculate will disappear, and he will lose from 15 to 30% of his erection. The female returns to penile stimulation after a few seconds and again applies the squeeze on her partner's signal. This can be repeated 4 times, at which time he can ejaculate. In this way, a period of 15 to 30 min of sex play may be experienced. This training session can be repeated for several days with the dual purpose of training the male to identify the sensations that occur just prior to ejaculation and for him to train himself to focus on his sensations rather than attempt to distract himself in an attempt to avoid ejaculating. It is suggested that he not concern himself with his partner's reactions at this point of treatment.

After several days, when it has become evident that the male can maintain an erection for some time, intercourse is attempted with the woman on top, her knees at her partner's nipple line, and it is recommended that she slide down on his penis, with minimal thrusting on either part. Again, he is to signal her when he recognizes that he is about to ejaculate, and she can slide off the penis 2 or 3 times and apply pressure. Again, this needs to be practiced until the male develops a feeling of control over his ejaculation. After a while, other positions can be tried, first the lateral, and then male on top.

The continuous time method is very suited to the treatment of premature ejaculation. However, it has been our experience that for the successful result to persist, the couple must continue to apply the "squeeze technique" or the "stop and start" method at regular intervals of time over a period of a year. We do not have sufficient experience to know how long beyond this it should be continued.

2. Ejaculatory incompetence: Ejaculatory incompetence can be divided into 2 groups:

a. Males who ejaculate rarely, if at all, whether through intercourse or with masturbation. Nocturnal emissions also are infrequent in this group.

b. Males who have little difficulty ejaculating with self- or partner manipulation but who cannot ejaculate within the vagina.

Both these categories are relatively rare, although some increase has been noted recently in the second group, and reversal rate is low. The continuous time method may be less suitable for this dysfunction.

Ejaculatory incompetence should not be confused with the normal physiological change which occurs in the older male; intercourse without ejaculatory demand which should be regarded as a normal development of aging by either the male or his female partner.

Ejaculatory incompetence also should not be confused with retrograde ejaculation which occurs when a man ejaculates into the bladder, rather than externally, a condition which follows prostatectomy. Retrograde ejaculation, also, is often an early symptom of diabetic neuropathy. It may occur occasionally in the older male.

The treatment of ejaculatory incompetence follows the initial phase of treatment described above, i.e., nondemanding sensate focus for both partners. When an erection occurs, vigorous manipulation by the female partner of the penis to ejaculation is recommended. This is particularly important for those males who have withdrawn in the past from direct female stimulation of their genitals.

Encouraging ejaculation near the vagina is often a next step, once external ejaculation has been accomplished by female manipulation. Then the female is advised to bring the male to the stage of ejaculatory inevitability by external stimulation and to quickly slide down on the penis while in the female superior position. Even if most of the semen is deposited externally, if the male feels a few drops have been deposited within the vagina, the psychological barrier against intravaginal ejaculation may be weakened.

If ejaculatory incompetence is not reversed, secondary impotence may develop, as it often does if premature ejaculation persists over a long period of time. If this does occur, the erectile difficulty should always be treated before any attempt is made to reverse ejaculatory incompetence or premature ejaculation.

It is generally accepted that the etiology of ejaculatory incompetence is related to psychological causes, such as fear of the vagina (the concept of the vagina dentata), male fear of pregnancy, hostility towards the female, etc. If sex therapy does not succeed in reversing the dysfunction, psychiatric referral should be considered.

The female partner of a male with ejaculatory incompetence often misinterprets his failure to ejaculate as a personal rejection, even though she may have experienced orgasm frequently as the result of the extended intercourse. Communication between the partners must be established before treatment is undertaken. Each stage of treatment may take considerable time, and this dysfunction may require more time than the 2-week period of rapid therapy.

Dysfunctions in the Female

Nonorgasmic Response in Females. Frigidity is a term still frequently used in the popular literature, and it conveys a total lack of bodily response to any stimuli. Since such a condition is almost totally nonexistent and carries a pejorative implication, the term, "nonorgasmic response," is preferred. This diagnostic category can be divided into two parts:

1. Primary orgasmic dysfunction: This condition is defined as follows: a woman has never experienced an orgasm at any time of her life from any form of stimulation, whether it was intercourse, masturbation, oral or manual manipulation, or fantasy alone.
2. Situational nonorgasmic response: Situational nonorgasmic response is defined as a female who has experienced at least one instance of orgasm response, regardless of the manner in which it was induced.

The majority of female patients present with the complaint of primary nonorgasmic response, infrequency of response, or difficulty in achieving an orgasm during intercourse. Many males complain of their inability to bring their wives to orgasm, reflecting the cultural swing from lack of concern with the female response to feeling overly responsible for the quantity and quality of her response. Each partner needs to feel that although he or she can provide opportunity for sexual pleasure, can enhance and share pleasure, each is ultimately responsible only for his or her own sexuality.

Primary nonorgasmic response, unlike most of the other sexual dysfunctions, initially can be approached by treating the female without partner involvement and is usually most successful if dealt with by a female therapist.

Because of cultural conditioning, negative early indoctrination about her female sexuality, religious orthodoxy and its threat of punishment for sexual feelings and thoughts, many women have displaced, denied, or inhibited their sexuality, as indicated in the oft-heard phrase, "I don't feel anything." In working with an accepting, nondemanding, permissive, and knowledgeable female therapist, such women often can he helped to allow their sexual feelings to emerge. The injunction "not to touch or to look" needs to be lifted by dispelling myths and misconceptions, correcting faulty information about physiological functioning, encouraging looking and learning about pelvic anatomy, and learning to touch and explore their bodies, particularly their external genitals, so that they can find out what pleases them. This information then can be transmitted to their partners. The female therapist can convey by her attitude that masturbation is permissible, that it is a normal, natural way of obtaining sexual pleasure. Specific instructions often need to be given as to how to masturbate. Sexual fantasy is encouraged, both in masturbation and in partner interaction, as a method of sexual arousal, and as a technique of distraction to reduce concern about the goal of orgasm. Films depicting female masturbation are often helpful in instructing the female how to masturbate.

Within the context of conjoint therapy, emphasis is placed on the female learning more about herself, not only to enhance her own sexual arousal and to be able to teach her partner what she likes, but also to point out that her arousal and excitement give pleasure to her partner as well.

In the treatment of both primary and situational nonorgasmic response, the couple is helped to understand that an orgasm, like an erection, cannot be willed or forced, but that each female must allow herself both to know and accept those stimuli that are arousing and pleasurable to her in paving the way for the orgasmic response. Most important, emphasis must be placed on immersing onself in giving and receiving pleasure rather than focusing on the goal of orgasm. Concern that the female have an orgasm, as an achievement for therapeutic success as well as the patient's gratification, can be counterproductive.

In working with female patients who present with nonorgasmic response, it is possible that the continuous time-limited method may make them feel pressured and serve to reinforce a goal-oriented focus. Where this method is required for one reason or another, therapeutic emphasis should be on enhancing sexual pleasure rather than on achieving orgasmic response.

Vaginismus. Vaginismus, a classic illustration of a psychosomatic condition, results from a spasm of the pubococcygeus muscle making penetration of the vagina extremely difficult, if not impossible. Most cases can be diagnosed at the time of the gynecological examination. The patient may forcibly keep her knees together and prevent the examining finger from entering the vagina. Another patient may attempt to cooperate by keeping her knees apart, but the involuntary spasm will persist. The gynecological examination does not always reveal the condition because some women may be relaxed in the clinical atmosphere of a doctor's office but will involuntarily throw the pubococcygeus into spasm when penile penetration is attempted.

Vaginismus may develop from psychological causes but may also be secondary to dyspareunia. This, in turn, may result from vaginitis, pelvic inflammatory disease, and other organic pathology. In turn, vaginismus may lead to impotence in the male if he repeatedly is prevented from penetrating the closed barrier. On the other hand, vaginismus may develop if the female is constantly disappointed by the male's inability to penetrate.

A physical examination with both partners and the male and female therapists (one of whom should be a gynecologist) present is of extreme importance in a case of vaginismus. The mere demonstration to the couple of the spasm of the vaginal muscle helps to focus the problem and prepares them to start immediate therapy. Often the couple is unaware before this demonstration of what is physically causing the barrier to penetration. When it is demonstrated that a gentle examination can be performed without causing pain, the husband is encouraged to place his finger in the vagina to demonstrate directly to him and his partner the severity of the involuntary constriction ring in the outer third of the vagina. He is instructed to repeat this at home and to try to insert two fingers, if his partner is willing. Communication is encouraged to determine some of the reasons why the female is reacting in this way. In addition to psychological factors related to her background and experience, she may have fantasies that need to be explored. For example, a female may fear penetration may tear her, or she may conceive the vagina as a bottomless pit in which the penis will be lost. Often it is the female therapist who can help the female patient express these fears which can then be dealt with. Extraordinary patience and gentleness on the part of the therapists must be employed, especially in the treatment of vaginismus.

Frequently, manual dilation is not sufficient, and graduated metal or plastic dilators must be used. The patient must be encouraged to insert these herself, even at the time of the examination, so that she can control the pace of insertion. She should be encouraged to use these at home, and her male partner can also insert the dilators which are increased in size at each visit. The female should guide her husbands hands when he inserts them to encourage intimacy and reduce her anxiety. She also should be encouraged to walk around the house for short periods to get used to the feeling of something inside her vagina. As therapy progresses, she can be encouraged to fantasy the penis inside her as she or her husband gently insert the larger dilators. This preparation for intercourse is extremely helpful, as is the woman's dilating her vagina with her fingers herself and exploring her genitals.

Often the couple is fitted for a diaphragm as another way of overcoming the female's resistance to penetration, to touching her genitals, and to indicate to the couple that the therapists are so convinced that they will succeed in having intercourse that they should be prepared. Also, the possibility exists that conscious or unconscious fear of pregnancy may be contributing to the vaginismus.

When the female is ready to insert the penis, she should do so in the female superior position so that she can guide the pace of insertion and control the direction of her pelvic movements. At first, these movements should be minimal so that she can learn how it feels to have a penis inside her and begin to focus on the potentialties for sexual enjoyment, rather than on the fears and anxieties of the past.

Occasionally a female may be so phobic that even the physician cannot examine the patient. The following case illustrates this and the use of the dilators:

> *Case 4:* A couple sought therapy for vaginismus. The woman stated that a week before she had literally jumped off the table during a previous examination. The physician assured her that at the present examination no one, including the physician, would touch her. A small 3-mm dilator was given her to place into her vagina. It took 1 hr for this to be accomplished. Her husband and the two therapists were present to encourage her. At the next visit it took ½ hr to put in the 5-mm dilator, and increasingly larger sizes were placed until a 30-mm dilator was inserted at the 4th visit. The patient was then able to permit her husband to put the larger dilators in at home, where she would walk around for 20 min daily with the largest dilator in place. Soon the husband was placing first 1, then 2, then 3 fingers into the vagina.

Not all cases of vaginismus require instrumental dilation. Instances of mild vaginismus often can be alleviated by manual dilation alone. Dilation under anesthesia is rarely indicated, is countertherapeutic, and has not been necessary in a long experience.

We feel that vaginismus will be overcome when a woman is fully convinced of her responsibility for her own sexuality. This should include dilating her own vagina manually as well as instrumentally.

Dyspareunia. Painful intercourse may be of three types:

1. Pain near the entrance of the vagina due to vaginitis, lacerations, unhealed episiotomy. This may result in vaginismus (and then produce impotence).
2. Pain deep in the vagina, often due to organic pelvic pathology (endometriosis, pelvic inflammatory disease, pelvic tumors).
3. Pain after intercourse due to pelvic passive congestion or uterine spasm.

Bilateral Dysfunction

The Unconsummated Marriage. Many couples have sought help because they were unable to have intercourse following marriage. The marriages ranged from 2 months to 8 years in length. With rare exception, the couple presented bilateral complaints: primary impotence and vaginismus. Both conditions were treated simultaneously.

General Sexual Incompatibility. In addition to patients who apply for treatment of the sexual dysfunctions described above, a number of couples seek help for general sexual incompatibility, even though neither of them suffers from any specific dysfunction. They complain of not enjoying their sexual experiences or that they have intercourse very infrequently. Sometimes they describe a disparity in their sexual needs or interests, which gives rise to conflict or withdrawal from each other.

A case illustration of this follows:

> *Case 5:* Barbara and Jack had been married for 4 years and had a 2-year-old child. Both were extremely attractive and well educated. They did describe an unusually close relationship with each other and an active life together. The one missing ingredient was that they had little sexual interest in each other and lived together almost as room mates, except for infrequent lovemaking. They had met in college where they were involved in an intense sexual relationship which ended shortly after marriage. They both felt dissatisfied with the present situation chiefly because they regarded it as unnatural. It soon became evident that the close relationship they described was based on very strong dependency needs, with each clinging to the other on an infantile basis. Each of them also continued to remain dependent on their parents, who played an active role in their lives. It was not possible for them to become involved in sex therapy before some of their individual problems were worked through.

In the treatment of an older couple, or for that matter any couple, it is important to repeatedly correct misconceptions and bring useful knowledge to their attention. For example, we spend considerable time explaining that sexuality in the older years is not an invention of overenthusiastic sexologists. It exists in one form or another in all individuals. This does not mean that it necessarily always expresses itself in the ability to have intercourse, for some it expresses itself only in the need for continued closeness, affection, and intimacy; in a continued intellectual interest in eroticism; or in the need for some romance in life.

There is a general prejudice toward older people and the widespread feeling that life, love, and romance are the province solely of the young. Thus, middle-aged individuals almost compulsively act as if they were still young adults, dressing, making up, and behaving as if they were in the same age group as their own children. The misconception that sexuality is solely dependent on a youthful appearance must be corrected.

Masters and Johnson (1970) found that among the 61 older women they studied (ranging in age from 40 to 78) both the intensity of physiological response and the rapidity of response to sexual stimulation were reduced with advancing years. The sex flush was more limited and restricted in the older women, there was less lubrication, there was delay in reaction of the clitoris to direct stimulation, reduction of duration in orgasm time, and the like. But they declared that they found "significant sexual capacity and effective sexual performance" in these older women. They concluded: "The aging human female is fully capable of sexual performance at orgasmic response levels, particularly if she is exposed to regularity of effective sexual stimulation. There seems to be no physiological reasons why the frequency of sexual expression found satisfactory for the younger woman should not be carried over into postmenopausal years. In short, there is no time limit drawn by the advancing years to female sexuality" (Masters and Johnson, 1970).

In the 39 older men studied (ranging from 51 to 89), Masters and Johnson found greater evidence that sexual response weakened with age, particularly after 60. Erection took much longer, ejaculation lacked the same force and duration, the sex flush was markedly reduced, greater time was required before another erection could be reached, etc. They added, however: "There is every reason to believe that maintained regularity of sexual expression coupled with adequate physical well-being and healthy mental orientation to the aging process will combine to provide a sexually stimulative climate with a marriage. This climate will, in turn, improve sexual tension and provide a capacity for sexual performance that frequently may extend to and beyond the eighty year level" (Masters and Johnson, 1970).

A study by the Duke University Center for the Study of Aging and Human Development found a tendency for a gradual decline in the reported frequency of sexual intercourse with age. They found 65% of men were having regular intercourse between the ages of 65 to 70 years, with a frequency approximately once in 12 days. We have reason to believe these figures can be improved with sex therapy. Ten to 20% of men aged 70 to 80 were having regular ejaculations.

It is true that certain changes occur in the menopausal and postmenopausal woman. The vaginal mucosa may atrophy and cause dyspareunia. Estrogen vaginal cream quickly alleviates this. The vaginal canal may narrow owing to atrophy of disuse and estrogen deficiency. This may require local estrogen therapy, oral estrogen-progestin replacement therapy, and even manual and instrumental dilation following the method described under vaginismus. It is uncommon for a male to lose his potency because of a hormone deficiency. However, if a man (usually beyond age 65 or 70) reveals atrophy and softening of the testicles and a shrinking of the penis, and a 24-hr urine specimen shows a gonadotropin (FSH) titre above 50 mg and a testosterone value below 30 mg a diagnosis of primary testicular atrophy then can be made and parenteral testosterone can be given.

We feel that counseling the menopausal couple, when both partners are seen together, can be very effective in opening up lines of communication and lifting earlier taboos and restrictions in the light of new scientific findings about sexual functioning (Zussman and Zussman, 1972). To sum up, the best way to assure a lasting meaningful relationship in the later years and to enjoy a continued sexual life, is to keep in mind the admonition: "Use or lose."

CONCLUSIONS

Whether therapy is based on the continuous or intermittent method, the treatment of sexual dysfunctions responds in many instances within a relatively short period of time. Because outcome studies (Masters and Johnson, 1970, O'Connor and Stern, 1972, and Schumacher, 1974) suggest that sex therapy may be the treatment of choice for couples suffering from sexual distress, certainly the techniques should be taught to a wide group of practitioners. Many couples may never go to sex therapy clinics or sex therapists in private practice but they will increasingly seek help from family practitioners, internists, gynecologists, etc. The techniques in themselves are relatively easy to master. It is often the resistances to treatment that produces obstacles to successful resolution of the problems, or the complexities of the interaction between the two partners. It is in handling these areas that skills need to be developed to be helpful to sexually dysfunctional couples.

Handling of underlying neurotic problems is sometimes necessary for a successful outcome, and certainly an understanding of dynamic principles influencing behavior contributes enormously to the treatment of any patient. For the most part, however, sexual problems seem to be due not to deep psychopathology but to poor cultural conditioning, ignorance about sexual functioning, faulty parental attitudes, and a lifetime of myths and misconceptions which can often he helped dramatically in the course of the rapid treatment we have described above.

REFERENCES

Caplan, G. 1961. *An Approach to Community Mental Health*. Grune & Stratton, New York.
Ellenberg, M. 1972. Physical and endocrinological factors in male sexual inadequacy. Presented at the Upjohn Seminar on Human Sexual Inadequacy, New York City.
Ellenberg, M. 1973. Impotence in diabetics: a neurological rather than an endocrinological problem. Med. Aspects Hum. Sexuality, 7: 12.
Mann, J. 1973. *Time-Limited Psychotherapy*. Harvard University Press, Cambridge.
Masters, W., and Johnson, V. 1966. *Human Sexual Response*. Little, Brown & Co., Boston.
Masters, W., and Johnson, V. 1970. *Human Sexual Inadequacy*. Little, Brown & Co., Boston.
O'Connor, J., and Stern, L. 1972. Results of treatment in functional sexual disorders. N. Y. State J. Med. 72: 1,927.
Reding, G., and Ennes, B. 1964. Treatment of a couple by a couple. Brit. J. Med. Psychol., 37: 325.
Saltzman, L. 1967. Recently exploded sexual myths. Med. Aspects Hum. Sexuality, 1: 6.
Schumacher, S. 1974. Preliminary report as presented at Masters & Johnson seminar on Future Trends in Sex Therapy.
Semans, J. 1956. Premature ejaculation, a new approach. South. Med. J. 49: 353.
Verwoerdt A., Pfeiffer, E., and Wang, H. S., 1969. Sexual behavior in senescence. II. Patterns of sexual activity and interest. Geriatrics, 24: 37.
Zussman, L. 1973. The climatric. Proc. R. Soc. Med. 66: 183.
Zussman, L., and Zussman, S. 1972. Conjoint counseling of the menopausal couple. Presented before the American Academy of General Practice, New York City.

The Short-Term, Intermittent, Conjoint Treatment of Sexual Disorders

CHESTER W. SCHMIDT JR., M.D. and JANE LUCAS, R.N.

This chapter provides a historical perspective and description of the short-term, intermittent conjoint treatment of sexual dysfunction. An attempt is made to describe the techniques and methodology of the treatment format, with an analysis of the therapeutic process. A theoretical base and a practical working knowledge of the treatment format are provided.

The history and theory are presented as a framework for understanding the development of the treatment format. A description of the rationale with advantages of this format as opposed to others is provided. The treatment method is described, including the criteria for selection, the treatment contract, and a general outline of the sessions. Common treatment problems are discussed; and suggestions about managing missed appointments, failure to follow the prescribed treatment format, and psychiatric side effects are proposed. Case examples are included to exemplify these problems. Transference and separation can become major therapeutic issues; thus, there is considerable emphasis on these and other psychodynamic issues. Finally, there is a brief review of our treatment results.

It is not the authors' intention to teach clinicians to do short-term, intermittent conjoint treatment but rather to provide an outline of a treatment modality which has evolved over a period of years and inevitably will continue to change.

PSYCHOTHERAPEUTIC COMPONENTS

Current interest in treatment methods of sexual dysfunctions is, to a considerable extent, due to the courage and work of Masters and Johnson. However, a variety of psychotherapies have provided essential elements to these treatment methods. In order to appreciate more fully the development of the treatment format to be described, the components will be briefly reviewed.

Psychodynamic Psychotherapy

Psychodynamic psychotherapy is the cornerstone of most psychotherapies and a fundamental influence on the authors' training and treatment experiences. By psychodynamics we mean that patient's earliest and continuing interactions with parents and/or significant others are repetitiously experienced, influencing the development of the patient's personality or character structure. From these interpersonal experiences a repertoire of thoughts, feelings, and behaviors is established which constitutes the unique character of each patient. Details of the history of past and current interactions with significant others, including the data which emerge from the patient's relationship with the therapist, make possible at times an explicit understanding of why the patient acts and feels as he does.

Conjoint Couple Therapy

The evaluation and treatment of marital units, as couples, had its beginning in American psychiatry in the late forties, when Mittelman (1948) reported the concurrent psychoanalysis of a married couple. Initially, marital therapy was considered ancillary to individual treatment. The method was recommended when individual treatment seemed to be failing (Haley, 1963). Within several years there was a rapid evolution of treatment methods culminating in conjoint couple therapy (Brody, 1961). The new form of couple therapy required the marital couple be evaluated and treated as a unit. Therapists reported the advantage of direct observation of the couple's behavior as compared to the distortions of individual reporting of behavior. Additional benefits such as direct observation of communication patterns, the couple's recognition of gaps in their knowledge about their partners, discrepancies in perception of shared experiences, opportunity for role-playing, and the value of male and female cotherapists as models emerged as therapists developed their skills in applying couple therapy.

Behavior Therapy

Additionally, many of the general principles of behavior therapy have been incorporated into our treatment format. The sexual dysfunctions are identified in specific, concrete, observable terms and associated affects are described and observed in behavioral terms. The environmental conditions that maintain behavior are objectively observed by the patients through detailed description and frequency counts of sexual behavior. This kind of analysis provides information about the functional relationship between sexual behavior and temporally related environmental events. Behavioral change is effected through a series of exercises which are prescribed by the therapists as successive small steps toward a chosen goal. Attempts are made to extinguish undesirable behavior at the same time the new behavior is being learned and reinforced.

Short-Term Therapy

Short-term or brief psychotherapy is the framework of our treatment format. Meyer (1967) and his coworkers are among a number of investigators who have studied the efficacy of this form of psychotherapy. The principle elements of brief psychotherapy include, first, a contract for treatment which has a definite endpoint which brings into sharp focus for the patient and the therapist the beginning, the middle, and the end of the therapeutic process. The second element, a result of the time constraint, is the necessity of selecting a limited number of specific therapeutic goals. Goals are selected mutually, following evaluation, and might include symptom relief of anxiety or depression, analysis of a significant relationship, alteration of function in day-to-day life situations, or review of important current life goals. In the treatment of sexual dysfunctions, the primary treatment goal is the reversal of the dysfunction with an emphasis on the mutual contributions to the sexual relationship. The third element of brief therapy is a reliance on the patients' own assets in problem-solving. The patients' coping abilities are supported by positive treatment results which come from total or partial achievement of the selected therapeutic goals.

Masters and Johnson

In the Masters and Johnson format (1970) of conjoint marital unit therapy, sessions are daily and last for 2 weeks. The first several days are devoted to evaluation and collection of data from the couple, as a couple and as individuals. At this time both partners receive physical examinations. The next phase of treatment is a review of the data with the couple. This review is called the "round table" and brings into focus the patients' own sense of sensual and sexual development, as well as descrepancies in the couple's knowledge about themselves and each other. Specific treatment goals are established at this point. The third phase of treatment is a series of exercises, designed to improve the couple's physical and psychological sexual and sensual awareness about themselves and each other. The touching exercises heighten sensual awareness and densensitise the patients to basic physical sexual experiences. Specific sexual techniques are introduced as the exercises progress for the purpose of altering the behaviors and psychological responses related to the dysfunction. Treatment success is measured in terms of reversal or initiation of reversal of the sexual dysfunction.

SEXUAL BEHAVIORS CONSULTATION TREATMENT FORMAT

Description

The treatment format developed by the Sexual Behaviors Consultation Unit is similar to the Masters and Johnson format in some respects but also different in significant ways. Elements of the psychotherapies already discussed have been brought together to form the treatment model. Inter- and intrapersonal psychodynamics are strongly emphasized. The duration of therapy has been increased from 2 weeks to 12 to 20 weeks. In addition, the therapy sessions are once per week (intermittent) rather than every day (continuous). As such, the format closely resembles a short-term or brief psychotherapy model. The duration of treatment and the intermittent sequencing of sessions are necessary components of the structure of the Sexual Behaviors Consultation Unit format. The resulting span of treatment time realistically permits therapeutic work on selected, important, psychodynamic issues which are usually related to the sexual dysfunction. Even though treatment is focused upon a sexual dysfunction, other aspects of the unit's relationship, as well as intrapersonal issues, will intrude into the therapeutic process. Certain of these dynamics can and should receive attention in order to further symptom reversal and in order to more fully integrate the new sexual relationship into the marital unit's over-all relationship. The intermittent sequence of sessions provides time between sessions for psychologically working through difficult issues and time for consolidating gains made by the unit. Even a seemingly simple issue translated into a concrete experience may require several repetitions before a behavioral change is successfully managed by the unit. In addition, there is time for multiple episodes of the touching exercises and for practicing specific techniques.

Advantages for the Therapists

The Sexual Behavior Consultation Unit format affords several advantages for the therapists. There is time to reflect upon the material being presented by the marital unit and to integrate the new data with the original data base. Treatment strategy can be developed along the way and adjustments of the treatment program made to suit the emerging data. For example, during the treatment of several couples a second sexual dysfunction was uncovered. Adjustments were made for therapeutic work on the "discovered" dysfunction.

Focus on the Unit's Relationship

The conjoint nature of the therapy emphasizes the relationship of the marital unit rather than the individual psychodynamics of the partners. Although each partner brings into the marriage and the treatment program his or her unique set of historical antecedents, it is their relationship which is really the focus of therapy. Often the marital unit will present themselves for evaluation stating or implying that one of them has a sexual problem and is, therefore, the primary patient. We attempt to alter this perspective immediately. Most couples initially accept the idea that they share the responsibility for the presenting complaint. However, during the course of treatment they often temporarily return to the point of view that one of them alone is the patient. Consistent, gentle pressure must be maintained on the couple to share, mutually, the responsibility for the dysfunction; otherwise, the partner who is designated the patient will eventually be "blamed" for the dysfunction. If this occurs, the mutuality of their relationship shifts, and there is a regression to the characteristic mode of relating, yielding a central component of the sexual dysfunction.

Cotherapy Teams

The use of female-male cotherapy teams is recommended by many clinics offering evaluation and treatment of sexual dysfunctions. There are no controlled studies to demonstrate cotherapy teams are the most effective means of providing treatment. However, our current impression is that cotherapy teams are beneficial to the patients. The presence of a female and a male therapist is helpful for the same sex partner. It is felt that a female can never know the orgasmic experience of the male, and a male cannot know the orgasmic experience of the female. The availability of a female and a male point of view may be essential. In addition, the pace of treatment is often rapid and two therapists are more likely to observe and record all that is happening during sessions. Sharing duties permits the therapists to alternate between active and observing roles. While in the observing role, behaviors and affects can be identified which are difficult to observe when immersed in the active, verbal process of treatment. Review of the treatment material by two therapists provides an additional perspective and opinion about the data for the purpose of developing treatment strategy. Although the cost of treatment is increased, usually 2-fold, by the charges necessary to cover both therapists' time, it is our opinion that the benefits afforded by the cotherapy team are worth the additional cost to the patients.

Patient Selection

Marital units present or are referred to our clinic with specific sexual dysfunctions, and, in addition, with a variety of individual and marital psychopathological conditions. Some couples present with a stated desire for a Masters and Johnson type treatment; others request consultation for the purpose of defining the quality of their sexual relationship. In each case we attempt to meet the requests of the patients. The initial evaluation usually takes 1½ to 2 hr, during which time the couple is seen together and then individually by the same-sex therapist. Case histories, physical examinations, and laboratory data from previous therapists or referring physicians are reviewed.

Selection Criteria

The first criterion is a mutual desire for treatment of a sexual dysfunction. On occasion the initial evaluation may reveal the partners do not agree on the need for treatment or have requested a consultation for purposes unrelated to a sexual dysfunction. A wife may bring her husband to the clinic for the avowed purpose of coming to grips with a sexual dysfunction; however, the covert issue may be his drinking. Or, a couple may come in for the treatment of a sexual dysfunction at a time when the wife is threatening divorce. Evaluation reveals the husband coerced his wife into coming to the clinic hoping we can change her decision about separating from him. A final example may be the couple who comes for treatment with one partner holding the other partner totally responsible for the dysfunction. Evaluation reveals the accuser is so threatened by the prospect of sharing responsibility that conjoint treatment is contraindicated.

The second criterion the marital unit must demonstrate, by history and by behavior, is a commitment to their continuing relationship. The problems in the relationship may be severe, with a great deal of anger on both sides, yet what is apparent in the evaluation is a sense of commitment to the relationship.

The third criterion is the presence of a sexual dysfunction. A marital unit may request treatment of a sexual dysfunction, but if the evaluation indicates the sexual difficulties are secondary to severe marital discord, not the result of a specific dysfunction, married couple therapy will be suggested.

The fourth criterion is that each partner must be in sufficiently good mental health to make use of the treatment program. Psychosis or severe neurosis in one or both partners would result in a referral for treatment for the psychopathological state. The opportunity for treatment of a sexual dysfunction at a later date would be offered to the couple when the psychiatric symptoms, evident during evaluation, were under control. Careful consideration should be given to couples in which one or both partners show evidence of a severe character disorder, such as antisocial behavior, alcoholism, drug addiction, or polymorphous sexual behaviors. Mild to moderate degrees of character pathology can be managed within our treatment program, although there is some risk that acting out behavior may appear as tensions build up during treatment.

The fifth criterion is that the couple have the ability to pay the cost of the treatment program. Our experience, in this regard, is similar to the experience of many other psychotherapists. The motivation for treatment is placed on the line when it comes to patients' meeting their obligations for payment. Although we have a limited experience with couples who are from lower socioeconomic groups, we have treated such (Hollingshead Class IV) couples with benefit.

Treatment Contract

Once a mutual decision has been made to engage in treatment by the therapist and the marital unit, a specific contract is negotiated. The contract should be clearly understood and agreed upon by all parties before the treatment begins. The first point of the contract is the duration of the treatment program. At present, depending upon the cotherapy teams, the number of treatment sessions may vary from 12 to 20. In our experience the absolute number of sessions is not critical as long as the ultimate number of sessions is within an agreed upon range. The second point of the contract is the length of each session. The sessions vary from 1 to 1½ hr, depending upon the preference of the team and the needs of the couples. The third point of contract is arrangement of the day, the time, and the place the sessions will be held. Once arrangements have been made it is a good rule to stick to the agreement unless extraordinary circumstances force changes. These concrete arrangements provide a structure or boundary within which the therapeutic work takes place. Changes in the boundaries during the course of treatment can create therapeutic problems. Since the format is limited in time, unnecessary, time-consuming problems are to be avoided.

The physical examination is the fourth contractual point. Some clinics stress the need for the therapists' involvement in the physical examination. We do not make this a requirement of the treatment contract but rather insist each partner have had a recent physical examination. Specific consultations are obtained, as indicated, either during the evaluation phase of the treatment or during treatment.

The last point of contract is an agreement about follow-up visits. Initially we offered 6-month and 1-year follow-up visits. We have shifted to a more flexible policy of varied schedules to suit the couple's needs. Most important, however, is an agreement to a schedule of follow-up visits.

Overview of Sessions

A detailed description of a session by session outline is included in another chapter (Chapter 5); therefore, an overview is presented here. The first 3 sessions should be planned to last for 1½ hr. Subsequently, 1-hr sessions seem to be adequate. Before seeing the couple individually, the cotherapists meet with the patient unit together to explain the format and discuss the contract. At this time instructions are given to refrain from all sexual activity until further notice. It is suggested that the individual interviews that follow not be discussed until the third session, when all four members will be together for that purpose. The rationale for this restriction is that, as each partner recalls and reports about his or her individual history and the history of the couple, it is desirable to have this material uncontaminated by the partner's input. The differences in the recall of shared experience is important clinical material to be discussed in the third session. The couple is then separated and each member is interviewed by the cotherapist of the same sex. Since an initial evaluation has already been done, this time is spent obtaining information about sensory awareness and the sexual endowment of the sensory experiences, and completing gaps in the history of the initial evaluation.

The second session again involves individual interviews, reversing cotherapists. This is an opportunity for the couple to expand, change, or add any new information which has been given in the previous interview. It is an additional experience of relating sexual material to a therapist of the opposite sex.

The third session is called the "round table" discussion and is a session devoted specifically to an attempt to get the dysfunctional couple to conceptualize the problem as they are experiencing it and to formulate the reasons and events leading up to the present problem. This is often a new experience for couples who have never openly or directly shared intimate historical material, views, and attitudes about sexuality.

Instructions for the sensate focus are given during this session. These include directions for touching each other with the specific goal of exploring, discovering, and heightening new sensory awareness. These initial exercises explicitly *exclude* the touching of breasts and genitalia. Thus a nondemanding experience is structured for the couple. Adequate time needs to be allotted for these instructions and discussion. The couple is instructed to engage in the sensate focus exercises at least twice before returning for the next appointment.

During the fourth session a detailed discussion of the exercises is encouraged. Many couples will begin to feel less anxious about discussing intimate sexual details. The cotherapists ask direct and detailed questions about the experience, including the emotional feelings arising out of the experiences. The first sensate exercises will often glaringly exemplify some very basic problems existing between members of the patient unit. Problems such as embarrassment about nudity, body image, sexual mythology, open communication, control, acquiescence, and mutuality may arise. The cotherapists should be able to make a judgement together in the session about whether the couple should go on to the next exercise or should spend the next week experiencing the touching. At this time, a didactic session about the anatomy and physiology of the male and female sexual response cycle is included. The female cotherapist describes the female response with subjective as well as factual material, and the male cotherapist describes the male response. Anatomical drawings, films, slides, and other visual aids may be used. There should be ample time for discussion and questions, and since sexual mythology is discussed here, this is often one of the most valuable sessions. Exercises including genital touching are prescribed in the next session. Intercourse is prohibited, and the emphasis again is on a nondemanding sensory experience. The couple is encouraged to use any other sensory stimulation available to enhance the experience such as the use of scented body lotion, lights or candles, music, and fantasy. There is consistent emphasis on the marital relationship as "the patient."

Additionally, the use of sexual performance is de-emphasized, while the level of new sexual awareness is emphasized. The affect and mood of the couple are discussed as the sexual relationship and the exercises progress.

The exercises progressively include penile containment, with specific positioning. Thrusting is prohibited so that the demand for orgasm from either partner is diminished. The various exercises for specific dysfunctions are described in detail in another chapter. These include such techniques as "the squeeze technique" for premature ejaculation and pelvic thrusting by the female only, in the female superior position, for anorgasmia. Often a reversal of the sexual dysfunction occurs within 6 to 8 weeks. The remainder of the sessions can then be used to encourage and reinforce the couple's new level of functioning. However, the intermittent time framework provides additional time, in case the exercises need to be repeated for a corrective experience.

Cost

A final advantage of the intermittent format is the cost, which ranges from $800 to $1,200 depending upon the number of treatment sessions and the fees of the therapists. Compared to the continuous form of treatment, this represents a considerable saving for the patients. Insurance coverage for treatment varies considerably among health insurance programs. Some insurance programs will pay for conjoint couple treatment; others will not. In those situations where the insurance program will not pay for conjoint couple treatment, the couple usually requests payment by their insurance company for the treatment of one member of the couple. The diagnostic label may, unfortunately, be important. Some insurance companies will pay for the treatment of "marital maladjustment", whereas others will insist coverage is only for neurotic or psychotic disorders.

COMMON TREATMENT PROBLEMS

Transference

During the course of any type of psychotherapy, the patient's relationship to the therapist is often distorted by unconscious thoughts and feelings that arise from the need to gratify initial infantile strivings for love and affection. Transference is the resulting "irrational" reaction to the therapist. Recognition of the transference by both the patient and the therapist, with an alteration of the patient's feelings and behaviors toward the therapist, is basic to psychodynamic therapeutic work. Analysis and working through of the transference are difficult during short-term psychotherapy because of the time constraints. One explanation of rapid improvement is a concept of a "cure" based upon the patient's positive transference feelings toward the therapist; that is, the patient directs loving feelings toward the therapist. In an attempt to please and in return be loved, the patient undergoes a reorganization of attitudes and behaviors which are suggested or implied by the therapist. Another explanation of patient improvement during short-term psychotherapy is that the patient and therapist find realistic solutions to the patient's problems. There is a reasonable probability that both forces are operating simultaneously to facilitate the cure.

Transference reactions are also present in couple therapy emanating from the couple as a unit. The therapeutic leverage gained from positive transference reactions is especially useful. A unit may resist carrying out exercises as prescribed, constantly performing fewer sets of exercises than requested by the therapists. The discussion may reveal the couple has difficulty in relating, as adults, to authoritarian figures. They assume a passive-aggressive mode whenever thus confronted. Identification of this transference reaction and an appeal for a change in their attitude and behavior can often be effected by calling upon the positive transference feelings. A change in the unit's behavior is necessary for the progress of treatment, and there may be a generalized effect upon behavior outside of the treatment situation.

Failure to follow the prescribed format is not always a transference issue, and at times it may be the result of poorly communicated instructions. In this instance it is often useful to have each member of the couple paraphrase the instructions so that there is no misunderstanding. The ability of the couple to accurately carry out instructions depends upon the quality of the instructions.

Living at Home during Therapy

Our treatment format permits the couples to remain at home during the course of treatment, and they are, therefore, subject to the viscissitudes of their daily routine. We have found the ordinary stresses of day-to-day living often contribute to the symptoms of the sexual dysfunction. The manner in which the marital unit characteristically manages daily routines, especially those which relate to their sexual relationship, provides essential data for the process of therapy and may appear only after several weeks of treatment. On occasion one partner of a marital unit may express a greater need for privacy than the other. Minor intrusions or distractions (such as the telephone, etc.) can completely block that partner's sexual responsiveness. If the other partner is not attentive to this need, or if the couple, as a unit, is not cognizant of this need, a significant number of their sexual experiences may have a less than satisfactory outcome. This kind of issue often emerges only after several weeks of treatment when the couple has been introduced to the exercises. The problem becomes apparent if the couple has difficulty complying with the therapists' request for completing the expected number of sets of exercises. Scheduling the exercises is found to be difficult if the couple cannot agree on a time and setting which is comfortable for both. Working through this particular problem is very helpful as it corrects a basic part of their sexual experience and also demonstrates the couple's ability to collaborate in problem solving.

Missed Appointments

The therapist must seriously regard missed appointments. At times the missing of appointments might be a transference issue, similar to the above example of passive aggressiveness. If the issue can be identified as a passive-aggressive way of dealing with authority figures, interpretation and confrontation, followed by corrective action, must be carried out. However, couples have missed appointments when they have not completed their exercises because of their fear or anxiety about anticipated anger that might be engendered in the therapists. Again, this is a transference reaction and should be worked through. On other occasions marital units have missed appointments because of the development of a significant psychoneurotic symptomatology in one or both partners, resulting from the couple's progress through the treatment format. In this circumstance, support and reassurance have usually allayed the symptoms so that the unit can continue in the treatment program. Finally, on occasion, either the couple or the therapists may have to cancel appointments because of vacations or illness, etc. Cancellations by therapists or patients should be announced in advance. Fees are normally not charged for canceled sessions, provided there is at least 24 hr notice.

Development of Psychiatric Symptoms During Treatment

The initial evaluation is usually sufficient for identifying psychoneurotic symptoms in either of the partners of the marital unit. However, psychoneurotic symptoms may emerge during treatment in one or both partners. The development of anxiety, depression, or somatization must be constantly assessed by the therapy team. In addition to the stress of the treatment process, the sexual dysfunction often has a dynamic utility within the marital relationship. Change in this equilibrium may also create a stress and can result in psychoneurotic or psychotic symptomatology with or without severe behavioral acting out. Mild to moderate symptoms or mild behavioral problems need not interrupt therapy. However, severe psychiatric symptomatology and/or severe acting out will usually require a change to another form of psychotherapy. Several case examples are illustrative of these points.

Case. 1. A couple, married 25 years, presented with a history of 25 years of premature ejaculation. The husband also had a history of several episodes of depression and during evaluation was considered to be moderately depressed. The couple gained control of the symptom of premature ejaculation. With control, the husband experienced a sharp reduction in his depressive symptomatology. Shortly after the husband's depression cleared, during the next session his wife displayed loosening of associations and paranoid thinking. We elected to continue the treatment program, and in the next session the paranoid thinking disappeared. Upon completion of treatment the couple had reversed the sexual dysfunction, the husband was no longer depressed, and the wife did not express any paranoid thoughts.

Case 2. Unfortunately, the treatment experience may have noxious side effects. A nonmarried couple who had been living together in a stable relationship for 2 years presented with the complaint of premature ejaculation. They gained rapid control of the presenting symptom, but the female partner began showing signs of depression. As treatment progressed, she became more depressed and during a tearful session she reported she was anorgasmic and fearful of the stability of the partnership. The therapists were supportive of her and encouraged open discussion of the possibility of separation. Her partner insisted their relationship would continue, and although she continued anorgasmic at the conclusion of treatment her depression had improved considerably. A 6-month follow-up revealed the couple had separated. Retrospectively, we think a disequilibrium was created by the male partner gaining confidence through his new ability to control ejaculation. At the same time, the female partner experienced a loss of control over the relationship resulting in depression. The disequilibrium in their relationship was not corrected at the conclusion of treatment and eventually led to their separation.

During the course of treatment severe marital discord may develop which may necessitate termination of treatment if the couple is unable to comply with the format or is moving toward a rupture of their relationship. Other treatment modalities may be offered so the couple is not left without help. Another strategy is to terminate the treatment upon mutual agreement by the therapists and the couple.

Case 3. A young couple, married 2 years, presented with a history of anorgasmia. The wife had an extensive history of psychiatric treatment which had been helpful in achieving a stable vocational status and considerable comfort in her marital relationship. Individual treatment had been of no help for her anorgasmia. Evaluation revealed the husband to be a narcissistic, demanding person, who, despite considerable psychological sophistication, blamed the sexual dysfunction on his wife. As treatment progressed and the mutually shared responsibility for the dysfunction was emphasized by the therapists, the husband became increasingly agitated over the idea that he shared responsibility for the dysfunction. His wife was more assertive in the sessions. He unexpectedly threatened an extramarital affair. His threat caused the wife a great deal of anguish, and she retaliated with the threat of separation. The couple suddenly resolved the crisis by the wife acquiescing to the husband's demands for a relationship that, theoretically, permitted extramarital affairs. They reported they were both orgasmic and suggested they required no more treatment. We agreed to end treatment, although the contract called for six more sessions, because we did not think the husband could follow the program without destructively acting out his anxiety.

Finishing Treatment—Separation

As treatment approaches termination, subtle changes in the feelings, thoughts, and behavior of the couple may occur. Couples who have made good progress may revert to old patterns of interaction, including the reappearance of the sexual dysfunction with which they presented. The reason for regression is often the fear, on the part of the couple, that they will not be able to keep their new relationship and behaviors without the support and direction of the therapists. Discussion about the couple's fears and anxiety of functioning without the guidance of the therapists should be openly done. It is usually reassuring for the couple to know these feelings are almost universal in treatment situations. Not all couples will act out their anxiety about separation; many will be able to state their concerns, but at the same time, maintain the newly acquired skills and behavior they have learned in treatment. The availability of follow-up visits in our experience does little to alleviate the anxiety about ending the weekly sessions. Mann (1973), in his book on brief psychotherapy, suggested that follow-up visits interfere with the process of separation. Since he considers successful separation an important treatment experience, he withholds the availability of follow-up visits in order to prevent the interference with feelings about separation. We have not found this to be a significant problem, and therefore we have offered all of our couples follow-up programs, depending upon their needs and availability.

Conduct of Therapists

The working relationship and conduct of the cotherapy team has obvious important effects upon the treatment program and therapeutic outcome. Mutual agreements between cotherapists, with regard to fees, time and place of treatment, should be reached before the treatment contract is arranged with the patient. An understanding and acceptance of each other's points of view with regard to male-female sexual value systems is essential. Such an understanding allows for different points of view which become expressed in the process of treatment and must be respected and tolerated. The cotherapists must be able to compromise both on the concrete issues of the therapy contract and on their interpretations of the more abstract material that evolves during the therapeutic process. The spirit of collaboration and compromise is a role model for the couples. Since the concept of mutuality is a key factor in long-term relationships, the behavior of the therapists with regard to mutuality must be consistent with their verbal messages. During the course of treatment there will be many opportunities for differences about interpretation of the couple's behavior and the dynamics of their relationship. They may find themselves siding with the partner of the same sex. The therapists' working through a disagreement along male-female biases is often a prelude to a significant, positive therapeutic step by the marital unit.

Other behaviors of the cotherapy team also present role models for the couple. Sharing the responsibilities of conducting the therapy sessions such as taking turns giving instructions for the sensate exercises and discussing the contractual arrangements concerning time, money, place, and treatment is similar to the shared responsibilities the couples must carry out during the exercises at home. Adequate time needs to be built into the treatment sessions for the cotherapy team to spend some time before each session to discuss the treatment strategy for that session, and likewise a postsession discussion is necessary for sharing and reviewing the treatment hour. Included in these discussions should be the continuous examination of the interaction of the therapy team itself.

Couples are often sensitive to, and curious about the relationship of the cotherapy team. These concerns will, at times, emerge during the treatment sessions in the form of personal questions directed toward one or both members of the cotherapy team. Responses to these questions are determined by the nature of the questions themselves and the conditions under which they are made. At times the team may respond by providing minimal amounts of data about themselves; at other times the questions may be interpreted and thus redirected back to the marital unit. None of our cotherapy teams is comprised of husband and wife teams; therefore, there is always some curiosity on the part of the marital unit as to the nature, if any, of the sexual relationship between the cotherapists. The personal and professional respect the therapists give to each other is the primary indication to the marital unit of the nature of the relationship between the cotherapists; as such, the cotherapists' relationship, outside of the treatment session, does not intrude into the treatment situation, if they are respectful of each other.

Follow-up Visits

The issue of follow-up visits has already been discussed briefly. At present, follow-up visits are offered to all couples, whether they complete the treatment program or drop out. The timing or sequence of follow-up visits is, to a large extent, dependent upon the patients' needs and their geographic availability. As has already been mentioned, we have moved from a rigid schedule of 6-month and 1-year follow-ups to a more flexible schedule. We do insist that the follow-up visits be conducted by the cotherapy team which treated the unit, and that both members of the unit be present for the follow-up session. The length of the session is usually at least 1 hr. The fees for these sessions are the same as those charged by the cotherapy team during treatment. Some teams make themselves available at any time for consultations related to regression of the sexual dysfunction, or as a resource for other marital difficulties. Should problems arise within the marriage, the team might offer consultation to the married couple. If an alternative form of treatment is indicated, the team refers the case to other therapists in order to preserve their (the team's) role with the couple.

BRIEF REVIEW OF TREATMENT RESULTS

A study from the Sexual Behaviors Consultation Unit by Meyer, Schmidt, Lucas, and Smith (1975), based upon the evaluation of 52 marital units and the treatment outcome of 16 of those 52 units, (both treated and followed over an average 7-month period), reported an initial failure rate (return to baseline condition or worse) of 19%. This is comparable to the initial failure rates reported by Masters and Johnson (1970). Immediately following treatment 25% of the units were judged "markedly improved," 25% were judged "improved," 31% were judged "equivocally improved," and 19% were judged to show no improvement. On follow-up, 19% of the couples were judged to show continued "marked improvement," 19% were judged "improved," 25% judged "equivocally improved," and 37% judged as showing "no improvement." In no instance did a marital unit report better results on follow-up than they reported at the time of treatment completion. Three of the units who reported equivocal improvement initially reported regression to the original dysfunction on follow-up. Over-all, our results were similar to those that might be expected from other psychotherapeutic modalities; however, it must be kept in mind that the statistics were those of a small sample. It would appear important to recognize that a variety of modalities are useful in the treatment of sexual problems, dependent upon the individuals and the particular type of dysfunction. Rather than a preconceived bias toward one particular treatment mode or another, the specific technique should be selected according to the unit's capacities, symptomatology, character traits, lifestyle, motivation, and therapeutic goals.

SUMMARY

Historical antecedents of short-term intermittent conjoint treatment of sexual dysfunction include psychodynamic psychotherapy, couples' therapy, behavior therapy, time-limited brief psychotherapy, and Masters and Johnson time-limited conjoint couple therapy, with special focus on sexual dysfunction.

Our treatment format is intermittent, meaning 1 visit per week for a period of 12 to 20 weeks. The rationale for the intermittent aspect is, in our opinion, that the increased span of time provides needed opportunities for therapeutic intervention within the framework of short-term therapy. The conjoint nature of the program emphasizes the relationship of the marital unit, provides both a male and a female perspective, and affords the opportunity to alternate between an active and an observing role.

Patient selection is based on an evaluation to determine the criteria for utilizing the treatment format: (1) mutual desire for treatment, (2) commitment to the relationship, (3) absence of severe psychopathology in either partner, (4) the presence of a sexual dysfunction, and (5) ability to pay for treatment.

The treatment contract includes the agreement about time, place, fees, length of treatment, and follow-up visits.

The treatment format includes a specifically designed set of sensate exercises prescribed to be carried out by the patients in the privacy of their own home. These experiences and the affects surrounding them are then explored and examined in the sessions. Psychodynamic issues often arise and, with some limitation, can be effectively dealt with during treatment. The transference phenomena are regarded as unavoidable and can be an asset in treatment. The transference, in fact, is regarded as a major therapeutic tool. In relation to this phenomenon, separation is always an issue to be dealt with continuously during the treatment.

Some common problems include failure to follow the format, missed appointments, and psychiatric side effects in various degrees. All of these behaviors and symptoms should be assessed on a continuing basis by the cotherapists. Interpretation, corrective experiences, and support are ways of dealing with some of these issues in treatment. Occasionally, treatment may need to be interrupted should noxious side effects occur.

The conduct of the cotherapists has an effect on treatment. Mutuality, compromise, and allowances for differences are issues which should be settled by the cotherapists before embarking on a treatment contract with a marital unit. The professional and personal relationships of the therapists are of interest to the patients and should provide unambiguous models of mutual respect.

REFERENCES

Brody, S. 1961. Simultaneous psychotherapy of married couples. In: Masserman, J., ed., *Current Psychiatric Therapies*, p. 139. Grune and Stratton, New York.

Haley, J. 1963. Marriage therapy. Arch. Gen. Psychiatry, 8: 213.

Mann, J. 1973. *Time Limited Psychotherapy*. Harvard University Press, Cambridge, Mass.

Masters, W., and Johnson, V. 1970. *Human Sexual Inadequacy*. Little, Brown and Co., Boston.

Mittleman, B. 1948. The concurrent analysis of married couples. Psychoanal. Q., 17: 182.

Meyer, E., Slaughter, R., Pollack, I. W., Weingartner, H., and Novey, S. 1967. Contractually time limited psychotherapy in an outpatient psychosomatic clinic. Am. J. Psychiatry, 124: 57.

Meyer, J. K., Schmidt, C. W., Jr., Lucas, M. J., and Smith, E. 1975. Short-term treatment of sexual disabilities: interim report. Am. J. Psychiatry, 132: 172.

Behavior Therapy Techniques in the Treatment of Sexual Disorders

ARNOLD A. LAZARUS, Ph.D. and
RAYMOND C. ROSEN, Ph.D.

Over the past two decades an approach to psychotherapy called *behavior therapy* or *behavior modification* has been developing within the scientific framework of applied experimental psychology. Initially, this approach to treatment was limited to methods based on Pavlovian and Skinnerian conditioning, but today it is viewed as a broad experimental approach to the alteration of disturbed and deviant behavior. In essence, behavior therapists are most interested in applying methods, generated by experimental psychologists in the study of normal behavior, to the study and change of abnormal behavior. One area to which the application of behavior therapy has proved especially successful is the field of sexual problems. Numerous successful treatment outcomes have led clinicians to develop a new set of assumptions about the best means of dealing with sexual problems. Perhaps the central issue in this regard concerns the relative importance or unimportance of "insight." The various insight-oriented therapies assume that disturbed behavior can be alleviated and changed by enabling patients to understand the dynamics underlying their behavior. Insight therapists also believe that increased awareness will lead people to feel better and to behave more adaptively. Yet there is now a spate of evidence indicating that people can often acquire a full understanding of the dynamic reasons for their distrubed behaviors and still remain unable to change their specific disturbances.

Behavior therapists regard the path between "insight" and behavior change as extremely complex. In some instances, it is necessary for insight or self-understanding to precede behavior change; in other cases, a change in behavior will lead to the

disabilities, methods and techniques which involve the graded and systematic implementation of various sensual and sexual assignments have proved the most successful. The present chapter underscores some of the most relevant behavioral tactics and strategies for treating sexual disabilities. Common pitfalls are discussed, as well as the development of a more comprehensive behavioral orientation known as "multimodal therapy."

INTRODUCTION

It has proved useful to distinguish "sexual inadequacy" from "sexual deviance." Lazarus (1969) proposed that the term *sexual inadequacy* include the following conditions: (1) complete or partial absence of sexual arousal or desire; (2) total or partial aversion to sex (despite feelings of arousal); (3) loss of sexual interest or arousal before achieving orgasm; (4) inability to achieve orgasm; (5) absence of pleasure during sex (including ejaculation without sensation); (6) premature ejaculation; (7) various degrees of pain or discomfort during coitus (dyspareunia, vaginismus).

The term, *sexual deviance*, on the other hand, refers to those disorders characterized by idiosyncratic, or societally unacceptable object choice. Typical examples include fetishism, transvestism, pederasty, sadomasochism, pedophilia, exhibitionism, as well as more unusual acts such as coprophilia or bestiality. Prevailing attitudes tend to regard homosexuality as an alternative orientation, rather than a form of deviance (Davison and Wilson, 1973; also see Wilson and Davison, 1974). There are, however, numerous homosexually oriented individuals with sexual inadequacies, just as there are persons who function in a heterosexual context but who are nevertheless troubled by certain "perversions" or "fixations." Furthermore, clinicians are frequently consulted by homosexuals who ardently desire to effect a heterosexual adjustment.

BEHAVIORAL TREATMENT OF SEXUAL INADEQUACY

The conceptual framework on which behavior therapy rests is known as "social learning theory" (Bandura, 1969). The basic tenet of this approach is that *behavior is a function of its consequences.* A fundamental assumption is that most persistent behavior patterns are maintained by positive and negative reinforcers. Repetitive responses endure because they promote pleasure and/or avoid pain. Consonant with the principles of social learning, specific treatment procedures are viewed as reeducative experiences that call for active participation. Thus, written materials, audio tape cassettes, films, and especially graded homework assignments are all important elements of the educational and specific behavioral retraining. The main emphasis is upon unlearning negative habits and acquiring a repertoire of adaptive feelings and responses in the here and now.

In accounting for the development of sexual inadequacies, psychogenic causes constitute, by far, the most prevalent etiological factors. A basic premise of the behavioral approach is that dysfunctions which are learned and maintained by environmental determinants can be overcome through the appropriate reeducative experiences. Sexual inadequacy seems often to be the result of learned inhibitions, especially anxiety. Interpersonal conflict is another major source of dysfunction. Recent research (Rosen, 1973) has also demonstrated the possibility of direct suppression of sexual responses through instrumental learning. This finding suggests that anxiety might often be the consequence, rather than the antecedent cause of a specific sexual dysfunction.

Two principles of learning that seem especially cogent in overcoming sexual inadequacy are (1) the principle of contiguity, and (2) the law of recency. *Contiguity* implies that if two events occur in close succession, the recurrence of one is inclined to produce the other. *Recency* is the "postulate that a given item is more likely to remind a person of some recent associate than of one more remote in time" (English and English, 1958).

In applying the foregoing principles to a behavioral sex therapy program, the first step is to instruct one's client(s) to make no coital attempts whatsoever until all preliminary procedures have been completed successfully. This stops the frantic, clumsy, sometimes desperate attempts to effect sexual union which escalates anxiety and undermines all or nearly all joy and pleasure. Instead, visual and tactile explorations of nonerogenous body zones are prescribed. Back rubs, shoulder massages, head stroking, and similar relaxing "togetherness exercises" begin to elicit contiguous feelings of pleasure from one amorous encounter to the next. The recency effect then promotes feelings of positive anticipation.

Next, pleasuring responses are gradually broadened to include the manipulation of genitalia and other erogenous areas. Arousal expectations are carefully excluded in order to avoid performance anxieties. Clients are asked to try and examine those manipulations that produce pleasant feelings—with or without sexual arousal. If clients are too hasty, negative elements are generally reintroduced and carry over via contiguity and recency effects. For this reason, clients are urged to "make haste slowly." *Successive approximation* is the important learning principle involved here.

The next step involves increasing the intensity and duration of genital stimulation. Should the enjoyment be lessened by any tension or anxiety, clients are advised to revert to a formerly pleasant interchange (*e.g.*, go back to massaging his or her shoulders) and are instructed to ascertain that each session ends on a positive note. The latter instruction is especially important to prevent negative expectations from generalizing.

Sexual arousal, often culminating in orgasm, is commonly reported by clients when the protracted genital manipulation phase is practiced. If orgasm is not achieved (as is sometimes the case with nonorgasmic women), the therapist needs to establish whether adequate lubrication is being applied, and whether the use of a vibrator might enhance orgasmic potential. LoPiccolo and Lobitz (1972) have described a program in which the initial experience of orgasm through masturbation is gradually transferred to intromission and intercourse. The knowledge that satisfaction can be attained without coitus is important in alleviating performance anxieties.

Behavior therapists regard such graded sexual assignments as a form of *in vivo desensitization*. The latter is the basis of the much publicized Masters and Johnson (1970) approach to sexual dysfunction. By means of systematic instruction and guidance, couples are encouraged to increase their range of intimate and erotic exchanges. Care is taken to avoid any demands or performance anxiety, misconceptions are corrected, and a general educational regimen deals with more subtle prejudices and myths. The upshot of these endeavors is that sexual inadequacies are no longer regarded as indubitable symptoms of deep-seated personality disorders. The tendency to deflect attention from current sexual problems to the presumed dynamics and underlying historical origins has not proved too successful (Moore, 1961). The behavioral treatment of sexual dysfunction has become an independent specialty, with short-term, goal-specific approaches to therapy (Lobitz and LoPiccolo, 1972).

Strategies and Tactics

Although originating from a limited number of learning principles, behavior therapy (when properly applied) takes cognizance of idiosyncratic needs and personalistic demands (Lazarus, 1971). It is not a mechanistic system which is invariant for all cases of sexual dysfunction. While basic treatment strategies for overcoming performance anxiety have been well documented (*e.g.*, Masters and Johnson, 1970), it is nevertheless possible for therapists to make tactical errors that undermine therapeutic progress. Thus, *strategic and tactical* considerations need to be carefully elucidated.

The major strategic considerations in overcoming sexual inadequacy are as follows: (1) Performance anxiety is removed by teaching the client to avoid the spectator role. The emphasis is entirely upon giving and receiving sensual pleasure. (2) Fear of failure is overcome first by expressly advising clients *not* to engage in coitus during the initial stages of therapy, and later by ensuring that they are capable of giving and receiving orgasmic release through a variety of oral, manual, and genital interchanges. (3) In certain dysfunctions (*e.g.*, premature ejaculation or vaginismus) additional techniques are administered (*e.g.*, the "squeeze technique," or relaxation training with graded dilation procedures). In cases where severe anxiety is present, the somewhat laborious technique of *systematic desensitization* has been shown to produce effective results (Obler, 1973). A more rapid and efficient variation of this procedure has been described by Brady (1966), who used Brevital, a fast-acting muscle relaxant, instead of extended practice in self-induced relaxation.

With respect to *tactical* considerations, therapeutic subtleties abound. As Lazarus and Davison (1971) pointed out: "The clinician, like any other applied scientist, must fill out the theoretical skeleton. Individual cases present problems that always call for knowledge beyond basic psychological principles" (p. 208). Let us consider a case in point.

Harry and Gloria, both 25 years of age, had been married for 2 years. While premarital sex was reported by both of them as satisfactory, problems crept into their sexual relations soon after marriage. Gloria complained of dyspareunia (pain during penetration), and Harry began experiencing loss of erection on some occasions and premature ejaculation on others. The couple decided to limit their sexual activities to mutual masturbation. All went well for several months until problems crept into this area as well. Harry complained that Gloria often hurt him while fondling his scrotum, and Gloria maintained that Harry would insist on fondling her breasts even when they were tender and painful at certain times of the month. For the past 6 or 7 months they had both resorted solely to self-stimulation. Their ostensible reason for seeking therapy was because they both wanted to have children.

Even from this brief description, any clinician would be alerted to the likelihood of a dyadic struggle that used sex as a battleground for more basic conflicts. After the couple had filled out a detailed life history questionnaire, clarification was sought concerning several background factors, whereupon the discussion focused on their antipathies and possible animosities. Both Gloria and Harry denied that they were angry with each other, and they insisted that apart from the sexual area, they related very well together. It soon became apparent that to pursue this line would only mobilize their "resistance" and truncate any useful therapeutic interventions. Accordingly, they were given the behavioral rationale for graded exposure, and they were requested to spend the next week engaging in various "sensate focus" experiences.

When they returned the following week, they both reported having been "too busy" to practice the sensual exchanges. The possibility was explored that their level of anxiety was so high that the initial treatment step was too demanding. This seemed unlikely. Instead, it appeared that their reluctance stemmed from a feeling that they were being treated "like guinea pigs." Moreover, they both seemed very unmotivated to follow any therapeutic directives.

In order to overcome such "resistances," we decided to employ a technique developed by Milton Erickson known as "paradoxical communication" (Haley, 1973). After reemphasizing the well documented virtues of *in vivo* desensitization (to refute the guinea pig allegation), the couple was provided with more detailed descriptions of several sensual exchanges with which they might begin their program. At this point the therapist deliberately ended the session by suggesting: "You know, I'm really looking forward to seeing how the two of you manage to sabotage the program this coming week." At the next session they both reported enjoying an eminently successful range of sensual experiences, and Gloria actually added "Sorry to disappoint you!"

Throughout the course of therapy, Harry and Gloria seemed to react adversely whenever the therapist was "up front" with them. For example, when they reached the point of applying genital stimulation for pleasure rather than for arousal, Harry began pressuring Gloria to have an orgasm. When the therapist stressed the importance of nondemanding, nonperformance-oriented sex play, Harry only intensified his demands. However, the following sort of remarks always produced desired therapeutic effects: "You're doing a great job of getting Gloria uptight and of extinguishing your hopes for any sexual gratification. Now the next time you two practice any intimate acts, why not do a really good job and bite her nipples off, or mutilate her in some other way, if she does not perform to your full satisfaction?"

It is worth mentioning that upon achieving a good sexual readjustment, the couple elected to remain in therapy in order to develop a more *assertive*, rather than a passive-aggressive *modus vivendi*. At this time they have maintained their sexual adjustment for over 5 months and are now displaying more open and authentic interpersonal styles.

Purists may object in theory to the use of tactics derived from nonbehavioral sources (*e.g.*, Gestalt therapy, cognitive theory, transactional analysis, or existential psychology), but the practicing clinician often has little choice in matters of this kind. If he wishes to maximize his therapeutic impact, it is imperative to be flexible, personalistic, and technically eclectic (Lazarus, 1971, 1972). At times, behavioral techniques need to be adapted to the particular demands of a dyadic situation (Rosen and Schnapp, 1974). Even though the basic conceptual framework is social learning theory, effective therapeutic *tactics* can be drawn from any source.

Common Pitfalls

Throughout this chapter we have emphasized that despite the apparent straightforwardness of the various sexual retraining techniques employed by behavior therapists and other action-oriented sex counselors, considerable clinical acumen is required for the adequate assessment and implementation of appropriate personalistic treatment programs. We remain skeptical of the general efficacy of any "prepackaged" programs for overcoming sexual difficulties. The treatment of premature ejaculation provides an excellent case in point.

A threshold training technique originally described by Semans (1956) was elaborated by Wolpe and Lazarus (1966) and later extended and refined by Masters and Johnson (1970). Known as the "squeeze technique," this procedure consists of 2 steps. With the male in a relaxed, supine position, the female stimulates his penis manually. At the "moment of inevitability" he signals her, whereupon she immediately squeezes the penis just below the coronal ridge. This pressure is maintained for about 20 sec and has the effect of terminating orgasm and ejaculation. It also results in a partial loss of erection, at which time the female again stimulates the male until erection and arousal are achieved, once more applying the squeeze at his signal. Couples are asked to repeat this process no less than 3 times at each love-making session. When the man is readily able to control ejaculation via this procedure, the female sits astride the male and stuffs his penis into her vagina. By actively thrusting her pelvis, she brings her partner to erection. When he experiences the sensation premonitory to ejaculation, he signals, she removes the penis, and immediately applies the squeeze. Masters and Johnson (1970) have reported a success rate of better than 90% with the use of this method.

The pitfalls to which we alluded now come to the fore. As consultants to various agencies, we have been asked to supervise therapists who wished to acquire expertise in these techniques. Among our trainees, a common error was the assumption that 90% of cases of premature ejaculation would respond positively if simply given the correct instructions for carrying out the threshold training. Yet many premature ejaculators are highly anxious and require anxiety reduction by means of relaxation training (Jacobson, 1964) and/or massage training (Downing,

1972). (In some cases, heightened anxiety appears to be causally related to premature ejaculation; in other instances the connection appears to be simply correlational.)

The level of anxiety may even be sufficiently high to justify the formal technique of systematic desensitization. Thus, one premature ejaculator whom we recently treated was so hypersensitive to criticism, rejection, disapproval, and failure that an elaborate series of desensitization and role-playing techniques had to precede specific sexual retraining. He was loaned a series of cassette tapes on progressive relaxation (Lazarus, 1971A) and was asked to practice the relaxation exercises twice daily. Within 2 weeks he was able to relax sufficiently to overcome minor tensions in his day-to-day encounters. The desensitization procedure consisted of having him deeply relaxed while vividly picturing several scenes, statements, events, and incidents that made him feel tense, upset, anxious, or otherwise disturbed. He was told to practice relaxing and letting go of all tensions before picturing unpleasant or upsetting events. In this manner, he soon found himself able to contemplate many situations with equanimity that had previously proved upsetting to him. Thus, as the tension and anxiety receded, he was willing to take psychological risks such as asserting his rights and speaking his mind. Most important from a sexual retraining perspective, he was finally able to ask his girlfriend whether she would be willing to embark on a mutual sex counseling program.

Other cases of premature ejaculation have required couples' communication training (Stuart, 1969). Sexually dysfunctional couples often display poor communication in several interpersonal areas, especially with regard to specific sexual needs and preferences. In many of these cases negative and hostile feedback seems to predominate over any constructive suggestions. The "squeeze technique" will prove quite ineffective in an atmosphere of interpersonal strife. It is a truism that personal discord must be resolved before sexual counseling is likely to succeed. In general, we would maintain that a therapeutic program which focuses primarily on establishing open verbal and nonverbal communication between partners and secondarily upon the mechanics of sexual performance is more likely to succeed and endure than treatments which emphasize mechanics over and above the context of overt and covert communication.

A BEHAVIORAL APPROACH TO SEXUAL DEVIANCE

Essential to the behavioral view of deviance is the notion of cultural relativism (Ullmann and Krasner, 1969). Fetishism, voyeurism, exhibitionism, transvestism, pedophilia, and homosexuality, the most common forms of sexual deviance in this culture, are only "abnormal" to the extent that they contravene the accepted mores of the society. Nevertheless, the pressures for conformity are sufficiently powerful that such individuals are often highly motivated to change their behavior. Organizations such as the Gay Liberation Movement and the Mattachine Society have done much to publicize the need for acceptance of alternative sexual orientations, and they seem to be having considerable impact on the mental health professions (Kameny, 1971; Marmor, 1971; Davison and Wilson, 1973).

There are two basic behavioral approaches to the treatment of sexual deviance: (1) In order to eliminate or reduce the probability of future occurrence of the unacceptable response, behavior therapists have utilized a variety of *punishment* techniques. To this end, sexual "deviates" have been "treated" by emetic drugs, electric shocks, and aversive imagery. These stimuli are typically administered in line with the principles of classical conditioning (with or without positive retraining), and instrumental escape and avoidance training, often employing ingenious schedules of intermittent reinforcement. Feldman and MacCulloch (1971) have authored a comprehensive text on the use of such procedures. (2) An alternative, although less well described approach, has emphasized *reorientation* to more culturally acceptable contexts, or treatment of concomitant sexual inadequacy as outlined in the previous section. To the extent that heterosexual skills are developed, the client's sexual options are increased.

Masturbatory reconditioning is a technique which epitomizes this second approach. The technique, which has also been called "Playboy Therapy" was illustrated in a well known case study (Davison, 1968). In order to develop an "appropriate" sexual orientation, the client masturbated to orgasm while controlling his fantasies. The following case illustrates the important steps to follow:

> Gary, a 22-year-old male junior college student, was unmarried and still a virgin. He had vacillated for 6 months before seeking therapy for fear of being considered "crazy." During the initial interview he revealed that all his sexual fantasies consisted of "bondage" scenes, in which he used vivid images of tying up most of the young women that he had ever known. Gary thought that such fantasies were probably symptomatic of a serious personality problem. After eliciting most of the relevant developmental material, a decision was made to attempt masturbatory reconditioning.
>
> His first "bondage" experience had taken place at the age of 12. Gary was playing a game with a group of friends, and while vigorously tying up a young female friend, he had ejaculated. Although he had previously attempted to masturbate, he had not yet successfully climaxed. After the "bondage" incident, however, he began masturbating frequently (4 to 7 times per week) with frequent

recollections of his first experience. At the age of 15 he bought a magazine in which numerous color photographs represented all aspects of the "bondage" ritual. From that time on all his sexual fantasies involved images of bondage.

Gary had hardly dated during his previous 2 years of college for fear of what he might be impelled to do on one of his dates. At the time he came in for therapy, he was becoming increasingly withdrawn from male as well as female friends. The first therapy assignments involved increasing the frequency of his social contacts. No specific sexual assignments were suggested, however, until his initial anxiety had been overcome.

The first phase of the reconditioning technique involved having him masturbate with his typical fantasies up until the moment of ejaculatory inevitability. At that point he shifted his attention to the nude centerfold in a popular men's magazine while experiencing the sensations of orgasm. He then began shifting his attention to the picture progressively earlier in the self-stimulation sequence. When it was possible for him to masturbate entirely without the "bondage" fantasies, he was encouraged to introduce images of real women in his life. This procedure, which took no more than 4 weeks, changed his self-concept markedly. He was completely reassured, and the focus of therapy shifted to his interpersonal relationships. Gary was forewarned that the "deviant" fantasies would probably recur again at some point in the future, but he was encouraged to use the reconditioning technique again whenever the need should arise.

Barlow (1973) has recently reviewed several such techniques for increasing heterosexual responsiveness. He concluded his review by questioning whether aversion therapy techniques are necessary in the treatment of sexual deviance and by implying that positive reorientation techniques may suffice in the majority of cases. We are of the opinion that ethical considerations demand that aversive procedures be reserved for situations that offer no therapeutic alternatives.

THE MULTIMODAL ORIENTATION

Emphasis has been placed upon the fact that unless a sufficiently complete and personalistic evaluation is conducted, inadequate and incomplete treatment procedures are likely to be administered. Lazarus (1973) has indicated that unless 7 separate, but interrelated, modalities are specifically investigated and altered, treatment will be incomplete. And incomplete treatment produces "half-baked" cures in which relapse is ever-present.

The modalities to be covered are: *behavior* (pays close attention to maladaptive responses and also remedies gaps in the patient's social repertoire); *affect* (deals with the elimination of unpleasant feeling states—anger, anxiety, depression—and the cultivation of positive emotions); *sensation* (teaches clients to experience the here and now by enhancing visual and auditory perception and by promoting a positive range of tactile, kinesthetic, olfactory, and gustatory pleasures); *imagery* (examines the "mental pictures" and fantasies that diminish the well-being of the individual, as well as those images that can be used to increase adaptive functioning); *cognition* (parses irrational ideas and integrates cogent plans, decisions, values, attitudes, and beliefs); *interpersonal relationships* (takes cognizance of the fact that most emotional problems are a function of, and exist within, person-to-person interactions, especially within dyadic and family settings); and *drugs* (a "medical modality" which recognizes that in many cases diagnosed as "highly anxious," "depressive," or "psychotic" the use of medication is often essential). The clinical consequences of attending to each of the 7 modalities is to ensure comprehensive and thorough therapeutic intervention.

The forementioned modalities can be succinctly expressed by the acronym, BASIC ID. Again, let it be emphasized that comprehensive assessment and therapy calls for the investigation and modification of problem Behaviors, Affective processes, Sensations, Images, Cognitions, Interpersonal relationships, with or without the use of Drugs or other medical procedures. While change within one modality influences all other modalities, it is nevertheless necessary to devote specific attention to each modality if long lasting therapeutic changes are to accrue.

Perhaps the simplest way of expressing the multimodal rationale is to underscore that comprehensive psychotherapy at the very least requires the correction of irrational beliefs, unpleasant feelings, deviant behaviors, stressful relationships, intrusive images, negative sensations, and possible biochemical imbalance. Instead of searching for a core construct or a critical modality, the multimodal approach emphasizes that patients are usually troubled by a host of specific problems which need to be corrected by a similar multitude of specific treatments. This approach vitiates the notion of any general "treatment of choice." It negates the search for a panacea.

An important question that arises from the foregoing is whether *every* patient should be offered the complete BASIC ID treatment. The answer, in a word, is "no." A functional analysis of the seven modalities seems to be necessary in every case, but unless specific problems are brought to light in each modality, only those areas that require therapeutic attention are actually included. But to a "multimodal therapist," the reason for ignoring a potential therapeutic zone is not because he or she does not work within that modality, but because problem identification has revealed no need to intercede in a given area.

By way of illustration, a 24-year-old man was unable to consummate his relationship with his girlfriend despite having undergone an extensive sex therapy treatment program which emphasized *in vivo* densensitization via graded exposure. A multimodal analysis revealed that he was unduly squeamish about female genitalia, and that he responded with high anxiety and withdrawal to images of menstruation. Obviously, a man who is squeamish about female genitalia *per se* is most unlikely to respond favorably to graded retraining until his specific aversions have been overcome. A BASIC ID or multimodal assessment process prevents therapists from ignoring seemingly peripheral problems that turn out to be central impediments to therapeutic progress. The reader who wishes to read a detailed description of the foregoing case may consult Lazarus (1974).

CONCLUSION

Sex therapy from a behavioral perspective draws on established concepts of experimental psychology (especially pragmatic principles of learning). In treating sexual inadequacies, the major clinical tactics and strategies involve the elimination of inhibitions (especially anxiety) as well as the facilitation of new techniques and responses. The treatment of sexual deviance, although often associated with sexual inadequacy, is nevertheless sufficiently distinctive to merit specific techniques. In this regard, while some behavior therapists have emphasized aversive procedures, we have stressed the importance of developing appropriate heterosexual alternatives. Finally, comprehensive therapy usually necessitates a multimodal assessment and intervention in order to maximize the durability of treatment outcomes.

REFERENCES

Bandura, A. 1969. *Principles of Behavior Modification*. Holt, New York.

Barlow, D. H. 1973. Increasing heterosexual responsiveness in the treatment of sexual deviation: a review of the clinical and experimental evidence. Behav. Ther. 4: 655.

Brady, J. P. 1966. Brevital-relaxation: treatment of frigidity. Behav. Res. Ther., 4: 41.

Davison, G. C. 1968. Elimination of a sadistic fantasy by a client-controlled counterconditioning technique. J. Abnorm. Psychol., 73: 84.

Davison, G. C., and Wilson, G. T. 1973. Attitudes of behavior therapists toward homosexuality. Behav. Ther., 4: 686.

Downing, G. 1972. *The Massage Book*. Random House, New York.

English, H. B., and English, A. C. 1958. *A Comprehensive Dictionary of Psychological and Psychoanalytical Terms*. Longmans, New York.

Feldman, M. P., and MacCulloch, M. J. 1971. *Homosexual Behavior: Therapy and Assessment*. Pergamon Press, Oxford.

Haley, J. 1973. *Uncommon Therapy: The Psychiatric Techniques of Milton H. Erickson, M.D.* Norton, New York.

Jacobson, E. 1964. *Anxiety and Tension Control: A Psychobiologic Approach*. Lippincott, Philadelphia.

Kameny, F. E. 1971. Gay liberation and psychiatry. Psychiatr. Opin., 8: 18.

Lazarus, A. A. 1969. Modes of treatment for sexual inadequacies. Med. Aspects Hum. Sexuality, 3: 53–58.

Lazarus, A. A. 1971. *Behavior Therapy and Beyond*. McGraw-Hill, New York.

Lazarus, A. A. 1971A. *Relaxation Exercises* (Cassette Tape-Recordings). Instructional Dynamics, Chicago.

Lazarus, A. A. (Ed.). 1972. *Clinical Behavior Therapy*. Brunner/Mazel, New York.

Lazarus, A. A. 1973. Multimodal behavior therapy: treating the BASIC ID. J. Nerv. Ment. Dis., 156: 404.

Lazarus, A. A. 1974. Multimodal therapy: BASIC ID. Psychol. Today, 7: 59.

Lazarus, A. A., and Davison, G. C. 1971. Clinical innovation in research and practice. In Bergin, A. E., and Garfield, S. L., eds., *Handbook of Psychotherapy and Behavior Change*. Wiley, New York.

Lobitz, W. C., and LoPiccolo, J. 1972. New methods in the behavioral treatment of sexual dysfunction. J. Behav. Ther. Exper. Psychiatry, 3: 265.

LoPiccolo, J., and Lobitz, W. C. 1972. The role of masturbation in the treatment of primary orgasmic dysfunction. Arch. Sex. Behavior, 2: 163.

Marmor, J. 1971. "Normal" and "deviant" sexual behavior. J.A.M.A., 217.

Masters, W. H., and Johnson, V. E. 1970. *Human Sexual Inadequacy*. Little, Brown, and Co., Boston.

Moore, B. E. 1961. Frigidity in women. J. Am. Psychoanal. Assoc., 9: 571.

Obler, M. 1973. Systematic desensitization in sexual disorders. J. Behav. Ther. Exper. Psychiatry, 4: 93.

Rosen, R. C. 1973. Suppression of penile tumescence by instrumental conditioning. Psychosom. Med., 35: 509.

Rosen, R. C., and Schnapp, B. J. 1974. The use of a specific behavioral technique (thought-stopping) in the context of conjoint couples therapy. Behav. Ther., 5: 261.

Semans, J. H. 1956. Premature ejaculation: a new approach. South. Med. J., 49: 353.

Stuart, R. 1969. Operant-interpersonal treatment for marital discord. J. Consult. Clin. Psychol., 33: 675.

Ullmann, L., and Krasner, L. 1969. *A Psychological Approach to Abnormal Behavior*. Prentice-Hall, Englewood Cliffs, N.J.

Wilson, G. T., and Davison, G. C. 1974. Behavior therapy and homosexuality: a critical perspective. Behav. Ther., 5: 16.

Wolpe, J., and Lazarus, A. A. 1966. *Behavior Therapy Techniques*. Pergamon, New York.

EIGHT

Sexually Graphic Material in the Treatment of Sexual Disorders

OLIVER J. W. BJORKSTEN, M.D.

The use of sexually graphic materials has become increasingly prevalent in sex education and therapy over the last few years. Yet, even though more and more people are advocating the therapeutic uses of these materials, there is very little research evidence demonstrating their direct therapeutic efficacy. It is the purpose of this chapter to review some of the over-all effects of "pornography" on normal people; to describe the therapeutic uses of sexually graphic material, including methodology, indications, and contraindications; and to discuss group process and therapist issues related to their uses. Where there is direct research evidence to bear on various aspects of the discussion, it will be mentioned. Since the various uses to which these materials are being put is rapidly increasing, this review will be out of date soon.

SEXUALLY GRAPHIC MATERIAL

There are many kinds of "sexually graphic materials." Probably the most frequently thought of is photographs of explicit erotic subjects. There are many other kinds as well: movies, slides, models, paintings, sound recordings, and literature. Other types which are less obvious include the induction of fantasy either by direct suggestions (*e.g.*, by painting a word picture) or by omission (*e.g.*, by telling someone that a part of the material they are about to see has had explicit material deleted from it) (Tannenbaum, 1970). What makes these stimuli "graphic" is not only the content which is depicted, but also the *expectation* by the observer that these materials will be explicitly sexual.

Unique Features

There are a number of unique features of sexually graphic materials which mainly have to do with the way in which sex is viewed in our society. Because of the widespread belief that many aspects of sex are "dirty" and immoral, it follows, then, that those aspects should be kept hidden. As a result of this secretiveness, people know less about sex than they could, the information they get tends to be vague (or by contrast "dirty"), and paradoxically, when given the opportunity to obtain accurate sexual information, people tend to respond with anxiety, indignation, and avoidance. Most professionals, as products of our society, suffer from these same learnings and attitudes. Contrast the reaction which a medical school class may have to seeing a movie of cholecystectomy versus seeing a movie of a sex change operation. While both movies may upset the students, there would probably be much more anxiety as a result of the latter film. Even if the latter film were one of heterosexual intercourse, there would be much more discomfort in the students if they were asked to react *publicly* to the film (Mussen and Scodel, 1955). Thus, one unique feature of sexually graphic films is the moral dilemma into which they throw the viewers. Needless to say, the intensity of the moral dilemma depends on the particular person, his background, the social context, etc. Especially relevant factors are religion, family morality, subcultural mores, local laws and their enforcement patterns.

The moral issue is of concern in the therapy situation because it can easily cause a therapist to be unnecessarily vague in his discussion with patients. Many gynecologists have models of the female reproductive organs in order to explain aspects of anatomy, but very few of them have models to demonstrate aspects of genital sexual activity.

The second unique feature of sexually graphic material is that it is, in fact, explicit. One can try to describe a pattern of sexual behavior, but nothing can communicate to others more exactly what happens than for them to witness it directly, or indirectly through movies. This becomes especially important for professionals who are supposed to be knowledgeable about a wide variety of sexual behaviors, many of which may not be their own preferred pattern. It would seem advisable for professionals to have at least witnessed various sexual behaviors before they seriously consider the psychodynamics of people who engage in those behaviors. The explicitness of these materials becomes very useful therapeutically not only for education of patients, but for desensitization as well.

Therapy, in its usual connotation, implies the presence of a patient (with a malady), a therapist (with a remedy), and some kind of relationship between these people. Education implies a student (lacking some knowledge), a teacher (possessing some knowledge) and some kind of relationship between the two. The end point of the therapeutic situation is the "cure," and, in the educational situation, the "learning." Both imply satisfaction of the patient/student as the main goal. The purpose of contrasting these two situations is to try to focus on what happens in "sex therapy." Commonly the patient is "suffering" from a lack of learning or a mislearning. Thus, the most important therapeutic factor may be education. What should we call the situation then: therapy or education? The implication of this distinction has to do with the therapist's behavior and responsibility. If the situation is one of an educational nature, as many of the "sex workshops" advertise themselves to be, then the "leader" has a limited responsibility to the participants, and it is questionable whether or not usual medical ethics would apply. On the other hand, if the situation is of a therapeutic nature, in the sense of a standard doctor-patient relationship, then all the professional standards and responsibilities should apply. Needless to say, this has medicolegal implications which sex therapists must consider, especially when they are conducting "educational" or "workshop" programs.

As Mussen and Scodel (1955) have shown, the permissiveness of the atmosphere affects the freedom of response which people will exhibit to sexual topics. Thus, if the therapist behaves in a very austere, aloof, "professional" manner, patients will tend to be reluctant in their expression of sexual ideas. On the other hand, if the therapist behaves more like a teacher who is warm, open, and friendly, there will tend to be much more openness on the part of the clients. Thus, the way the professional thinks of himself, as a therapist and/or a teacher, may directly affect his behavior and, in turn, the patients' response but, on the other hand, lead to the ethical dilemma described above.

The Place of Sexually Graphic Material in Sex Therapy

Sexually graphic material, as used by the Division of Family Study at the University of Pennsylvania Department of Psychiatry, is strictly an adjunct to sex therapy. It is never used alone for the treatment of any marital unit which suffers from a sexual dysfunction. Since we see, at most, 20% of couples presenting to us, as having what might be considered a primary sexual problem, we consider sex therapy to be a part of the broader field of marital therapy. Therefore, sexually graphic materials are used in only a very small percentage of our cases. Before considering how sexually graphic materials are used in our practice, it is relevant to review briefly the effects of "pornography" on normal individuals.

Effects of Sexually Graphic Materials on Normals

In considering the studies which have examined the effects of "pornography" on people, there are a number of problems which emerge. First, the exact nature of the stimulus situation varies from study to study (*i.e.*, the materials used, the context, etc.). Second, the people studied are usually not representative of the population (those most frequently studied are college students). Third, few longitudinal studies have been done on the effects of pornography. Fourth, no studies have been found which examine the effects of pornography on sexually dysfunctional couples. Finally, it appears that the question of whether it is the pornography or the experimental situation itself which causes effects has not been adequately explored (for a notable exception see Mann, Sidman, and Starr, 1970). The last problem is especially relevant to the sex therapy situation where it is common for workshops not only to show sexually graphic materials, but to have group discussion as well. It is unclear whether it is the group discussion or the sexually explicit material, or some interaction, which exerts the most important effect.

A person's response to pornographic material depends on many factors some of which are:

1. Stimulus
   a. Reality of the materials
   b. Duration
   c. Intensity
   d. Perceived intention
   e. Theme
2. Context
   a. Place: home, theatre, laboratory
   b. Other People: alone, presence of others, who is present
   c. Social factors: permissiveness of atmosphere
   d. Demand characteristics of situation
3. Need state of the person
4. Personality
   a. Sex guilt
   b. Sexual identification
   c. Attitudes

5. Socialization: learned sex role differences; background
6. State of consciousness
   a. Intoxicants
   b. Fatigue
   c. Medication
   d. Generalized arousal

The literature has not systematically explored each of these variables, but there is information on some of them.

Levitt (1969) has attempted to study systematically the arousal value of various sexually explicit photographs. He and Hinesley (1967) were able to rank order 19 sexual themes (see Table I). For men, the more explicit the representation of heterosexual coitus, the more arousing they find the photograph.

Kinsey (Kinsey, Pomeroy, and Martin, 1948; Kinsey and associates, 1953) found the same thing by interviewing men and women about their response to erotica. In contrast, however, Kinsey found that, for women, more arousal occurred from material that was less explicit and allowed more fantasies (*e.g.*, reading materials and commercial films).

Levitt found not only that certain themes were more arousing than others for men, but also that the perceived intent of the stimulus mattered. Thus, a picture showing what seemed to be an "accidental" view of a woman's underpants was more

TABLE 8.1

Rank Ordering of Sexual Arousal Properties by a Group of Male Graduate Students[a]

1. Heterosexual coitus in the ventral-ventral position
2. Heterosexual coitus in the ventral-dorsal position
3. Heterosexual petting, participants nude
4. Heterosexual petting, participants partly clad
5. Heterosexual fellatio
6. Nude female
7. Heterosexual cunnilingus
8. Masturbation by a female
9. A triad of two females and one male in conjunctive behavior involving coitus and oral-genital activity
10. Partly clad female
11. Homosexual cunnilingus
12. Homosexual petting by females
13. Sadomasochistic behavior, male on female
14. Homosexual fellatio
15. Sadomasochistic behavior, female on male
16. Masturbation by a male
17. Homosexual anal coitus
18. Nude male
19. Partly clad male

[a] Reprinted with permission from Levitt and Hinesley, 1967.

arousing for men than one which was clearly designed to stimulate, such as a picture of a woman masturbating.

The reality of the stimulus can be considered in two ways, both of which are relevant to the amount of arousal of the observer. First, the stimulus may be graphically more or less realistic (*i.e.*, a photograph versus a drawing); generally, the more realistic, on this dimension, the more arousing a stimulus will be (Goldstein, Kant, and Hartman, 1973). Second, stimuli may be either realistic, in the sense of portraying events which could actually happen, or fantasy-like, portraying scenes which tend to be wish-fulfilling. There appears to be little experimental data bearing on this dimension, but it is noteworthy that much pornography on the market depicts fantasy themes; one could guess that this must be arousing to at least one segment of the population.

The context in which pornography is viewed appears to be quite important as a determinant of the response. Clark (1952) and Mussen and Scodel (1955) studied this question and gathered evidence which would support the common sense notion that the more permissive the atmosphere, the more freely subjects will express sexually oriented ideas. There have been few, if any, studies which examine the freedom of response as related to the subjects' relationships with other audience members. In other words, how would a person respond if he viewed erotic material with his wife, mother, sister, brother, father, close male friend, strangers, etc. present, either all together or with various combinations of these people present? Few studies have examined the effect of the physical location in which pornography is viewed, although there are some notable exceptions (Clark, 1952; Glide Foundation, 1970). Most studies have used a laboratory setting which leaves the generalization of results open to question.

The demand characteristics of the situation in which pornography is viewed also appear to be quite important in determining the response. If the situation is one in which the person is told that the materials he is about to see are pornographic, he will be expecting one kind of stimulus, but if he is told that it is not pornographic, he will be expecting a different kind. Moreover, the value system which he applies in evaluating what he is seeing, and how he "should" respond, may be quite different in the two situations. Expectations and value systems will differ, and there is evidence that when someone is told that a film has been censored he will tend to supply his own erotic scenes where he thinks they have been deleted by censors. These self-supplied scenes may be even more pornographic than the actual scenes which have been censored (Tannenbaum, 1970). Needless to say, these considerations could easily apply to the current practice by the motion picture industry of rating their films for the "protection" of minors. These ratings simply create an expectancy of what will be seen or might have been seen.

The need state of the observer of pornography at the time of the viewing appears not to have been studied. Thus, a person's response to pornography may be quite different if he has just had a satisfying sexual experience rather than a prolonged period of abstinence. The results of several investigations (Schmidt and Sigusch, 1970; Schmidt, Sigusch, and Meyburg, 1969; Sigusch, Schmidt, Reifeld, and Weidermann-Sutor, 1970; Kutschinshy, 1970; Mosher, 1970) agreed that, after viewing pornography, married couples tend to have increased coitus and single people have more sexual fantasies and/or masturbate more. However, the prior sexual behavior of the subjects was not taken into account. These investigators found that this "stimulating" effect of pornography is: (1) short lived, lasting usually no more than 24 hr; (2) does not produce any unusual sexual practices, *i.e.*, the subjects engage in their usual sexual pattern, (3) produces no increase in extramarital sex, and (4) appears to cause little, if any, modeling of what occurs in the films.

Usually, investigators have been interested in what a person will do after exposure to pornography; they have not adequately investigated such factors prior to viewing the erotic material as: successful versus unsuccessful sexual encounter, last sexual release prior to viewing material, attitudes toward pornography, etc. We are left with the interesting question of the relative amount of reinforcement which pornography has: if a person has a high need state, views pornographic material, and then has a sexual encounter which is satisfying (and thus reduces the need state), will the person be reinforced and thus seek out more pornography? If he is reinforced, is it because of the pornography *per se*, or the association between the pornography and the reinforcement of tension reduction due to the satisfying sexual experience (whether it is masturbatory, coital, or any other pattern)?

The personality of the observer of sexually graphic material is related to response. The two factors which have received most attention are sex guilt and sexual identification. Mosher (1970) found that sex guilt, (*i.e.*, guilt about one's sexual impulses and activities) does not preclude arousal but rather causes people not to seek out pornography in the first place. If a person has much sex guilt, he will tend to rate films as more pornographic than those people with lower guilt; he will also rate films as less enjoyable and more disgusting, will tend to feel that scenes of oral-genital behavior are abnormal, and will have more negative affective states after viewing the material. People with higher sex guilt tended to be less sexually experienced in Mosher's study. Further, he has reported that married males and females tend to be rather similar in their ratings of disgust with pornographic materials. This is not the case with single people, among whom females report substantially more disgust than males. High guilt married people generally tend to report less satisfaction with their sexual relationship than low guilt couples. The men in the high guilt group also report more masturbation than low guilt males. Finally, Mosher found that males with high sex guilt were less likely to use exploitive techniques to gain intercourse from their dates and tended to be less successful when they did try to use these techniques than males with low sex guilt. Males who were sexually "calloused" toward women (*i.e.*, believed in exploitive and/or forceful techniques to gain intercourse) tend to be lower in manifest sex guilt.

The strength of a subject's sexual identification may influence his or her response to erotic materials. For effeminate men (Miller and Swanson, 1960) and for masculine-identified women (Goldberg and Milstein, 1965; Loiselle and Mollenauer, 1965) it appears that viewing "threatening" photographs of nude females causes some disorganization of thinking or a greater degree of "perceptual defense." The question of effeminate males' and masculine-identified females' response to nude males appears not to have been investigated. One aspect of sexual identification, a person's sex role learning, is apparently a powerful determinant of the kind of stimuli that a person considers erotic.

Kinsey and associates (1953) found differences between men's and women's interest in erotica, observing that men tended to prefer more direct portrayals of erotic scenes and women preferred portrayals which allowed them to use fantasy (*i.e.*, literary passages, etc.). This finding has since been supported by other investigations (Jakobovits, 1965). Mosher (1970) found that men and women were equally aroused by films of coitus, but men were more aroused than women by films showing oral-genital relations. Generally, the women in this study reported more negative reactions (disgust, etc.) toward the films than did the men.

Socioeconomic background has not been thoroughly studied as a variable in response to erotic stimuli. However, Kinsey and associates (1948) and Gebhard, Gagnon, Pomeroy, and Christensen (1965) both felt that interest in erotica is greater in more highly educated men. Reasons cited for this finding range from greater ability to purchase pornographic materials by wealthier men, to greater need for these materials by higher socioeconomic class men because of the greater prohibition against premarital intercourse.

One group of variables which has received little attention is that related to a person's state of consciousness when exposed to sexually explicit material. Without even considering such substances as the psychedelics, one can question the effects of alcohol and medications (*e.g.*, antidepressants, tranquilizers, sympatholytics, etc.) on arousal from erotica. Clark (1952) attempted to examine this variable by observing men's reactions to erotica when intoxicated at a party or not intoxicated in the classroom. He found, as one might expect, that there was more free expression of response to erotic materials at the party than in the classroom. However, it appears that many variables have been confounded in this study, and this question is still open.

Tannenbaum (1970) has tried to integrate findings from various research efforts concerned not only with the effects of observing sexually graphic materials, but also materials which portray aggression. The unifying concept is that of generalized emotional arousal which can occur from a variety of sources ranging from viewing films of aggression (Berkowitz, Corwin, and Heironimus, 1963; Berkowitz and Rawlings, 1963), to physiological manipulations (Schachter and Singer, 1962; Schachter, 1964), to viewing films or erotic material (Tannenbaum, 1970). Once a person is in a state of generalized arousal, the theory postulates that it is the cognitive cues from the environment which help the person interpret which emotion will be experienced. Thus, for example, Tannenbaum found that if subjects were shown an arousing erotic film and then put in a situation in which an aggressive response was appropriate, they would aggress more than if the subjects were shown either a neutral film or an aggressive film which was not particularly arousing. Thus, some general state of undifferentiated excitement is postulated which can be channeled in various directions which the subject and environment determine. This has direct relevance to a person's response to sexually graphic material because this theory would suggest that the response is to some extent determined by the amount of initial arousal that the person is experiencing at the time the materials are presented. If a person were very fatigued and was experiencing low arousal, the response could be minimal. (It is this rationale that some therapists use when they use techniques of "implosion" or "desensitization" in their sex education workshops.) On the other hand, if a persons' initial level of arousal were very high (*e.g.*, from being very anxious about the materials they were about to see), their response to the materials could be even stronger than it otherwise would be. Moreover, if their initial arousal were caused by some "irrelevant" emotion (*e.g.*, anger at not being able to find a parking place), it could still add to the arousal produced by the film stimuli. It appears that one of the most useful aspects of this theory is that it is not only based on a considerable amount of experimental work, but also offers an explanation for a large number of divergent observations.

Finally, the question of the long-term effects of pornography must be considered. Most studies have investigated subjects' response up to 24 hr after exposure and find a brief increase in sexual behavior, in the usual pattern, if a partner is available. Mosher (1970) found that some attitudes became altered as measured 2 weeks after exposure to pornography (specifically, single people became somewhat more liberal about premarital sex, and married people became more liberal about extramarital sex). Howard, Reifler, and Lipton (1970) studied 23 college mens' responses to being exposed to pornography for 90 min a day for 15 days as compared with nine control subjects who did not see pornography. Physiological measures included: penile erection, heart rate, urinary acid phosphatase, skin temperature, and respiratory rate. They found that this repeated exposure to pornography led to a diminished response, as measured by the above parameters, less interest and reported sexual arousal, and no harmful psychological results, as measured by a battery of psychological tests administered both before and after the exposure to pornography. The total duration of this study was 5 weeks, and, at present, it appears to be one of the longest longitudinal, prospective studies on the effects of pornography. Mann, Sidman and Starr (1970) found no changes in behavior 28 days after married couples had been exposed to pornography or during the month (once a week) that the couples were being shown these materials.

This review has not attempted to be exhaustive but merely highlights our knowledge on some relevant issues. For more complete surveys see Cairns, Paul, and Wishner (1962); Cairns (1970); and Mann (1971).

THERAPEUTIC USES FOR SEXUALLY GRAPHIC MATERIAL

The following therapeutic uses have been found for sexually graphic materials. It will be obvious from examination of these uses that the distinction between educational and therapeutic uses becomes blurred, but it is felt that frequently the two overlap (see discussion above).

Because of the highly charged nature of sexual topics with the consequent secretiveness so frequently found in our society, there is little chance for accurate learning about sexual matters. There is also very little opportunity for people to exchange ideas openly in a safe atmosphere that can provide an opportunity for attitudes to be reexamined. It is often necessary for a therapist to be extremely active in keeping people focused on uncomfortable subjects, such as sex. One way in which people can clearly be "kept to the point" is by showing them sexually explicit materials before a group discussion. Even though avoidance behavior is extremely common after this kind of exposure, it is less easy to maintain than if films are not shown. Moreover, by systematically showing many varieties of sexual behavior, people can become aware of attitudes and conflicts about which they had not known before.

Example 1: The couple presented to the clinic for marital counseling because of frequent disagreements and less frequent sexual contact than the two desired. He is a 45-year-old business executive who is successful at present, after severe prior business reversals, and is married for the second time after his first wife died. He brings 2 children to this marriage. She is 30 years old, was briefly married before, and has 1 child by the present marriage. In the course of marital therapy it became clear that the husband was a rather anxious man who had extreme performance concerns and suffered from premature ejaculation to which he would not admit. The wife was an extremely emotionally labile person who was angry most of the time, resentful at her husband's passivity and sexual inhibition, but also angry when he was decisive. The couple requested that they be referred to a "sexual enrichment workshop" which they then attended over a weekend. They were exposed to explicit erotic film materials and group discussions with other couples. The major effects of this experience on this couple were (1) a transitory sense of well being and closeness; (2) briefly improved sexual relationship; and (3) the realization by the husband that he was extremely inhibited about masturbation.

Even though a thorough sex history had been obtained early in the course of treatment, it was not clear either to the therapist or to the husband the extent of his inhibition about self-stimulation. The couple has sabotaged all attempts to deal with the sexual problem directly and at present, over 1½ years after treatment began, still has the same sexual and relationship difficulties.

The main point of this example is that even though the sexually graphic materials had no over-all effect on the clinical course of this couple, it had a dramatic effect on the husband by clearly demonstrating to him some inhibitions of which he was unaware.

Another common occurrence is that when professionals have occasion to observe sexual patterns they have learned about, their attitudes about those patterns begin to loosen and become redefined. For example, when mental health professionals are shown the National Sex Forum film, "Soma Touch," of a male masturbating in a rather dramatic manner, many of them will often diagnose the male as "homosexual." When asked what they actually saw which led them to this diagnosis, they usually cite such evidence as: "narcissism," "exhibitionism," "self-preoccupation," and "flamboyancy." When confronted with the fact that there is no actual homosexual behavior in the film and that, by definition, any person who masturbates must be "self-preoccupied," the professionals are forced to rethink exactly what criteria they use to decide the nature of a person's sexual identity.

It is not infrequent that professionals define every film they see, in a sequence of films, as in some way abnormal. Finally, when they have seen every variety of sexual behavior that they can imagine, including the pattern they engage in, they are forced to rethink their definitions of normality and consider the interaction of their own inhibitions and past learnings on their clinical judgement.

Needless to say, there are many attitudes and feelings which people have about sexuality which they can scrutinize when given the chance. The few examples cited above are frequent ones which we have seen.

Education

Sexually graphic materials can serve a very useful educational purpose for patients. These materials can provide information more rapidly than an explanation and often more accurately as well. It is quicker and more accurate to show a man a picture of the vulva and point out the location of the clitoris than to try to explain it to him. Sexually graphic materials can be extremely useful in teaching patients about their anatomy. This is important not only for people with birth defects but for those with normal anatomy as well (Money, 1970).

Example 2: A couple in their late twenties presented at the clinic with the complaint that the wife had never had an orgasm in her entire life by any means at all. They had been married for 7 years and have 2 children. Both have doctoral level degrees in biologically related fields. During the first session it became apparent that neither one knew the location or the function of the clitoris. To verify this finding, they were shown a picture of the vulva, and neither knew the anatomy beyond the most rudimentary level. The clitoris was pointed out and the couple was instructed to try to locate it "*in vivo*." They returned the next week and reported that not only had they found the clitoris, but that she found it so enjoyable when it was touched, that she had been orgasmic several times. After 2 years, the woman is still orgasmic with no further sexual counseling. The marriage, however, deteriorated and the couple separated 1½ years after they were initially seen and after 1 year of marital therapy.

Couples can learn more about their anatomy, about coital techniques, and about therapeutic techniques as well. For example, the film produced by the National Sex Forum, "The Squeeze Technique," demonstrates this technique more accurately in 12 min than many therapists can in an hour. (Showing the film also requires no therapist time.) New films are being produced to demonstrate such things as the "sexological examination" to professionals.

Couples report two other educational effects from seeing erotica. First, they are often forced to develop an effective vocabulary referring to sexual matters after they have been exposed to these materials; and, second, seeing other couples engaging in sexual relations in the films gives the observing couples a feeling that permission has been given to them to enjoy sex and provides them with some people after whom they may model themselves.

Fantasy Building

One of the many prohibitions which people may experience is that against sexual thoughts and fantasies. It is reasonable that if sex is "dirty and immoral," one should not dwell on it unnecessarily. A consequence of this is that a number of men and women have a paucity of sexual fantasies, which has the effect of causing lack of continuity in sexual relationships. In other words, during a sexual encounter a person may have a hard time providing his own internal cues which make arousal feel continuous and instead depends entirely on external stimulation, which, no matter how sensitive, can never be as smooth, fulfilling, and continuous as internal fantasies (Stanley, 1974).

Another consequence is that some people with sexual fears may actively inhibit the fantasies of the things of which they are afraid (*i.e.*, internal avoidance), even if those things are, by most standards, commonplace.

Example 3: A 24-year-old single male presented to the clinic with the problem that he wished to engage in heterosexual relationships but was homosexual. The patient had never had a heterosexual experience, and he had been exclusively homosexual since the age of 16 when first seduced by his brother some 4 years older. After many months of developing a therapeutic relationship with the patient, and exploring his feelings about his interpersonal relationships, it became apparent that his major problems involved: (1) lack of knowledge about how to engage in heterosexual relationships (*i.e.*, he felt that women were completely different from men and that none of the skills he had in interpersonal or sexual relations with men applied to women); (2) fear of women's genitals; and (3) difficulty with intimacy with men such that even though the patient engaged in sex with men, he had no close friends who were male.

Two approaches were used. First, the patient was taught how to sexually approach a woman. This was done by having him develop a hierarchy of sexual approach; he was shown pictures of nude women (something he had never seen before). It was clear that the patient could not have sexual fantasies of women if he had never seen nude women. He was asked to grade pictures of nude women on the basis of whether they were stimulating or aversive to him, mainly for the purpose that he really look at the pictures. (In fact, the patient found the pubic hair to be the most distasteful thing but only when there was a direct view of the perineum.)

The erotica were used to lend reality to the sexual approach hierarchy which was then presented to the patient after he was in a state of deep muscular relaxation. He was able to visualize all steps of the hierarchy rapidly. During a homosexual encounter (which had never been prohibited), he felt confident that he could have intercourse with a woman. A few weeks later he had successful intercourse with a woman friend, and he eventually formed an intense relationship with her which lasted for 8 months.

Since that time he has been able to form normal sexual relationships with women, but he has spent most of his time over the last 2 years in therapy working on his relationship with men.

The point of this example is that it is impossible for a person to have fantasies about things to which he has never been exposed. One might question why it was that this patient was never exposed to nude women, either by pictures or by experience. It is probable that the same family background which led to his massive inhibition to being aggressive and assertive (and with women, thus "nasty") led him to avoid exposing himself to the very things which could help him overcome those inhibitions. It also helped him to feel that heterosexual objects were bad and to be avoided, which he did, in deed as well as thought.

Performance anxiety is one of the most common causes of sexual dysfunction. One common form of performance anxiety is the fear that one's fantasies are abnormal, such that if, during a sexual experience, certain things cross one's mind, then one is "sick." This forces people into the difficult position of trying to control their thoughts but, more commonly, of feeling badly after they have already had the "bad" thoughts. By viewing sexually explicit materials, these people often experience that permission has been given to them to think about what they please.

Trigger Films for Group Discussion

It can be most helpful for people to discuss sexual matters in a group situation, but they tend to avoid this most embarrasing subject. Sexually graphic materials can be used to trigger group discussion about sex. Once sex has been talked about, it seems that many other issues become easier to discuss. The result is the sense of a successful experience and usually a subsequent increase in group cohesiveness.

Behavior Therapy

There are at least two applications for sexually explicit materials which have not been discussed. Both of these are forms of behavior therapy: aversive conditioning and desensitization. In aversive conditioning, sexually explicit pictures which represent the patient's sexual object are paired with some noxious stimulus (such as electric shock), such that the person learns to associate an unpleasant feeling with the image of the sex object (Feldman and MacCullock, 1967; Cautela, 1967). The purpose of this procedure is to change patients' sexual patterns which utilize "undesirable" sex objects, such as children, fetish objects, etc.

Desensitization is a widely used technique in behavior therapy and is gaining more and more acceptance as a technique in the therapy of sexual disabilities. The technique of systematic desensitization, developed by Wolpe (Wolpe, 1974; Friedman and Goldstein, 1974), involves the graded exposure of the patient to things he is afraid of, while he is in a state of deep muscular relaxation. This is usually done by developing a hierarchy of intensity of the fearful object with the patient's cooperation. After this hierarchy has been agreed upon, the patient is put into a state of relaxation by one of many techniques including brevital (Brady, 1966), or Jacobsen's progressive relaxation (Jacobsen, 1938), and the hierarchy is presented, beginning with the least feared step first. The patient is kept in the relaxed state by trying never to expose him to a step in the hierarchy which is "too big," *i.e.*, creating more anxiety than can be overcome by the relaxed state the patient is in. Wolpe (1974) has described variants of the desensitization technique when ideal circumstances are impossible to create. One of these variants is "desensitization *in vivo*" in which the patient actually lives out the stepwise progression along the hierarchy, instead of using fantasy. It is this variant that is used in some forms of sex therapy, including the use of explicit erotic materials.

There are several methods by which sexually graphic materials are used, and the exact method may desensitize different things.

These various methods will be described below but suffice it to say that most methods involve either simply the viewing of explicit materials, or both the viewing and then discussion of them. Some methods involve the gradual exposure of people to more and more explicit materials, and other methods attempt to bombard the audience with massive input of erotica, which is a form of "flooding," or "implosion" rather than systematic desensitization. As mentioned above, if sexually graphic materials are shown with little or no discussion, they have little long-term effect. If desensitization were to occur, one might expect it to alter: (1) anxieties about sexual behaviors; (2) the person's disgust with certain sexual fantasies or behaviors; and (3) anxieties about a person's self-image. As a consequence of these changes in feelings, a person's attitude may change to make him more open to varieties of sexual values. Prolonged exposure to erotica has been shown to lead to a lessening of arousal (Howard, Reifler, and Liptzin, 1970) and might be considered an example of habituation rather than desensitization. The point is that simply showing erotica could not be expected to desensitize more than what the materials depict. For example, it could not be expected to desensitize a person to the social aspects of the sexual situations, such as talking about sexual topics, social inhibitions, etc.

If exposure to sexually graphic materials is followed by discussion, either in a group situation or with a therapist, one could expect desensitization of not only all the things suggested above but the anxiety about discussion of sexual topics as well. In other words, secretiveness about sex, which is a norm in our culture and produces embarrassment when people try to talk about the subject, may be directly attacked by desensitizing the anxiety surrounding *discussion* of sexual topics. This has particular relevance for sexual partners who wish to communicate more freely with each other and for professionals who are expected to be able to obtain accurate and specific sex histories from their patients. Unfortunately, there are no studies available which clearly demonstrate which is more important: desensitization of anxiety about sexual behavior by observing erotica or desensitization of anxiety about *discussion* of sexual topics. If desensitization of anxiety surrounding the discussion of sexual topics is more important, then the use of sexually graphic materials may be unnecessary in this situation.

Special emphasis should be placed on the importance of teaching experiences, which are aimed at improving students' "comfort level" with discussion of sexual topics with their patients. Studies at the University of Pennsylvania (Vines, 1974) have demonstrated that exposure of medical students to both sexually graphic materials and group discussion in a 2-day "workshop" can significantly reduce their anxiety when taking a sexual history as compared with controls. Anxiety was inferred from four dimensions which were rated by independent observers of videotaped interviews.

METHODS OF USING SEXUALLY GRAPHIC MATERIALS

The method that one chooses by which to expose people to sexually graphic materials depends on one's goals for treatment. No matter which method one picks, however, it is important that the presentation be done well, since many seemingly minor or extraneous factors can have a huge impact on the audience. For example, if music accompanies the presentation of a sexually explicit film, the exact composition is important; the quality of the film, the comfort of the seating (on chairs, on the floor, etc.), and the general atmosphere of formality or permissiveness all dramatically affect the manner and degree to which an audience will respond. Thus, most groups which use these materials strive for smooth, technically perfect presentations, and they often develop rather sophisticated equipment and technical finesse.

The various methods used today can generally be divided into those which utilize a "workshop" format and will be called "massed presentations" or those which divide exposure of the materials into segments separated by a longer period of time, called "spaced presentations." Needless to say, there are gradations between the two types of presentations.

Massed Presentations

The rationale for using a massed method of presentation ranges from a rapid form of systematic desensitization to downright implosive bombardment. Most groups which utilize these methods hope that the anxiety response, which is greatest early in the experience, will be fatigued by the end of it, such that the participants are more comfortable with their own sexual thoughts and with discussion of sexual topics. Since most massed experiences occur over a period of 1 or more days, they are a convenient way of rapidly obtaining a change in the participants. There are some indications that because of the massing of input these methods may actually be more effective at increasing comfort level than the spaced methods.

General characteristics of massed methods include: (1) at least a 1-day format; (2) a large amount of sexually graphic material shown in a relatively short period of time; (3) a special environment; (4) group discussions; (5) group and workshop leaders usually not being therapists of the participants (although this is by no means always true, nor is it necessarily harmful); (6) group leaders experienced in group process and who utilize methods of group dynamics and group psychotherapy; (7) partners encouraged to attend workshops together; (8) use of various group exercises to facilitate communication, etc.; and (9) exposure to a considerable amount of educational material.

Types of Massed Methods

All of the specific models described below have evolved since their inception and are continuing to be refined. Therefore, all of these descriptions should be viewed as examples of methodologies, and the centers whose names are associated with the descriptions are their originators.

1. National Sex Forum Model. This model originated in San Francisco at the National Sex Forum and has been refined not only at the University of California Medical School, San Francisco, but at the University of Minnesota Medical School as well. Many other centers employ this model today, and there are probably numerous variants of it. It was probably the first workshop of its kind.

The audience, which may range in size from small numbers of people to over 100, and may consist of either individuals alone or with their partners, meets in a very comfortable, large theatre. Large pillows are used for the participants to sit on and an atmosphere of informality is encouraged. After an introduction, in which the purpose of the workshop is explained and the audience is put at ease as much as possible, they are shown various audiovisual materials. Usually the presentation begins with materials which are not too sexually explicit, but it soon includes nudity and then other forms of sexually graphic materials. Interspersed with these presentations may be various lecture inputs to the audience. After the first session there is a small group discussion in which up to 12 people can share their reactions to the program. After a break, this same process continues, ending with a small group, followed by a presentation known as the "sexorama" in which the audience is bombarded with a large number of sexually graphic materials simultaneously for a period of hours (usually 1 to 2 hr). Depending on the time available, a 2nd or 3rd day may be provided. On some occasions the 2nd day may be very similar to the 1st, but, on others, much more didactic information may be presented (*e.g.*, for professionals who are trying to learn as much as possible about human sexuality) or the opportunity to work on relationship issues may be provided. Currently, emphasis is placed on the small group discussions which generally occur 3 times each day of the workshop.

The National Sex Forum has been extremely effective in the development of new audiovisual materials and literature for their programs, and it has produced a series of sexually graphic films which are widely used. These films are usually referred to as the "Glide Films" (since the National Sex Forum was originally a service of the Glide Foundation of the Glide Methodist Church in San Francisco). A description and evaluation of the effects of their early programs appear in Volume V of the Technical Reports of the Commission on Obscenity and Pornography.

After seeing an extremely massed presentation of sexually graphic materials, as is typical in these programs, the participants experience extreme fatigue and are not surprised or anxious at seeing almost any kind of erotica. They are much more able to discuss sexual topics freely with one another and much more receptive to accurate information about sexual matters, since they are less likely to distort facts by their anxiety. It is noteworthy that there have been no harmful effects reported from these programs.

2. University of Pennsylvania Model. The model developed at this center differs from the previous one in that it: (1) presents smaller segments of sexually graphic material at a time; (2) intersperses small group discussion more frequently; and (3) was developed by using a population which was in marital therapy for a variety of problems, some of which included sexual difficulties. Only later was this model expanded to serve more educational purposes. Since they were developed primarily with clients in therapy, the workshops tend to remain smaller, consisting of 10 to 15 couples.

Typically, 10 couples in marital therapy are referred by their therapists to these weekend workshops, and they have not met prior to the experience. Early on the 1st day there is a brief introduction which explains the purpose of the workshop and attempts to set the participants at ease. They are then shown a number of segments of audiovisual materials which follows a more or less psychosexual developmental pattern: first, a segment relating to fantasies and cultural issues, then masturbation, followed by homosexuality. After these segments follow ones contrasting sensuality (a film on dance therapy with autistic children) and crass sexuality ("hard-core" pornography films, slides, etc.). Finally, there are segments on heterosexuality and pleasuring.

Each audiovisual segment is followed by a small group discussion led by male-female coleaders. There are no more than 10 members in any group, and couples are split in such a way that partners are not in the same group. It is felt that by splitting the partners they will not only get twice as much group experience (by being exposed to 18 other people instead of only 8), but they also can set aside some of their immediate relationship problems and focus on their own sexual feelings and attitudes more effectively. The 1st day usually begins at 9:00 a.m. and ends about 6:00 p.m. Couples are encouraged to spend more time alone together that evening, but most return home.

The next morning begins with a small group discussion during which participants can relate their reaction to the previous day's experience, as well as what occurred with their partner that evening. Following this small group discussion, the entire group convenes for a general discussion of human sexuality. This is usually conducted by all the leaders and is mainly a question and answer period. During the small group discussions, factual material is not discussed since it often fosters avoidance of emotional issues. These factual questions are deferred to the morning discussion of the 2nd day. The workshop ends at noon of the 2nd day. The following is a specific agenda:

SAMPLE WORKSHOP FORMAT

Day 1		*Day 2*	
8:30	Introduction	9:00	Small group discussion
9:00	Genesis slides* Unfolding	10:00	Plenary session—open discussion of any questions on human sexuality
9:20	Small group discussion		
10:00	Soma touch Susan (or Shirley)	11:45	Evaluation
10:30	Small group discussion	12:00	End of workshop
11:15	*vir amat* Holding		
11:45	Small group discussion		
12:30	Lunch		
1:30	Looking for me "pornography" slides		
2:00	Small group discussion		
2:45	Rich & Judy Free		
3:15	Small group discussion		
4:00	Erogenists, squeeze technique Give to get		
4:30	Small group discussion		
5:15	Touching		
5:30	End of day 1		

* All materials produced by the Multimedia Resource Center (540 Powell Street, San Francisco, Calif. 94108).

There are many effects that these workshops have on the participants, but all of the following effects do not occur on any given person or couple. (1) Immediate effects on the individual participants include: sexual arousal; acute sense of failure that they cannot be uninhibited like the people in the films and that their relationships with their partners are not like they imagine those in the films to be; and the feeling that they have been given permission to be sexual people. (2) Immediate effects on the couples include: dramatically increased communication. This is the single largest effect of these workshops. Couples open up about secret thoughts and feelings that may have to do with any area of their lives, not necessarily sex. (If one can talk about "dirty" subjects with strangers, one can talk about anything with one's partner!) The couples tend to feel less isolated; they become much more interested in each other's bodies and in sensuality; and finally, in some couples, the dysfunction (either marital or sexual) is exacerbated, thus preventing denial of the problem. (3) Long-term effects on the individual include: increased knowledge about sex; decreased belief in sexual myths; decreased social inhibition; and the feeling that permission has been given to be social. (4) Long-term effects on the couple include: increased communication; more effective utilization of therapy; and increased contact and openness with other couples. The effect on marital therapy can be dramatic, and therapists who refer clients to these workshops estimate that they can reduce up to 30% of a couple's time in marital therapy.

A great concern was whether or not these workshops could be harmful to the participants since they were by definition not "normal, healthy" people, at least in their present relationships. A long-term follow-up study is being conducted with 65 couples who have participated in these workshops. Of these couples, there were no casualties, as defined by acute depression or anxiety lasting longer than 3 weeks or an acute psychotic episode. Although several of the participants became acutely upset, this tended to change the nature of their marital relationship, which was productively used in therapy. All of the couples' therapists were questioned and no later casualties, unseen at the time of the workshop, appeared. Generally, those who became upset had an acute sense of failing to live up to the performance, behaviors, and relationships portrayed in films. This follow-up study will be reported in detail when completed.

After experience with several hundred clients, there have been less than five casualties to the best of our knowledge. Thus, it is felt that these workshops are not harmful to couples in marital therapy and to many patients in individual psychotherapy.

3. University of Texas Medical School, Galveston, Model

(Pullian, Croft, Powell, Cruson, and Blakney, 1974; Powell, Blakney, Croft, and Pullian, 1974). It appears that at the present time, this model is the one most strictly devoted to the direct treatment of sexual dysfunction and involves the widest variety of techniques. Each couple that is to participate in the workshop is selected on the basis of having a sexual dysfunction and undergoes not only a history and physical examination, but also a "sexological" examination prior to the workshop. The purpose of the sexological examination is not primarily to examine the patients' sexual areas but to educate them about their own bodies and the bodies of their partners.

The workshop typically begins at noon of the 1st day and occurs in a setting in which there are facilities for showing audiovisual materials and small group discussion and where each couple can have complete privacy as well. The workshop team consists of a multidisciplinary group (psychiatrist, psychologist, gynecologist, etc.) and has at least one member "on call" in the workshop area, day and night, to handle crises. Each other staff member is available at home if needed by his or her patients. This close supervision is planned not only as part of responsible patient care, but it has been experience of this group that rapid treatment often produces some stage of crisis in their patients. (This is the same observation which Masters and Johnson (1970) have made in their rapid treatment of sexual dysfunctions.)

There are five main components of these workshops: exposure to sexually graphic materials, small group discussion, sex education, practice sessions, and meetings between each couple and the workshop leader responsible for them in particular. After an introduction explaining the basic format, goals, and types of materials the couples can expect to see, some humorous materials are shown, and anatomy and physiology of sexual functioning are discussed with the emphasis being placed on sex as a natural biological function. It is clear that this group is able to maintain a concerned, hopeful, and lighthearted atmosphere in their workshops by the appropriate use of humor. This is probably one very important factor in their success. Following this discussion and exposure to audiovisual materials, the couples are given their first assignment to carry out alone: go to their private rooms, undress as much as possible (the amount is not crucial), discuss childhood learning about sex, and the principles on which the workshop is based (a list of "principles" is given to each couple prior to the workshop), and compose "turn-on" lists of things they find pleasurable. They then reassemble, fully clothed, in the main group room to have a group discussion of sexual myths, body image, and more sexual physiology. The ground rules of these groups are such that individuals do not have to share information from their pasts. The next exercise that each couple is assigned to do in private consists of undressing as much as possible (hopefully more than the last time if it was a problem), facing each other, and touching each other's face. After this, the couple stands in front of a mirror and each person tells what he or she likes about the other's body.

The men and women then meet as single-sex groups to discuss face touching and sensuality in general. The whole group then convenes to see films on "pleasuring." The use of body oils is then explained to the couples, and they are asked to have a third private session together to begin nongenital body caressing, with the ground rule that the receiver must tell the giver what he or she does not enjoy. The next meeting is of the whole group for a discussion of sexual fantasies and observation of erotic films which focus on sexual fantasy, followed by a fourth private couples' session which consists of nongenital body caress during which the receiver tells what does feel good. This ends the formal program for the 1st day, except that after dinner, each couple is seen alone to discuss the happenings of the workshop up to that point. Crises tend to occur most often during this 1st night, varying according to the relationship of the partners.

The 2nd day has the same format as the 1st and begins with exposure to films showing masturbation. During the fifth private couples' session (*i.e.*, the first one of the 2nd day) which follows the film sequence, permission is given to the partners to touch each other's genitals in an exploratory manner, in which no response is required. A noon break is followed by a discussion of the "squeeze technique" and a film is shown of it. The couples then retire for the sixth time, and the female partner does the "squeeze technique" on the male. This is encouraged for all couples regardless of whether premature ejaculation is a problem because it requires the male to be a passive observer of himself and the situation. This is felt often to be of great use to the men. Further group discussion and audiovisual input is followed by the seventh private couples' session in which nondemanding pleasuring and possibly vaginal stuffing of the partially limp penis are permitted. The 2nd day ends with more individual sessions for each couple. In general, the atmosphere is much less tense by this point in the workshop.

The 3rd day begins with a group meeting of all the couples to discuss their progress, information about positions used in sexual relations, oral-genital sexuality, and other patterns of sexual behavior. During the eighth private couples' session, the partners are given permission to have intercourse if they wish. This session is followed by a meeting of the whole group to discuss the problems of reentry, how to discuss sex with their children, their "turn-on" lists, and finally the principles which were originally presented to them.

This model has been developed over the last 1½ years and seems to represent a synthesis of many methods of treating sexual dysfunction. The over-all principle, however, appears to be to expose the participants to a carefully patterned sequence of events which are progressively more anxiety-provoking, and thus represents an *in vivo* desensitization process. Of all the models with which I am familiar, this one seems to be the most carefully designed with respect to this desensitization sequence and probably helps to account for its high initial success rate.

Follow-up studies are being conducted on the outcome of this workshop model, and at the present time data are available from 30 couples. These 30 couples had 38 sexual symptoms, most of which were premature ejaculation and situational orgasmic dysfunction. Of these 38 symptoms, 36 were reversed by the end of the workshop (and 1 reversed the following week). Of the 30 couples, 6 have sought more marital therapy and 2 have since divorced. The particupar dysfunctions which appear most amenable to this treatment are premature ejaculation and situational orgasmic dysfunction.

There are a number of issues which need to be resolved with respect to the "mechanism of action" of these workshops. First is the question of the effect of viewing one sexually graphic film at a time versus exposure to many inputs simultaneously. Proponents of the former method would argue that by showing many films simultaneously, a person could always shift his attention away from scenes which are uncomfortable and instead watch more pleasant ones, thus diminishing the impact of the sexually graphic material. They would further suggest that by showing one film at a time, this visual avoidance would be prevented and fewer materials would be necessary since each input would have more impact. Proponents of the second method would argue that by bombarding a person with more input than he can process, it would not matter if some avoidance occurred because the person is overloaded anyway such that his defenses are bypassed and the anxiety response fatigued (*i.e.*, a form of the technique in behavior therapy called "flooding"). It is clear that both methods work in the hands of the groups which use them, but this theoretical question may have practical relevance for clinicians who cannot produce bombardment sequences because of lack of money, technical assistance, or facilities.

Second is the relative importance of the sexually graphic

materials versus the group discussions that all these workshops provide. From our earlier discussion it became clear that simply showing sexually graphic materials does not have a prolonged effect on couples. On the other hand, although group discussions of sexual topics without the use of sexually graphic materials may be helpful, there is some question as to whether they have as much impact as when these materials are used. Thus the most plausible hypothesis at present seems to be that the maximal effect occurs if both elements are used together. The sexually graphic materials may provide the focus (as does the group leader) and the generalized arousal, and the group discussion provides the opportunity to reevaluate attitudes and desensitize anxiety surrounding discussion of sexual topics. Again this issue, while theoretically important, has practical relevance in that its consideration may help the clinician to plan workshops which have a maximal impact with minimal facilities.

Third, an issue which may anticipate the following discussion, is how massed or spaced the exposure must be in order to produce any effect and/or a maximal effect. This is really a question of determining a threshold of effect, as well as the speed of habituation of exposure to these materials. Even from the description of the massed methods it should be clear that the amount of exposure varies a great deal, ranging from bombardment to occasional inputs. In general, it can be concluded that showing several hours of sexually graphic materials in 1 day will produce desensitization. How much less than this is also effective? Howard, Reifler, and Liptzin (1970) showed 1½ hr of material daily for 15 days and observed a significant decrease in arousal (this may be different from desensitization of anxiety surrounding sexual behavior and discussion). At least they observed an effect. Studies at the University of Pennsylvania (Vines, 1974) compared three conditions in their effectiveness in desensitizing anxiety surrounding discussion of sexual topics (specifically, taking a sex history by 3rd year medical students): first, massed exposure and group discussion (U. of Pa. Model); second, weekly exposure of the same sexually explicit materials in the context of lectures to medical students but also in conjunction with small group discussion; and, finally, no exposure to either audiovisual materials or group discussion (control group). A significant difference was found in anxiety level between the massed condition and the controls but not between the spaced condition and the controls.

Even though this study could not determine whether the group discussion or the sexually graphic materials was most important in producing desensitization, what it did help to clarify was how little one can do and still get a significant effect (*i.e.*, weekly 2-hr exposure to group discussion and sexually graphic materials is not effective). Again, from the clinical point of view, one may not need to utilize a bombardment workshop in order to effectively produce desensitization, but one cannot space the exposures too far apart either.

Finally, an issue which is of crucial importance is the prior experience and attitude structure of the participants in workshops. This issue has received little research attention and in our experience greatly affects a person's response. One plausible hypothesis is that the more conservative a group of people, the greater tendency for them to become anxious when exposed to sexually graphic material. If this is true, the practical significance is that for those groups it would be more effective to expose them only *gradually* to sexually graphic materials, consistent with systematic desensitization. Massive exposure might be expected to cause such an intense reaction that they would have a strong tendency to avoid the situation by either leaving, not paying attention, or "making their minds up" and sticking to old attitudes "no matter what." Conversely, for people who have had a good deal of prior exposure to sexually graphic materials, spaced presentations may be "old hat" and not very interesting. It would be expected that those groups would require a more intense presentation of these materials.

Spaced Presentations

Spaced presentations are those situations in which sexually graphic materials are used only occasionally or with a significant period of time between exposures. The issue of how spaced is "spaced" has been discussed above. The rationale of most intermittent presentations is that showing is better than telling, *i.e.*, the materials are used as a demonstration and not to alter anxiety or attitudes.

Characteristically, spaced presentations as part of an ongoing therapy tend to be relatively short (*i.e.*, less than an hr), are presented by the patient's own therapist, and demonstrate some point in the therapeutic process.

Some examples of spaced presentations include: showing anatomical models to patients to educate them about anatomy; showing films to demonstrate pleasuring, the squeeze technique, or various sexual behaviors; or showing sexually explicit material to patients who have a paucity of sexual fantasies of a particular type. These materials are often used as part of lectures given to students taking courses in human sexuality.

The therapeutic effectiveness of spaced presentations of sexually graphic material on patients' sexual problems has not been studied. Our experience has been that they are seldom necessary and, when used, are best received after the couple has first had the chance to try out for themselves whatever the films portray. Thus, for example, when the couples see films of pleasuring (*i.e.*, body caress), they will hopefully have the reaction "Oh, that is what we did, there's nothing so special about that film." This tends to create a success experience rather than a performance anxiety (that they will not do as well as the couple in the film). The most effective use for these materials, in our experience, is for education of couples with respect to anatomy and sexual behavior.

Even though less sexually graphic materials are used in the spaced methods, there are probably more therapeutic issues raised by them than when patients attend workshops. The crucial factor is that the couple's own therapist is the person who is responsible for exposing the patients to these materials; in a workshop, the leaders are not in the same kind of relationship with the patient as their therapist. Generally speaking, when these materials are used judiciously and for a clear purpose, the therapeutic relationship is strengthened (Alger, 1969). Often the patients feel that the therapist is trying to use all available means to help them. Therapists probably have more reservations and fears about using these materials (as well as direct means of intervention in general) than do patients. They tend to be embarrassed about being associated with "dirty" materials, feel they may insult "respectable" patients, fear that the patients may begin distorted rumors about them and that the therapeutic relationship will be destroyed.

There are some genuine concerns, however, that any responsible therapist must consider. If an expressive form of psychotherapy is being used (*e.g.*, psychoanalytically oriented psychotherapy) in which one hopes that a transferance relationship will develop, it is likely that the patient will perceive the therapist as advocating a position if he utilizes these materials, and the transference will be altered in an undesirable direction. Even in direct intervention therapies transference occurs but in a somewhat different form than in expressive therapies. Use of sexually graphic materials can cause this transference to become more sexualized than the patient or therapist can effectively handle. For example, couples often perceive a therapist to represent the "perfect partner!" They may wish they had the therapist instead of their own partner, and when the therapist shows them sexually graphic materials, this fantasy is further elaborated to include a "perfect" sexual relationship with the therapist. The other partner may easily perceive this feeling and become jealous, angry, or depressed. Unless the therapist is most adept at balancing the therapeutic relationship with the couple, this can lead to the couple leaving therapy.

The therapist's own motivations must also be scrutinized when he decides to utilize sexually graphic materials. If the therapist finds himself attracted to one of the partners he is counseling, not only may he permit the "perfect partner" fantasy to continue but may also act out his own fantasy by deciding to have a vicarious sexual relationship with the patient via erotica. The therapist may also dislike one partner of a couple and utilize these materials to act out his aggressive feelings if he senses that exposure to them may precipitate performance anxiety in the patient. The therapist must also consider his own narcissistic and exhibitionistic impulses when he is responsible for showing erotica to patients.

Therapists may be reassured, on the other hand, that purposeful exposure to erotica may expose more of the therapist's value system in a way which strengthens the relationship. Finally, if the therapist responds to the erotica with some measure of arousal, he may become quite guilty and unnecessarily question countertransference feelings. Therapists should be reassured that some degree of arousal *from the materials* being shown is not harmful and may be expected, unless they are totally habituated to the materials, which is rare.

GROUP PROCESS ISSUES

Small group discussions form an important part of most workshops which utilize sexually graphic materials. It is important for the leaders to have a thorough knowledge of the principles of group dynamics and psychotherapy. While it is impossible to explain "how to lead a group" in the space available here, an attempt will be made to outline some of the relevant group issues. The assumption will be made that the reader has some familiarity with the group dynamics; for those who do not, valuable references include: Yalom (1970), Cartwright and Zander (1968), and Kaplan and Sadock (1971).

Discussion groups usually follow exposure of the participants to the sexually graphic materials, meet in a separate room, and consist of between 8 and 12 members. Couples may or may not be separated, but usually attempts are made to have both sexes in the groups. Generally, dual sex coleaders are preferred, and the length of the session may vary from 30 to 90 min. The number of group meetings may vary greatly from workshop to workshop, depending on the goals.

The leaders' behavior tends to differ some from that typical in psychotherapy groups, in that they are more self-disclosing, are more responsive to the participants, and do not necessarily pursue and explore psychodynamic leads or make many massed group interpretations. They will allow the group to be more "dependent," early in its existence, by breaking silences and facilitating discussion. Since the life of the group is, by definition, short, and the over-all goal is for participants to share immediate feelings and thoughts, not explore depth material, the leaders must attempt to quickly reduce anxiety and create an atmosphere of friendliness, openness, and acceptance of differing points of view. They must take an active role in setting desirable norms and altering undesirable ones.

Norms may be thought of as rules or expectations which occur in groups and can develop extremely rapidly. It is the norms which are felt as "what you can do," or "what you can't do" in the group. The following are considered desirable norms: (1) here and now discussion of feelings, thoughts, and attitudes (*i.e.*, discussions of whether sexually graphic materials should be shown to children, how the cameraman must have taken that shot, or lengthy stories of "movies I saw 20 years ago," are all considered undesirable); (2) an atmosphere of personal attitude reevaluation and a stance that one's own attitudes and opinions may differ from other peoples'; (3) safety that one will not be belittled for expressing different points of view (if people do not feel safe, they will tend to be silent or remain at a story-telling level); (4) use of specific words when discussing thoughts and reactions to the material; (5) encouragement of humor; (6) openness and some self-disclosure by the leaders to serve as a model for other group members; and finally, (7) cohesiveness.

Norms considered to be most undesirable are: (1) judgemental statements (*i.e*, "it is wrong to believe such and such"); (2) autocratic leader behavior (*e.g.*, it is not the place of the leader to proselytize his or her personal point of view, except to allow for the relativity of attitudes; a person has as much right to his conservative attitudes as to his liberal ones); (3) arguing with expressed attitudes (one's attitudes usually cannot be defended on a factual basis because they were learned over years of experience); (4) avoidance of open discussion of feelings (usually by rational discussions of peripheral topics such as technique of film production, efficacy, or uses of the materials, or excessive openness, and finally, (5) the use of vague, general vocabulary in the discussion.

These norms are only some of the many which develop in groups, but they are considered to be the most important ones for these particular group situations. Whenever there is a system of norms, it is possible for a person to break the norms (rules) and the group must deal with him in some way. The following are some of the more common ways that people can stand out in these groups. (1) Excessive moral indignation: although most people who have not been exposed to sexually graphic material are somewat upset by them and may have considerable moral concern, they leave some room for a change in attitude. Some people feel, however, that they are being personally attacked by the workshop (and in a sense they are) and fight back to maintain their moral position. The leader's goal in this situation should be to encourage the individual to maintain his viewpoint, if he wishes, but defer vigorous defense of it in the group. On the other hand, the group must be encouraged to tolerate this individual's particular position since he has a right to it. (2) Excessively liberal views: some participants have "seen it all" and believe that everything is acceptable, even beyond reasonable limits. They throw all judgement to the winds and "let it all hang out." As often as not, this is another, quite effective way of avoiding discussion of one's real feelings and thoughts. It can also mislead other group members. Thus, the leader's goal in this situation is to encourage the use of reasonable judgement by the individual and group in response to these expressed views. (3) Excessive defensive avoidance of discussion of here and now feelings by using "intellectualization" (*i.e.*, rational discussion). This is a very common form of avoidance used by highly educated participants. The leaders goal is to discourage its use, often by directly asking that the participants not discuss these issues in the small group but defer these valid issues until later. (4) Excessive self-disclosure may occur if some participants enter the small groups with the expectation that the purpose of this group is for psychodynamic exploration. This often represents a misunderstanding of the ground rules and requires that the leader simply explain them. On occasion, this deep self-exploration is a way of avoiding immediate reactions to the materials, since for these people talking about their relationship with a sibling at age 5 is easier than discussing current feelings about sexual topics. Pearsall (1974) devised the following list of other reactions to erotic films by an item analysis of the reactions of 300 mental health professionals.

A. Subjective Orientation toward Erotic Films

1) Neutralizer: "I've seen it all before; that was not very impressive"
2) Isolator: "I don't get the point; what are the films trying to prove?"
3) Teacher: tends to use big words: "Did you notice this or that?"
4) Primary voyeur: watches the films, but doesn't get involved himself

5. Secondary voyeur: watches everyone else watching (doesn't really see the films himself)
6) Tertiary voyeur: watches himself watching; "I think that I felt excited by that last film," (doesn't really see the films himself)
7) Accelerator: tends to make the first comment in the group: "Okay, when do we see the real stuff? "
8) Shocker: "Did you ever see 50 horses doing it together? "
9) Panicker: "Oh my God . . .! " That is all they can express
10) Innocent: "I can't imagine anyone ever seeing that stuff"

B. Objective Orientation toward Erotic Films

11) Film critic: comments on the quality of the sound track, story line, etc.
12) Artist: sees a symbolic message in every action in the film
13) Competitor: "I can make films much better than that"
14) Validifier: "It's not what I do, so it cannot be real"
15) Actor: tries on many different reactions, but does not consistently have one of his own (like the "as if" person)
16) Withdrawer: doesn't talk at all, (these people never seem to desensitize)
17) Executive: talks about his career, schedule, etc.
18) Diagnostician: labels everything that he sees in the films
19) Parent: tries to protect other group members from the horrible things they are seeing
20) "Gone": this person does not come to the group meeting after seeing the films

INDICATIONS FOR THE USE OF SEXUALLY GRAPHIC MATERIAL

An attempt has been made to describe the over-all purposes of the various methods of exposure to sexually graphic materials. Each of the different methods is particularly suited for dealing with certain kinds of problems. By way of summary, assuming there are no contraindications, the indications for the use of sexually graphic materials are:

1. Inability to discuss sexual matters using specific terms, due to inhibition
2. Anxiety about sexual behaviors
3. Anxiety about having sexual fantasies
4. Paucity of sexual fantasies
5. Excessively restrictive conservative attitudes about one's own sexual behavior
6. Naivete and ignorance about sex
7. Unrealistic expectations of sexual performance in self or partner
8. Sexual identity confusion
9. Sexual enrichment of couples with no specific dysfunction ("humdrum" marriage)
10. Couples with communication difficulties.

("Communication" problems are a currently fashionable complaint, not without some valid basis. The indications for these workshops, however, assume a specific and clear-cut inhibition to communication with the partner.)

CONTRAINDICATIONS TO THE USE OF SEXUALLY GRAPHIC MATERIALS

It is the general consensus of people who work with sexually graphic materials, as well as the research literature, that exposure to these materials is very safe. Our work at the University of Pennsylvania with couples in marital therapy has also shown that exposure of this group of people to sexually graphic materials is safe. There are three major contraindications to the use of sexually graphic materials which we observe. (1) Psychosis, usually schizophrenia and organic brain syndromes. (Manic-depressive illness is not necessarily a contraindication especially if controlled with lithium carbonate.) Of greatest concern is the possibility of precipitating an acute schizophrenic episode or helping to elaborate a delusional system. (2) Severe depression accompanied with feelings of performance inadequacy. Seeing "beautiful" people having a "beautiful" relationship may make the person feel even more inadequate which, although tolerable in a nondepressed person, may be quite harmful for someone already severely depressed. (3) A person with strong, nondefensive moral indignation for the public display of sexually graphic materials should not be put in the position of being in a group in which he is almost by definition a deviant. Our experience with the few of these people we have encountered has been that nothing either particularly good or bad happens to their sexual attitudes, but they often are poorly tolerated by a group that may not be as charitable as they are.

CONCLUSIONS

The use of sexually graphic materials represents a new and potentially useful tool for sex education and sex therapy. Like many new techniques, it has rapidly gained wide popularity and is currently being used and misused as a panacea for all the "sexual hangups" from which our culture suffers. There are indications, however, that this fad is reaching its peak and will soon subside to leave in its place another method which has its indications and contraindications, as most therapeutic procedures do. And like most therapeutic procedures, the use of sexually graphic materials requires that the clinician have some knowledge, skill, experience, and competence in their application.

REFERENCES

Alger, I. 1969. Therapeutic use of videotape playback. J. Nerv. Ment. Dis., 148: 430.

Berkowitz, L., Corwin, R., and Heironimus, M. 1963. Film violence and subsequent aggressive tendencies. Public Opin. Q., 27: 217.

Berkowitz, J., and Rawlings, E. 1963. Effects of film violence on inhibitions against subsequent aggression. J. Abnorm. Soc. Psychol., 66: 405.

Brady, J. P. 1966. Brevital-relaxation treatment of frigidity. Behav. Res. Ther., 4: 71.

Cairns, R. B. 1970. Psychological assumptions in sex censorship: an evaluative review of recent (1961–68) research. Tech. Reports Comm. Obsenity Porno., 8: 252, U.S. Gov't. Printing Office, Wash., D.C.

Cairns, R. B., Paul, J. C. N., and Wishner, J. 1962. Sex censorship: the assumptions of anti-obsenity laws and the empirical evidence. Minn. Law Rev., 46: 1,000.

Cartwright, D., and Zander, A. 1968. *Group Dynamics*, Harper and Row, New York.

Cautela, J. 1967. Covert sensitization. Psychol. Rep., 20: 450.

Clark, R. A. 1952. The projective measurement of experimentally induced levels of sexual motivation. J. Exper. Psychol., 44: 391.

Feldman, M. P., and MacCullock, M. J. 1967. Aversion therapy in the management of homosexuals. Br. Med. J., 1: 594.

Friedman, P., and Goldstein, J. 1974. Chap. 6, Phobic reactions, in: Arietti, S., ed., *American Handbook of Psychiatry*, Vol. III, Ed. 2, Chap. 6, p. 110. Basic Books, New York.

Gebhard, P. H., Gagnon, J. H., Pomeroy, W. B., and Christenson, C. V. 1965. *Sex Offenders: An Analysis of Types*. Harper and Row, New York.

Glide Foundation. 1970. Effects of erotic stimuli used in national sex forum training courses in human sexuality. Tech. Rep. Comm. Obsenity Porno., 5: 354, U.S. Gov't. Printing Office, Washington, D.C.

Goldberg, P. A., and Milstein, J. T. 1965. Perceptual investigations of psychoanalytic theory concerning latent homosexuality in women. Percept. Mot. Skills, 21: 645.

Goldstein, M. J., Kant, H. S., and Hartman, J. J. 1973. *Pornography and Sexual Deviance*. Univ. of Calif. Press, Berkeley.

Howard, J. L., Reifler, C. B., and Lipton, M. B. 1970. Effects of exposure to pornography. Techn. Rep. Comm. Obsenity Porno. 8: 97, U.S. Gov't. Printing Office, Wash., D.C.

Jacobson, E. 1938. *Progressive Relaxation*. Univ. of Chicago Press, Chicago.

Jakobovits, L. A. 1965. Evaluational reactions to erotic literature. Psychol. Rep., 16: 985.

Kaplan, H. I., and Sadock, B. J. Eds. 1971. *Comprehensive Group Psychotherapy*. Williams & Wilkins, Baltimore.

Kinsey, A. C., Pomeroy, W., and Martin, T. 1948. *Sexual Behavior of the Human Male*. W. B. Saunders, Philadelphia.

Kinsey, A. C., Pomeroy, W., and Martin, T. 1953. *Sexual Behavior of the Human Female*. W. B. Saunders, Philadelphia.

Kutschinshy, B. 1970. The effect of pornography: a pilot experiment on perception, behavior and attitudes. Tech. Rep. Comm. Obsenity Porno. 8: 133, U.S. Gov't. Printing Office, Washington, D.C.

Levitt, E. E. 1969. Some new perspectives on an old problem. J. Sex Res., 5: 247.

Levitt, E. E., and Hinesley, R. K. 1967. Some factors in the valences of erotic visual stimuli. J. Sex Res., 3: 63.

Loiselle, R. H., and Mollenauer, S. 1965. "Galvanic skin responses to sexual stimuli in a female population. J. Genet. Psychol., 73: 273.

Mann, J., Sidman, J., and Starr, S. 1970. "Effects of erotic films on sexual behavior of married couples. Tech. Rep. Comm. Obsenity Porno., 8: 170, U.S. Gov't. Printing Office, Wash., D.C.

Mann, J. 1971. An experimental induction of human sexual arousal. Tech. Rep. Comm. Obsenity Porno., 1: U.S. Gov't. Printing Office, Wash., D.C.

Masters, W. H., and Johnson, V. E. 1966. *Human Sexual Response*. Little, Brown and Co., Boston.

Masters, W. H., and Johnson, V. E. 1970. *Human Sexual Inadequacy*. Little, Brown and Co., Boston.

Miller, D. R., and Swanson, G. E. 1960. *Inner Conflict and Defense*. Holt, Rinehart and Winston, New York.

Money, J. 1970. The positive and constructive approach to pornography. Tech. Rep. Comm. Obsenity Porno., 8: 252, U.S. Gov't. Printing Office, Wash., D.C.

Mosher, D. 1970. Psychological reactions to pornographic films. Tech. Rep. Comm. Obsenity Porno., 8: 255, U.S. Gov't. Printing Office, Wash., D.C.

Multimedia Resource Center, 540 Powell Street, San Francisco, Ca. 94108.

Mussen, P. H., and Scodel, A. 1955. The effects of sexual stimulation under varying conditions on TAT sexual responsiveness. J. Consult. Psychol., 19: 90.

Pearsall, P. 1974. Personal communication.

Pullian, G., Croft, H., Powell, C., Creson, R., and Blakney, P. 1974. Personal communication.

Powell, C. C., Blakney, P., Croft, H., and Pullian, G. 1974. Rapid treatment approach to human sexual inadequacy. Am. J. Obstet. Gynecol., 119: No. 1, 89.

Schachter, S., and Singer, J. 1962. Cognitive, social and physiological determinants of emotional state. Psychol. Rev., 69: 378.

Schachter, S. 1964. The interaction of cognitive and physiological determinants of emotional state. In Berkowitz, L., ed., *Advances in Experimental Social Psychology*, Vol. 1. Academic Press, New York.

Schmidt, G., and Sigusch, V. 1970. Psychosexual stimulation by films and slides: a further report on sex differences. J. Sex Res., 6: 268.

Schmidt, G., Sigusch, V., and Meyberg, U. 1969. Psychosexual stimulation in men: emotional reactions, changes of sex behavior and measures of conservatives' attitudes. J. Sex. Res., 5: 199.

Sigusch, V., Schmidt, G., Reinfeld, A., and Wiedermann-Sutor, I. 1970. Psychological stimulation: sex differences. J. Sex Res., 6: 10.

Stanley, E. 1974. Perspectives on the need for continuity of psychical stimulation in female sexual arousal. Med. Aspects Hum. Sexuality, 8: 98.

Tannenbaum, P. 1970. Emotional arousal as a mediator of erotic communication effects. Tech. Rep. Comm. Obsenity Porno., 8: 326, U.S. Gov't. Printing Office, Washington, D.C.

Vines, N. 1974. Unpublished doctoral dissertation.

Wolpe, J. 1974. The behavior therapy approach. In Arieti, S., ed., *American Handbook of Psychiatry*, Vol. 1, Ed., 2, Chap. 48, p. 497. Basic Books, New York.

Yalom, I. 1970. *Principles and Practice of Group Psychotherapy*. Basic Books, New York.

Effects of Drugs on Sexual Arousal and Performance

CAROL SUE CARTER, Ph.D. and JOHN M. DAVIS, M.D.

NINE

In human sexual functioning, drug-induced alterations have been reported at the following levels: (a) changes in sexual desire or subjective pleasure, (b) changes in potency with or without alterations in sexual desire, (c) failure to ejaculate with otherwise apparently normal subjective responses, and (d) reproductive failure due to gamete infertility. The present survey will focus on the first three of these. For all of the above reproductive functions, the available observations are most complete for the male. However, the paucity of specific reports of drug effects in the human female may not be interpreted as evidence for absence of drug effects on female sexual functioning.

In the present survey we are forced to rely primarily on reports from two sources. One involves case studies and anecdotes regarding side effects of various medical drug treatments. The second is based upon similar accounts from persons involved in the use of illicit drugs or purported aphrodisiacs. Psychological factors may activate or depress sexual responsivity in both sexes. The problems, therefore, associated with placebo effects in such reports must, of course, not be ignored. Little direct experimental evidence exists, and conclusions regarding the effects of any drug or class of drugs on human sexual performance must be correspondingly tentative.

A variety of drugs may alter human sexual responses. In addition, laboratory research is available examining the pharmacological basis of sexual behavior in animals. Unfortunately, at the present time the intersection between information from these sources is very limited. Most contemporary theories regarding the biochemical basis of sexual behavior are based primarily upon data from the laboratory rat. These will be described at points where the correspondence to the human findings is most striking.

Historically the earliest references to the use of chemicals to alter sexual behavior come from reports of attempts to find the perfect aphrodisiac or love potion. The modern usage of the term aphrodisiac generally refers to a substance capable of exciting sexual desire or drive.

Among the first substances used for the purposes of increasing sexual drive (Benedek, 1971; MacDougald, 1973) were derivatives of parts of plants which in some way resembled the reproductive organs and in particular the phallus or testes (following the so-called "doctrine of signatures"). Pliny and Dioscorides (1st century, A.D.) described the reputed passion-enhancing ability of satyrion (also known as priapiscus) and orchis. Both herbs were prepared from bulbous plant roots. Similar powers have been attributed by the Chinese to ginseng root. To our knowledge there is no evidence that any of these plants possessed true aphrodisiac powers.

Also prescribed among the early treatments for decreased libido were compounds prepared directly from various animal parts. Most commonly recommended were preparations derived from the testicles or penis of domestic animals. The most famous medical example of such a treatment was the widely publicized report by the aging physician, Brown-Séquard, that his self-administered testicular extracts produced marked rejuvenation. Although Brown-Séquard's injections of aqueous testicular extracts were not physiologically active, interest in this work stimulated studies of the effects of hormones on behavior (reviewed Carter, 1974).

More modern attempts to increase male sex drive through the use of active forms of male hormones also have been generally unsuccessful (Cooper, 1971; Benkert, 1973). In cases in which lowered sexual drive is due to hormonal insufficiency (for example, following reduced testicular output or castration), androgen treatments may restore sexual behavior; but for the individual who has physiologically normal circulating levels of androgen, exogenous hormones usually have not been reported to be of benefit. In addition, of some theoretical interest are reports that androgens may activate sexual interest in the human female (Salmon and Geist, 1943; Waxenberg, Drellich, and Sutherland, 1959). These changes have been attributed to increases in genital blood supply and sensitivity and/or to more direct effects on the central nervous system and behavior.

Benedek (1971) has also compiled a list of substances recommended as aphrodisiacs in at least two American or English text books of medicine between the years of 1890 and 1920. Included were alcohol, cannabis (marijuana or hashish), cantharidin (Spanish fly), capsicum (South American cayenne pepper), cimicifugin (black snakeroot), cubeb, damiana, ergot (to be injected into the dorsal vein of the penis), lecithin, nux-vomica (or its active alkaloid, strychnine), sanguinaria (bloodroot), yohimbine, gold chloride, iron arsenate, and zinc phosphide.

Specific aphrodisiac properties have also been attributed to several foods including oysters, truffles, and potatoes. Aside from their nourishment value these foods are apparently without merit as aphrodisiacs and probably owe their reputations in this regard to the "doctrine of signatures."

Compounds that reduce social inhibitions and/or alter sensory perceptions or general arousal are still in use by persons seeking modern day love potions. The ability of any of these compounds to specifically enhance sexual desire or pleasure remains controversial.

The most readily available reputed aphrodisiac is alcohol. It is generally accepted that low doses of alcohol may reduce social inhibitions in both sexes. In this regard, alcohol has received wide use in both modern and primitive cultures as a means of facilitating initial sexual expression (Horton, 1943; Berreman, 1956). However, there is no direct evidence that alcohol actually enhances sexual pleasure. Furthermore, large doses of alcohol may inhibit or eliminate sexual performance. In rats, also, high doses of alcohol may eliminate sexual performance at the level of the spinal reflex while leaving sexual interest intact (Hart, 1973).

Cannabis has also gained a reputation as an aphrodisiac, presumably owing to its ability to alter sensory awareness and social behaviors (Gay and Sheppard, 1972). Any aphrodisiac properties of either marijuana or hashish are at best temporary and long-term use of these drugs may in fact, decrease libido by reducing testosterone output (Kolodny, Masters, Kolodner, and Toro, 1974; Maugh, 1974). In addition, in male rats THC (an active component of marijuana) decreased sexual interest and performance (Merari, Barak, and Plaves, 1973).

Among the compounds which have been reported capable of enhancing sexual enjoyment is amyl-nitrite ("Poppers"). This is a volatile substance which causes vasodilation and according to the reports of users may intensify the feelings associated with orgasm. Amyl-nitrite also seems to reduce sexual inhibitions and may delay ejaculation (Everett, 1972). However, the compound is potentially dangerous with side effects including headaches and, in rare cases, cardiovascular distress.

There are also anecdotal reports from the drug culture that a variety of other compounds may reduce inhibitions and subjec-

TABLE 9.1

Drugs with Reported Ability to Increase or Facilitate Some Aspect of Sexual Activity

Drug	Reported Behavioral Effects
Alcohol	Reduced sexual inhibitions, vasodilation
Marijuana or hashish	Reduced sexual inhibitions, altered sensory awareness
LSD	Reduced sexual inhibitions, altered sensory awareness
MDA	Reduced sexual inhibitions, altered sensory awareness
Amyl-nitrite (poppers)	Altered sensory awareness, especially in genital area
Amphetamines	Altered sensory awareness, CNS stimulation, slight increase in potency
Yohimbine	Altered sensory awareness, CNS stimulation, slight increase in potency
Strychine (nux-vomica)	Altered sensory awareness, CNS stimulation, slight increase in potency
Cocaine	Altered sensory awareness, CNS stimulation
L-dopa	CNS stimulation, slight increase in potency, general improvement in health

tively prolong or intensify sexual pleasure or orgasm (Gay and Sheppard, 1972). Specifically described as aphrodisiacs are intravenous injections of amphetamine or MDA (an amphetamine-related hallucinogen, known as the counter culture "love drug"). Both drugs reportedly reduce inhibitions and enhance or prolong sexual experiences in both sexes. Following amphetamine injection a few females reported immediate orgasm and more than half of the males interviewed by Gay and Sheppard reported spontaneous erections following injection. Amphetamines may also increase aspects of male sexual behavior in rats (Butcher, Butcher, and Larsson, 1969; Leavitt, 1969; Ahlenius, Eriksson, Larrson, Modigh, and Södersten, 1971) but have been reported to be inhibitory in female rats (Meyerson, 1968). Also popular as an aphrodisiac in drug subculture is intravenously injected cocaine. Drug-induced sexual exhilaration and, less frequently, spontaneous erections have been reported following cocaine injection. Amphetamines, MDA, and cocaine probably all act in part through their central nervous system stimulant properties. Psychedelic drugs, such as LSD, mescaline, psilocybin, and STP are also reportedly associated with reduced sexual inhibitions and, in some cases, increases in sexual interest. However, the effects of the psychedelic drugs in humans are apparently closely related to situational considerations, and under some circumstances these drugs reportedly inhibit sexual behavior. In rats low doses of LSD may facilitate and high doses may inhibit male sexual behavior (Bignami, 1966; Malmnäs, 1973), while in female rats LSD has been observed to be generally inhibitory (Eliasson, Michanek, and Meyerson, 1972; Eliasson, 1974).*

Abuse of several drugs has also been reported to decrease libido. In particular, long-term use of or addiction to heroin, morphine, opium, or barbituates is usually accompanied by a loss of sexual interest (Gay and Sheppard, 1972). This may be in part a general effect of the abuse of such agents, but it is reported that sexual behavior may wane even in relatively healthy heroin users. Reduced gonadal function is also indicated following prolonged heroin addiction (Cushman, 1973), and changes in sexual behavior may be related to altered hormone levels. Some methadone users also report decreased sexual interest; however, the effects of methadone are typically less debilitating than those seen during heroin use, and relatively normal function is usually recovered during methadone maintenance (Cushman and Dole, 1973; Mintz, O'Hare, O'Brien, and Goldschmidt, 1974).

CHANGES IN POTENCY WITH OR WITHOUT ALTERATIONS IN SEXUAL DESIRE

The term, sexual potency, may be used to describe the ability to achieve penile erection and as such refers only to the male. It is most typically applied to human functions since in other species penile erections may be less easily observed or sperm transfer may be achieved by other means. Impotence refers to the inability to achieve an erection under appropriate conditions and may represent a serious clinical problem. Impotence can result from disruptions in either central or peripheral nervous system function, but the causes are typically difficult to identify (Cooper, 1971; Belt, 1973).

Several substances with reputations as aphrodisiacs are able to produce priapism (a sustained and sometimes painful erection). Presumably drug-induced priapism is a function of chemical alterations in the normal autonomic control of erection and detumescence. Penile erection is a parasympathetically (cholinergically) controlled function involving vasodilation and engorgement of the penile vessels. With increased sympathetic

* Meyerson, Carrer, and Eliasson (1974) have proposed, based upon data from animal research, that female behavior is inhibited by serotonin. LSD and other drugs with the ability to potentiate central serotoninergic activity reportedly inhibit sexual behavior while drugs that reduce levels of serotonin may facilitate sexual behavior in female rats.

activity (involving adrenergic function) these vessels constrict and the erection subsides.

One of the most widely known aphrodisiacs is the substance known as "spanish fly" (tincture of cantharides). In use since the 16th century and prescribed as a treatment for impotence in the early 19th century (Benedek, 1971), "spanish fly" is extracted from a beetle. This compound irritates the urogenital tract and was once used as a diuretic. In sufficient doses it may result in priapism which probably earned for "spanish fly" its reputation as a sexual stimulant. There seems to be no evidence that the substance actually increases sexual desire in either sex.

Long in use both as an aphrodisiac and as an attempted treatment for impotence is nux-vomica. Strychnine is the active ingredient in the extract of seeds from *Strychnos nux-vomica*, and priapism may be associated with strychnine poisoning. Nux-vomica in low doses continues to be used in contemporary medical preparations for impotence (including, "afrodex" and "potensan-forte").

Yohimbine is another ancient treatment for impotence which has gained some modern acceptance. (Yohimbine is also an ingredient in "afrodex" and "potensan-forte.") Yohimbine is a diuretic and capable of stimulating genital hyperemia and thus penile erection. Attempts to increase sexual behaviors in rats with this drug have been unsuccessful (Johnson and Diamond, 1969).

The medical effectiveness of compounds such as "afrodex" and "potensan-forte" which contain both nux-vomica and yohimbine as well as an androgen (methyl testosterone) is limited although some improvement in cases of impotence has been reported with these agents (Cooper, 1971). Individuals who responded to such compounds often also improved with placebo treatments, emphasizing the importance of psychological components in treating impotence.

L-dopa, a dopamine precursor which is commonly administered to Parkinson patients, may also improve sexual functioning. Benkert (1973) reported specifically a slight increase in spontaneous or nocturnal erections following L-dopa treatment, but this effect was not reliable enough to serve as a clinical treatment for impotence. The general improvements in health following L-dopa may also account for some of the ability of this drug to restore sexual potency or interest (Bowers and Van Woert, 1972; Goodwin, 1971; Benkert, 1973).†

†The recent evidence that L-dopa may stimulate sexual responsivity in physically well male rats (Gessa and Tagliamonte, 1974) has been used in support of a more direct action for this compound or other catecholamines in male sexual function. Theories regarding the biochemical basis of sexual

It is not uncommon for decreases in sexual interest to be accompanied by impotence. Consequently, most of the drugs mentioned in the previous section which alter sexual desire may also reduce subsequent reproductive function. The converse is of course not always the case, and the inability to gain an erection in the presence of relatively normal sexual interest may be especially disturbing.

The clinician should be particularly sensitive to the problem of drug-induced impotence. This side effect has been reported at least occasionally after administration of the following: chloropromazine and related phenothiazines; monoamine oxidase inhibitors such as pargyline, reserpine, and other rauwolfian derivatives; heroin or morphine; and, to a lesser extent, barbiturates and anticholinergics (Belt, 1973). In addition, for heroin or methadone users premature ejaculation seems to be a problem during drug-free periods. The return to the use of either drug may delay ejaculation and to this extent may be viewed by some users as a desirable side effect (Mintz and associates, 1974).

FAILURE TO EJACULATE WITH NORMAL SUBJECTIVE RESPONSES

One unique symptom which is occasionally reported following drug treatment and in particular treatment with Mellaril (thioridazine) in the male is the absence of ejaculate following an otherwise apparently normal orgasm (known technically as aspermia; Shader, 1972b). The specific symptoms which may accompany aspermia include the absence of ejaculate during intercourse, masturbation, or nocturnal emission and, in some cases, the subsequent observation of "white" urine. In at least one Mellaril patient sperm has been observed in the urine (Shader, 1972b). Based upon these observations and reports of aspermia with other drugs. Shader has inferred that these compounds may cause a failure of the internal sphincter of the urethra to close during ejaculation which, particularly if the person is lying prone during this time, may allow the ejaculate to flow into the bladder. Specifically he has suggested that alpha-adrenergic blocking agents are likely to produce this effect.

Following Mellaril treatment Shader (1972b) has observed aspermia in less than 5% of his patients; however Blair and

---

behavior have been proposed based primarily upon research using the laboratory rat. These suggest that male behavior is facilitated by the catecholamines and, in particular, dopamine, and it is inhibited by serotonin (Gessa and Tagliamonte, 1974; Malmnäs, 1973). Increasing levels of catecholamines tend to be associated with behavioral activation, and sexual behavior may be facilitated by various methods of increasing general arousal in male animals (Sachs and Barfield, 1974).

TABLE 9.2

Drugs with Reported Ability to Decrease or Inhibit Some Aspect of Sexual Activity

Drug	Reported Behavioral Effects
Heroin, morphine, or opium	Decreased libido and potency
Methadone	Temporary decrease in libido and potency
Barbituates	Decreased libido and potency
Alcohol	Decreased potency after high doses
Phenothiazines (esp. Mellaril)	Decreased libido and potency, aspermia
Guanethidine	Aspermia
Pargyline	Aspermia
Phenoxybenzamine	Aspermia

Simpson (1966) estimated a higher incidence of the symptom (approximately 30%). A review of case studies also has linked aspermia to the following drugs: phenoxybenzamine, chlorprothizene, pargyline, guanethidine, and reserpine (Shader, 1972b).

Aspermia may be particularly distressing and thus clinically important if the patient observes the symptom but fails to report it because of personal embarrassment. This could be especially important in young patients who may notice aspermia during masturbation or as an absence of nocturnal emissions but may be reluctant to discuss the problem. Normal function has been reported restored if the treatment is discontinued or an alternative drug is administered.

REPRODUCTIVE FAILURE DUE TO INFERTILITY

Evidence continues to accumulate implicating biochemical changes and in particular the biogenic amines in the regulation of such reproductive processes as gonadotropin release (Kamberi, 1972). It is possible that virtually any drug capable of disrupting neurotransmission in areas of the nervous system involved in reproductive processes may have the potential to alter fertility.

For example, it has been recently suggested that reserpine (Shader, 1972a) and several of the phenothiazines (Beumont, Gelder, Friesen, Harris, MacKinnon, Mandelbrote, and Wiles, 1974a; Beumont, Corker, Friesen, Kolakowska, Mandelbrote, Marshall, Murray, and Wiles, 1974b) may alter endocrine function. In the female, amenorrhea has been linked to phenothiazine treatments, including chlorpromazine and Mellaril (Beumont and associates, 1974a).‡ In the male, slight reductions in

‡Galactorrhea may be another side effect of phenothiazine treatment, and prolactin secretion is frequently elevated in these patients.

testosterone levels may accompany phenothiazine treatments. However, these reductions are typically subclinical and are reversible following discontinuance of treatment (Beumont and associates 1974b). Related suppressive effects of reserpine have been noted, especially in animals (Shader, 1972a). However, for both reserpine and the phenothiazines, existing clinical reports do not generally suggest that the effects of these drugs are severe enough to produce infertility, and it should not be assumed that they are acting as contraceptives in either sex.

A recent survey of the side effects of marijuana suggested that both decreased sperm counts and hormone outputs may follow the chronic use of that drug (Maugh, 1974; Kolodny, Masters, Kolodner, and Toro, 1974). In female heroin or methadone usders, menstrual cycles are often irregular or attenuated (Santen, 1973). Related side effects have been observed on methadone maintenance in both sexes; however, the effects are typically less pronounced and of shorter duration than those observed with heroin use. The available litterature suggests that reproductive function usually returns to normal when a disruptive drug is discontinued, but careful long-term studies of the behavioral effects of most drugs are nonexistent.

SUMMARY

Increases in sexual behavior (particularly in the male) are more commonly associated with moderate doses of drugs which are central nervous system stimulants. In constrast, decreased libido is a frequent complaint following the use of depressants. Compounds which alter sensory awareness or social inhibitions may also be associated with sexual interactions. Drug treatments which produce improvements in general health may be, of course, accompanied by restored sexual interest. Whether any of these effects are reflections of specific changes in sexual function remains open to investigation.

Chemicals with the ability to alter autonomic function and thereby facilitate erection (or even produce priapism) have in some cases gained reputations as aphrodisiacs. The use of such agents to treat impotence is, however, generally unsuccessful. The clinician should be particularly sensitive to the potential ability of a variety of medications to disrupt potency or, for example in the case of Mellaril, to produce occasional aspermia (failure to ejaculate).

REFERENCES

Ahlenius. S., Eriksson, H., Larsson, K., Modigh, K., and Södersten, P. 1971. Mating behavior in the male rat treated with *p*-chlorophenylalanine methyl ester alone and in combination with pargyline. Psychopharmacologia, 20: 383.

Belt, B. G. 1973. Some organic causes of impotence. Med. Aspects Hum. Sexuality, 7: 152.

Benedek, T. G. 1971. Aphrodisiacs: facts and fable. Med. Aspects Hum. Sexuality, 5: 42.

Benkert, O. 1973. Pharmacological experiments to stimulate human sexual behaviour. In: Ban, T. A. *et al.*, eds., *Psychopharmacology, Sexual Disorders and Drug Abuse*, p. 489. North-Holland Publ. Co., Amsterdam.

Berreman, G. D. 1956. Drinking patterns of the Aleuts. Q. J. Stud. Alcohol 17: 503.

Beumont, P. J. V., Gelder, M. G., Friesen, H. G., Harris, G. W., MacKinnon, P. C. B., Mandelbrote, B. M., and Wiles, D. H. 1974a. The effects of phenothiazines on endocrine function: 1. patients with inappropriate lactation and amenorrhoea. Br. J. Psychiatry, 124: 413.

Beumont, P. J. V., Corker, C. S., Friesen, H. G., Kolakowska, T., Mandelbrote, B. M., Marshall, J., Murray, M. A. F., and Wiles. D. H. 1974b. The effects of phenothiazines on endocrine function: II. effects in men and postmenopausal women. Br. J. Psychiatry, 124: 420.

Bignami, G. 1966. Pharmacologic influences on mating behavior in the male rat. Psychopharmacologia, 10: 44.

Blair, J. H., and Simpson, G. M. 1966. Effect of antipsychotic drugs on reproductive functions. Dis. Nerv. Syst., 27: 645.

Bowers, M. B., and Van Woert, M. H. 1972. Sexual behavior during L-dopa treatment of Parkinson's disease. Med. Aspects Hum. Sexuality, 6: 88.

Butcher, L. L., Butcher, S. G., and Larsson, K. 1969. Effects of apomorphine, (+)-amphetamine, and nialamide on tetrabenazine-induced suppression of sexual behavior in the male rat. Eur. J. Parmacol., 7: 283.

Carter, C. S. 1974. *Hormones and Sexual Behavior*. Dowden, Hutchinson and Ross, Inc., Stroudsburg, Pa.

Cooper, A. J., 1971. Treatments of male potency disorders: the present status. Psychosomatics. 12: 235.

Cushman, P., Jr. 1973. Plasma testosterone in narcotic addiction. Am. J. Med., 55: 452.

Cushman, P., Jr., and Dole, V. 1973. Detoxification of rehabilitated methadone maintained patients. J. A. M. A., 226: 747.

Eliasson, M. 1974. Effects of LSD and monoamine synthesis inhibitors on hormone-activated copulatory behavior in the female rat. Brain Res., 66: 369.

Eliasson, M., Michanek, A., and Meyerson, B. J. 1972. A differential inhibitory action of LSD and amphetamine on copulatory behavior in the female rat. Acta Pharmacol. Toxicol., 31:Suppl. 1, 1.

Everett, G. M. 1972. Effects of amyl-nitrite ("Poppers") on sexual experience. Med. Aspects Hum. Sexuality 6: 146.

Gay, G. R., and Sheppard, C. W. 1972. Sex in the "drug culture." Med. Aspects Hum. Sexuality, 6: 28.

Gessa, G. L., and Tagliamonte, A., 1974. Possible role of brain serotonin and dopamine in controlling male sexual behavior. Adv. Biochem. Psychopharmacol., 11: 217.

Goodwin, F. K. 1971. Behavioral effects of L-dopa in man. Semin. Psychiatry, 3: 477.

Hart, B. L. 1973. Reflexive behavior. In: Bermant, G., ed., *Perspectives on Animal Behavior*, p. 171. Scott, Foresman, Glenview, Ill.

Horton, D. 1943. The function of alcohol in primitive societies: a cross-cultural study. Q. J. Stud. Alcohol, 4: 199.

Johnson, D. N., and Diamond, M. 1969. Yohimbine and sexual stimulation in the male rat. Physiol. Behav., 4: 411.

Kamberi, I. A. 1972. Biogenic amines and neurohumoral control of gonadotropin and prolactin secretion. Proc. 4th Int. Cong. Endocr. Int. Cong., series 273: 112.

Kolkodny, R. C., Masters, W. H., Kolodner, R. M., and Toro, G. 1974. Depression of plasma testosterone levels after chronic intensive marijuana use. N. Engl. J. Med., 290: 872.

Leavitt, F. I., 1969. Drug-induced modifications in sexual behavior and open field locomotion of male rats. Physiol. Behav., 4: 677.

MacDougald, D. Jr. 1973. Aphrodisiacs and anaphrodisiacs. In: Ellis, A., and Abarbanel, A., eds., *The Encyclopedia of Sexual Behavior*, p. 145. Aronson, New York.

Malmnäs, C. O. 1973. Monoaminergic influence on testosterone activated copulatory behavior in the castrated male rat. Acta Physiol. Scand. Suppl. 395: 1.

Maugh, T. H., LL, 1974. Marijuana: the grass may no longer be greener. *Science*, 185: 683.

Merari, A., Barak, A., and Plaves, M. 1973. Effects of $\Delta^{1(2)}$-tetra-hydrocannabinol on copulation in the male rat. Psychopharmacologia, 28: 243.

Meyerson, B. J. 1968. Female copulatory behavior in male and androgenized female rats after estrogen and amine depletor treatment. Nature, 217: 683.

Meyerson, B. J., Carrer, H., and Eliasson, M. 1974. 5-Hydroxytryptamine and sexual behavior in the female rat. Adv. Biochem. Psychopharmacol., 11: 229.

Mintz, J., O'Hare, K., O'Brien, C. P., and Goldschmidt, J. 1974. Sexual problems of heroin addicts when drug-free, on heroin and on methadone. Unpublished manuscript, Dept. of Psychiatry, University of Pennsylvania, Philadelphia.

Sachs, B. D., and Barfield, R. J. Copulatory behavior of male rats given intermittent electric shocks: theoretical implications. J. Comp. Physiol. Psychol., 86: 607.

Salmon, U. J., and Geist, S. H. 1943. Effect of androgens upon libido in women. J. Clin. Endocrinol., 3: 235.

Santen, R. J. 1973. How narcotics addiction affects reproductive function in women. Contemporary Obstet. Gynecol., 3: 93.

Shader, R. L. 1972a. Male sexual functon. In: Shader, R. L., ed., *Psychiatric Complications of Medical Drug*, Raven Press, New York.

Shader, R. L. 1972b. Ejaculation disorders. In: Shader, R. L., ed., *Psychiatric Complications of Medical Drugs*. Raven Press, New York.

Waxenberg, S. E., Drellich, M. G., and Sutherland, A. M. 1959. The role of hormones in human behavior. 1. Changes in female sexuality after adrenalectomy. J. Clin. Endocrinol. 19: 193.

TEN

Treatment of Sexual Dysfunction in Patients with Physical Disorders

ERNEST R. GRIFFITH, M.D. and ROBERTA B. TRIESCHMANN, Ph.D.

Management of sexual problems in the physically disabled is a complex task because of the multiple etiological considerations and the varied treatment strategies with which the professional must be familiar. Therefore, we discuss etiology in terms of primary and secondary conditions with the assumption that both must be evaluated in each individual treated. Principles of management are discussed in terms of who treats the patient, when the treatment occurs, where treatment is given, and interpersonal factors which must be noted. Emphasis in this chapter is placed on details of managing the primary dysfunction with the cautionary note that methods of treatment of secondary dysfunctions, described elsewhere in this book, are relevant to most cases of primary dysfunction also. Attention is given to special problems of the congenitally disabled.

DEFINITION OF THE PROBLEM

Any form of direct intervention in the treatment of sexual problems of the physically disabled requires a clear understanding of the distinction between primary and secondary dysfunctions. Evaluation of the problem requires a delineation of the primary dysfunction and any secondary dysfunctions since the treatment strategies will differ.

Secondary dysfunctions are those in which there is no evidence of organic impairment to account for the difficulty. Rather, attitudes and anxieties interfere with sexual satisfaction and thus the etiology is a behavioral one. These dysfunctions have received the most attention in the literature, and multiple intervention strategies have been developed of either a counseling-psychotherapeutic or behavioral nature. Most of the patients seen for treatment by the average sexual counselor have secondary dysfunctions and the patient initiates the referral, usually after suffering with the dysfunction for quite a while.

Primary dysfunctions have organic impairments (neurological, endocrinological, urological, gynecological, musculoskeletal, etc.) as their etiological base. Until very recently these dysfunctions have received little attention by either researchers or therapists, and thus the literature regarding therapeutic interventions is meager. Furthermore, as a criterion for treatment, most sexual therapists screen out anyone with a primary dysfunction and, consequently, have little to no experience with the psychosocial problems of the physically disabled. This is unfortunate since, in our experience, most primary disorders entail a secondary component, each aspect of the dysfunction requiring equivalent attention to maximize the probability of success.

Therefore, this chapter addresses itself to primary dysfunctions with secondary components (see Table 10.1). The etiology of the problem is physical with a behavioral component (premorbid attitudes toward sexuality along with anxieties and fears about the primary dysfunction itself). The goal of the therapy will be remedy or amelioration of the physical problem, behavior change, or both. The method of therapy will be physical (chemotherapeutic, local modalities, surgery, etc.), counseling, behavior modification, or all three. Few therapists can deal with the diagnostic and therapeutic complexity of these cases which often require medical, counseling, and behavior therapy expertise. Consequently, the team approach of physician and psychologist (or other professional skillful in behavioral and counseling techniques) is usually desirable and, at times, essential. The problem may be identified by a professional, by the patient, or by both. It is important to note that many professionals and patients have assumed that sexual functioning is impossible

TABLE 10.1

	Primary Dysfunctions with Secondary Components	Secondary Dysfunction
Etiology	Physical and behavioral	Behavioral
Goal of therapy	Remedy or amelioration of physical problem, behavior change, or both	Behavior change
Method of therapy	Physical (chemotherapeutic, local modalities, surgery, etc.) counseling, behavior modification, or all three	Behavior modification or counseling
Qualifications of therapists	Medical expertise, and expertise in behavior change and counseling techniques; team approach recommended	Expertise in behavior change and counseling technique
Detection of the problem	The professional, the patient or both; patient may not identify as problem	The patient

following many severe illnesses and disabilities. While the professional community gradually is reversing its opinion, many patients may not. Therefore, referral for treatment may be initiated by the professional and not by the patient, which has major therapeutic implications.

The secondary components to cases of primary dysfunction include the psychosocial and learned attitudes toward sexuality which influence everyone. Cultural, ethnic, and religious factors may have a significant impact on sexual functioning following a disability or illness if previously defined "proper" sex acts are no longer available and alternative methods of sexual gratification are considered to be taboo (Trieschmann, 1975; Pfeiffer and Davis, 1972). Early experiences with parental figures and peer groups influence attitudes toward relationships and sexuality and may become a problem only after onset of disability. Past social experience and general self-confidence are crucial in determining the patient's reaction to a disability and are critical in creating a social life as a disabled person (Trieschmann, 1974). One has to be able to interact comfortably with people in order to form a sexual relationship. Secondary dysfunctions which predate the onset of the illness or disability will further complicate postdisability sexual functioning. For example, an anorgasmic woman may see the physical disability or illness as an escape from sexual interactions. The male with a premorbid history of intermittent secondary impotence may have an exacerbation of the problem following a myocardial infarction.

Following the onset of the illness or disability, the individual is vulnerable to other secondary components. Devaluation and desexualization of the patient by himself and others occur frequently (Wright, 1960). The person who suffers a physical disability may tend to devalue himself because of the change in his (her) physical attractiveness or physical ability, and this sense of devaluation may be communicated to others he meets (Ford and Orfirer. 1967). Society prizes attractiveness, youth, and physical ability, and thus the patient's devaluation of himself may be confirmed by the reactions of others (Griffith and Trieschmann, 1975). Devaluation is often correlated with desexualization; the community may not recognize the person as a suitable sex partner and may believe that because a person is disabled, sex is no longer important in his life (Hohmann, 1975). All the patient's premorbid social experience and self-confidence will be required to combat the devaluation and desexualization phenomena, and therapists should be aware of these influences on sexual functioning. In addition, anxiety and fear about the primary problem can inhibit sexual satisfaction.

The person disabled congenitally or early in life is vulnerable to most of the secondary components outlined above (Brown, 1970). However, particular attention should be given to the influence of early experiences on adult functioning (Wright, 1960). For example, the disabled child may receive less mothering behavior (cuddling and other sensory stimulations), may be overprotected (fewer opportunities to develop self-confidence), and may be socially isolated (few opportunities to learn normal peer group and heterosexual behaviors). Devaluation, desexualization, cultural attitudes toward sexuality, and fears about the illness or disability may also influence sexual functioning.

EVALUATION OF THE PROBLEM

To evaluate a sexual problem in a person with a physical disability, one must consider premorbid function, present function, future expectations, and characteristics of the spouse-partner.

For the noncongenitally disabled, a thorough life history must be obtained to estimate self-perception and social skills prior to the onset of the disabling condition. Attention should be given to success and failure experience with family, friends, school, work, and leisure time activities. A sexual history should include attitudes toward various kinds of sex acts, "proper" sex roles for male and female, likes and dislikes, degree of experience, and value system. Cultural, ethnic, and religious sanctions and prohibitions should be elicited. A medical history along with records of previous relevant medical treatment should be obtained. Given a thorough background on premorbid functioning, a review of present physical, psychological, social, and vocational status will help to define the degree of change that the disability entails; what has been lost, what assets and liabilities remain. The physical assessment should include the various forms of mobility (walking, wheelchair, transfers to and from bed, capability of positional changes in bed) and self-care activities (dressing and undressing, bowel and bladder management, personal hygiene, and contraceptive use). A medical history focusing on associated conditions (cardiac disease, hypertension, pulmonary disease, diabetes, etc.) which might interfere with sexual function should be obtained. The physical examination should review the neurological, musculoskeletal, urological gynecological, and cardiovascular systems. In certain cases, measures of physical capacity may be indicated, such as monitoring of the cardiac patient with electrocardiograms during sexual activity, or objective measures of strength, range of motion of the joints and endurance. The present functional analysis must detail the physical dimensions of the disability as it pertains to previous preferences in sex acts and the over-all impact of disability as it pertains to sexuality—self-perception in relation to the opposite sex. To evaluate the physical disability without exploring the potential social disability will reduce the efficacy of any remedial action.

The congenitally disabled person should be evaluated on the same dimensions as described above except that the emphasis is not on loss or change, but on who he has learned to be and on what he has learned to do (Fotheringham, 1971). A sexual history must detail the behaviors in his repertoire, attitudes, perferences, and cultural taboos. The question of social skills should be carefully evaluated because the congenitally disabled may have a less active social life than the able-bodied person.

Future expectations must be considered from several points of view. Given the present physical and functional status of the individual, what is the prognosis for improvement or deterioration? What goals do the patient and partner have and what is their understanding of the problem? Careful attention should be given to eliciting misinformation, misconceptions, and fears surrounding the disability *per se* and their relationship to sexual functioning (Trieschmann, 1975). Evaluation of the problem requires an estimate of the course of the disability and associated complications over time, along with an awareness of the various types of intervention strategies outlined below. Not all of these interventions are equally appropriate at any one moment but may be considered as sequential treatment approaches depending on the course of the disability and the variations in the nature of the problem over time.

Optimal treatment effectiveness will depend on the presence of a partner and the complete participation of the partner in the evaluation and treatment process. A general social history with emphasis on the partner's self-perception and attitudes toward sex role should be obtained. A detailed sexual history should be elicited from the partner, with emphasis on activities, preferences, cultural, and religious attitudes.

The focus of the evaluation process is to define what sexual behaviors were in the couple's repertoire prior to disability, how many of these are no longer appropriate or possible, what sex acts are feasible now, how willing the individuals are to try new methods, and which sex acts they are willing to practice.

PRINCIPLES OF MANAGEMENT

The timing of treatment will influence the issue of therapist selection and the patient's receptivity to treatment. If the sexual dysfunction is identified soon after the onset of the disability or illness, treatment may be initiated during the rehabilitation phase by rehabilitation personnel; however, the patient may not be fully aware of the parameters of the dysfunction. Or treatment may be initiated after discharge from the hospital. Referral may be made to a therapist skilled in handling secondary dysfunctions, and the patient may be more aware of the impact of the primary problem on sexual functioning. Since sexual counselors have a variety of backgrounds, we would emphasize the necessity of obtaining the essential physical-medical data from a qualified specialist in the relevant areas: urology, cardiology, physiatry, internal medicine, orthopedics etc. Furthermore, a thorough understanding of the specific psychosocial problems of the physically disabled is invaluable (Shontz, 1971). Ideally, we would recommend a team approach to treatment based on professional discipline and sex, as advised by Masters and Johnson (1970). If treatment of the sexual dysfunction occurs in the rehabilitation milieu, the question of who treats the patient is less well defined since many rehabilitation centers do not have formal sexual counseling programs. Nevertheless, counseling can be given in uncomplicated cases by those members of the rehabilitation team who (1) are comfortable with their own sexuality, (2) are knowledgeable about the psychosocial and learned components of sexuality, (3) are aware of the various religious and cultural prohibitions of certain sex acts, (4) and are familiar with the relevant medical-physical factors of the individual case. It is essential that medical rehabilitation personnel be aware of the principles of counseling and the complexity of the psychosocial aspects of sexual behavior (Hohmann, 1972). We continue to recommend the team approach and would suggest that complex cases be treated in this manner.

Within the context of the rehabilitation setting, the topic of sexual functioning may be introduced in a general manner following the acute phase of treatment. An acquired disability may be accompanied initially by a period of psychic and physical shock where the focus of the intervention is survival. Following this phase, the professional may discuss with the patient the various components of a rehabilitation program, sexual functioning being one (Cole, 1975). This dialogue should be aimed at giving the patient permission to initiate questions about sexual functioning when he (she) is ready and informing the patient that sexual functioning is a relevant aspect of postdisability living. Even though granted such permission, many patients will not initiate discussion about sexuality, and the professional should be aware of the subtle cues which patients may send instead. Not only should professionals be aware of the patient's desire to discuss sexuality, but they should be equally sensitive to cues from the patient that he is neither ready for nor interested in sex at this point or in the future (Hohmann, 1975). Some disabilities may provide the individual with a convenient excuse to avoid sexual contacts, and this wish should be respected. To differentiate between embarrassment and disinterest in sex, the assistance of an individual skilled in counseling techniques may be sought.

In proceeding with treatment, ideally both patient and sexual partner should be included, but this is not always possible. A partner may be unwilling to participate, inaccessible, or nonexistent. Under these circumstances, the possibility of a surrogate partner may be considered. If the circumstances and conditions of such an arrangement are completely understood and acceptable to all responsible parties, it offers a further valuable dimension to the treatment process, as demonstrated by Masters and Johnson (1970).

Most disabilities do not necessarily affect the sex drive any more than they would affect hunger or thirst. The disability may influence the *type* of sex acts which would be feasible or advisable, but few disabilities preclude all sex acts (Trieschmann, 1975). Therefore, implicit in any discussion of the management principles is the meticulous appreciation of the value systems of the patient and the partner (Hohmann, 1972). No form of intervention that is inconsistent with these values should be imposed, no matter how compatible with the best judgements of the treatment staff. The value system should be elicited as part of the evaluation process, and the professional should be clearly aware of his or her own values regarding sexuality. When the patient's value system precludes alternate forms of sexual acts other than genital-genital intercourse, the goal of treatment would be to advise the patient of what methods of sexual satisfaction are available and to assist the patient at making a decision that he can live with. Perhaps this will result in the decision to abstain from sex acts (other than kissing), and this decision should be respected.

MANAGEMENT OF THE PRIMARY DYSFUNCTION

The ensuing discussion is restricted to physical disabilities affecting the locomotor system and chronic disease states commonly associated with these disabilities.

The Kinesiology of Sex Acts

Preparations. Preparatory activities require mobility skills so that the sexual behaviors might occur at an opportune place and time. If the disabled individual is not capable of independently transferring to a bed, couch, floor, or other suitable place, the sexual partner may be trained by the disabled individual or a physical or occupational therapist to assist in these transfers. In like manner, the disabled individual may require some assistance on the part of the partner for other preparatory activities such as undressing, positioning, and placement of contraceptives. For the arthritic, a preliminary application of superficial heat in the form of a shower or a bath, followed by limbering up exercises, may increase joint mobility or decrease pain (Erlich, 1973). The patient with chronic obstructive lung disease might improve respiratory function through the assistance of postural drainage, chest clapping, and respiratory assists prior to sexual activity.

In cases in which there is incomplete control over bladder and bowel functions (neuropathic bladder or bowel), routine emptying prior to sexual activity is a precaution against incontinence during intercourse. Occasionally, however, the male may require a semidistended bladder so as to stimulate or maintain erections (Bors and Comarr, 1960). Patients should be reassured that ordinarily there are no harmful effects of leaving an indwelling catheter in place. Men may be advised to double the catheter back over the penis and cover both with a condom for aesthetic purposes or as a precaution against the transfer of urethral infection. Women may tape the catheter back onto their abdomen so that it is up out of the way. Certain individuals or their partners may be taught to remove and replace the catheter shortly before and after sexual activities. It has been noted that responsibility for routine care of the excretory functions of the disabled individual may lead to an abhorrence of sexual acts by an otherwise loving and devoted mate (Rusk, 1964). Prophylactic medications will be discussed under the heading of "Drugs."

Contraceptive placement may require considerable assistance by the able-bodied partner where upper extremity function of the individual is reduced as with quadriplegia or peripheral neuropathies. Where vaginal lubrication is inadequate, as in Sjögren's syndrome (Erlich, 1973), local lubrication should be provided.

In neuropathic states where erections are not under cortical control, there are numerous techniques which may be tried, the success of each varying from individual to individual (Griffith, Timms, and Tomko, 1973). Gentle tactile stimulation of the penis, particularly about the glans and frenulum, may be adequate. Other dermal trigger points can be found in the perineal and adjacent areas. Light touch, tapping, scratching, hair pulling, pinching, slapping, massaging, vibratory stimuli, heat, cold, licking, sucking, and rectal digital stimulation may be effective in inducing or maintaining erections. Such trigger sites should be sought throughout the body. Women with spinal cord lesions appear to be reflexly or directly responsive to similar stimuli (Griffith and Trieschmann, 1975). Skin segments immediately about the level of sensory change or about the breasts have been found to be exquisitely sensitive. Vaginal lubrication, clitoral and breast engorgement, and sexual flushing have been observed in many women after these stimulatory activities (Cole, 1975). Production of a mass reflex, including erection, may sometimes be elicited by scratching the foot of the male with an upper motor neuron lesion. The semierect penis may further tumesce after intromission and active thrusting by the female partner (the "stuffing" technique). Another method of enhancing erections is the application of a rubber band around the base of the penile shaft (Jackson, 1972). *A cautionary note: this tourniquet should be released within ½ hr after application.*

Positions. Positional variations are of extreme importance in the performance of various sexual acts. The immobile or immobilized (as by extensive casting) patient usually must be in the passive supine or side lying position. The partner may require explicit instructions in supporting the individual with pillows or other padding A below-knee amputee rarely has a balance problem, but the above-knee amputee may require support to maintain a level pelvis or may wish to wear the prosthesis instead (Cummings, 1975; Mourad and Chiu, 1974). While the paraplegic may be capable of assuming a prone position, this is almost impossible for the quadriplegic with a complete lesion. A supine, oblique, or side lying position would be most appropriate in these cases. Hemiplegics and unilateral upper extremity amputees (Cummings, 1975) often prefer a side lying position with the unaffected extremity uppermost. In general, severe cardiac, hypertensive, or pulmonary patients should avoid isometric muscle activity associated with the prone position. Isometric contractions of this type tend to augment diastolic hypertension and consume additional energy (Eliot and Miles, 1973). Relatively more passive and comfortable positions such as sitting, supine, or side lying with adequate support are advisable. Partners of women with severe hip joint disease may find the posterior approach to intromission to be the only convenient or available posture (Erlich, 1973). This position is often the one of greatest comfort for patients with discogenic root compression or other chronic spinal disabilities where positions of extension aggravate pain (Rubin, 1972). Those with cervical root compression may find that recumbent positions enhance the pain. Hypertensive individuals may avoid rises in blood pressure by elevating the head of the bed (Howard, 1973). Conversely, by lowering the head of the bed and not immediately assuming the upright position after intercourse, they may prevent hypotension.

Alternate Sex Acts. For those who are unable to perform penile-vaginal intercourse, a repertoire of other activities is possible, provide that there are no psychological constraints upon either partner. Unquestionably, many couples have been satisfied with gentle expressions of affection: hand-holding, cuddling, and kissing (Hohmann, 1972; 1975). In other cases. the disabled member may become adept at stimulating the partner to orgasm by fellatio; cunnilingus; breast manipulation; manual masturbation; the use of implanted or external penile prostheses; or manual application of penile-shaped objects such as dildos, vaginal douche nozzles, or electric vibrators (Comarr, 1970; Griffith and associates, 1973). When a sex partner is unavailable, solitary masturbation by any of the above techniques is often an acceptable substitute.

Precautions. There are a number of precautions which should be noted regarding sexual activitiy in cases of illness or physical disability. Patients with decreased mobility and/or reduced sensation are susceptible to decubitus ulcers and must obtain relief from skin pressure over vulnerable bony prominences by periodic alterations of position. Individuals with spinal cord lesions above the midthoracic level are prone to autonomic hyperreflexia during sexual stimulation (Comarr, 1970) and during the late stages of labor (Bors and Comarr, 1960). This syndrome is manifested by sudden diastolic hypertension; slowed heart rate and other arrhythmias; flushed, warm, moist skin of the face and upper torso; pallid, cool, dry skin of the remainder of the body; throbbing headaches; nasal congestion; and pronounced "goose flesh" (Kurnick, 1956). The hypertension may be sufficiently severe as to be life-threatening. Vulnerable patients must be educated as to the cause, recognition of symptoms, and treatment of this reflex. All potential stimuli including sexual activity and bladder or bowel distension should be reduced or eliminated. The subject's head should be elevated. Rapid acting drugs such as trimethaphan, mecamylamine (Braddom and Johnson, 1969), or guanethedine (Young, 1963) should be administered by injection. The last two drugs are available in oral form and may be taken prophylactically.

Patients with osteoporosis, so common to long standing disorders of the locomotor system, must be warned of the hazard of fractures during sexual activities. Those with neurogenic disorders should be prepared for occasional fecal or urinary incontinence. Scrupulous perineal hygiene and frequent cleansing and deodorizing of urinary or fecal collection devices is recommended. Amputees may find the symptoms of the phantom limb, whether painful or not, inhibitory to sexual function (Cummings, 1975). Antihypertensive drugs, tranquilizers, sedatives, antidepressants, narcotics, anticholinergics, antihistamines, estrogen, corticoids, nicotine, alcohol, and digitalis have been implicated as inhibitors of sex drive, erection, or ejaculation. Cardiacs should be cautioned about the possible added stresses during intercourse occasioned by recent heavy meals, alcoholic excess, anxiety or guilt, physical fatigue, extremes of temperature or humidity, restrictive clothing, and hyperventilation (Eliot and Miles, 1973; Howard, 1973; Rubin, 1968). Individuals with a recent myocardial infarction, acute heart disease, congestive heart failure, or functional classification IV of the New York Heart Association are best advised against sexual intercourse. Hypertensives should be informed of positional, physiological (cardiovascular stresses of sexual excitement), psychic, and drug factors influencing blood pressure. Patients with advanced pulmonary disease having dyspnea at rest usually cannot tolerate vigorous sexual activity (Kass, Updegraff, and Muffly, 1972). Those with hip prostheses must avoid forceful abduction to prevent hip dislocation (Erlich, 1973). Subjects with back disabilities require instruction concerning the painful effects of sudden twisting, turning, or hyperextension of the torso (Rubin, 1972).

Penile Prostheses. Men with persisting unresponsive organic impotence who wish to continue penile-vaginal intercourse may be considered as candidates for external or implanted penile prostheses. An example of the external prosthesis is the Coital Training Device (C.T.D.) fabricated by the Fre-San Products Manufacturing Company (2903 Mayfield Rd., Cleveland, Ohio). This type of device is frequently rejected as being obstructive to sensation and aesthetically or psychologically unacceptable.

Several kinds of surgical implantation prostheses are available. Lash and colleagues have used a perforated acrylic rod (Loeffler, Sayegh, and Lash, 1964). Pearman described a silicone device to which a spring or Teflon rod was added (1972). Morales, Suarez, Delgado, and Whitehead (1973) developed paired polyethylene rods. Most recently, Bradley and coworkers have fabricated a hydraulic implant which allows "erection" and decompression of the penis (Grabstald and Goodwin, 1973). The major purpose of prosthetic implants is to allow easier intromission, ideally where partial erection and some penile sensation exist. Possible complications are infection, sloughing and extrusion of the prosthesis, and local pain.

Drugs. Most frequently the major beneficial effect of systemic drugs is the amelioration of physical complications of the primary disorder. Testosterone has been demonstrated to have a salutary effect in the recently injured male spinal cord patient (Cooper and Hoen, 1952). There are indications that endogenous androgen levels are temporarily depressed shortly following the injury. In cases where gynecomastia and testicular atrophy are associated with a severe catabolic state, the use of intramuscular testosterone may reverse these signs. There is no evidence, however, that the drug will directly modify sexual performance in these patients.

The use of testosterone with or without chorionic gonadotropin was advocated by Schoffling, Federlin, Ditschuneit, and Pfeiffer (1963) as an efficacious means of treating impotence associated with diabetes mellitus. No other study, to our knowledge, has duplicated these results.

Some studies indicate that spinal cord-injured women may have estrogen deficiency (Bailey, Checkles, and Johnson, 1968), but none demonstrates whether or not estrogen has a beneficial effect such as altering the menstrual irregularities that certain of these women have. It appears that sex hormones should be reserved for disabled subjects who have specific hormonal deficiencies provided that no contraindications exist.

Occasionally the impotence of uncontrolled diabetes mellitus or peripheral neuropathies secondary to recent nutritional deficiencies is reversible following specific corrective therapy (McDowell, 1968).

Effective combinations and well timed dosage schedules of antihypertensive drugs should allow most hypertensive subjects to be sexually active without excessive diastolic elevations. However, nearly all of these drugs have the potentiality of interfering in some way with sexual function. It is possible to reduce side effects by combining agents so as to lower the dosage of the major offenders (Oaks and Moyer, 1972). Another approach is to switch to drugs that have little or no influence on sexual performance. The combination of a diuretic, hydralazine, and propranolol is often useful in situations where potent antihypertensive effects are necessary (Howard, 1973). Propranolol reduces cardiac work and thus may relieve or forestall anginal attacks associated with sexual excitement (Eliot and Miles, 1973). The drug is contraindicated in those with bronchial asthma, incipient or frank congestive heart failure, bradycardia, or heart block. Short acting nitrates or nitrites have been used prophylactically just prior to intercourse in hypertensive or anginal subjects.

Pain accompanying chronic disabilities may itself reduce or inhibit sexual behaviors. Analgesics or anti-inflammatory agents may adequately control discomfort, especially if the dosage schedule is timed so that maximal effects coincide with planned sexual activity. The potential adverse side effects of narcotics and tranquilizers have already been noted. Corticosteroids continue to have a preeminent place in the management of the collagen disorders. The sexual implications of the cosmetic effects of Cushing's syndrome in the adult or adolescent are obvious. In addition, corticoids have produced decreased libido, impotence, testicular atrophy, and menstrual disturbances (Erlich, 1973).

Sedation, tranquilization, and a protective environment serve as modifiers of recurring impulsive or inappropriate sexual behavior in certain patients with cerebral dysfunctions (Ford and Orfirer, 1967) associated with vascular, traumatic, neoplastic, degenerative, or congenital disorders. People with temporal lobe seizures at times display either bizarre or decreased sexual behavior which may respond favorably to specific antiepileptic medication or ablative surgery (Hierons and Sanders, 1966; McDowell, 1968).

Spasticity occurring with upper motor neuron lesions in either sex may be severe enough to prevent or interrupt vaginal containment of the penis. Diazepam, dantrolene sodium, or a combination of the two should be initiated orally before bolder measures are sought. Installation of phenol solution into motor end plate regions of spastic muscles or into peripheral nerves innervating those muscles is a safe but usually temporary measure. Intrathecal administration of phenol or alcohol is a more vigorous neurolytic technique which may itself produce impotence (Griffith and associates, 1973).

Men with infertility secondary to spinal cord lesions have been subjected to several procedures which decidely improved their ejaculatory capability and sperm quality but rarely resulted in insemination of their partners. The methods described thus far include: penile stimulation with an electric massager (Tarabulcy, 1972), installation of prostigmine intrathecally (Guttman and Walsh, 1971), and intrarectal electrical stimulation (Bensman and Kottke, 1966). Since ejaculation is often retrograde, the sperm has been collected from the bladder. To reduce the spermicidal effects of urine, it may be alkalinized with sodium bicarbonate taken orally for several days before the time of collection (Rusk, Covalt, Fisher, Marks, Sullivan, and Diller,

1967). After the bladder is emptied by catheter, it is lavaged with Ringers solution, and ejaculation is attained by whatever technique is available. The sperm are collected by voiding or catheterization. The fresh specimen may either be inoculated directly into the vagina or stored in the frozen state by the liqud nitrogen method. These urological procedures are not fully developed at this time, and thus far they are relatively unproductive though promising techniques for fertilization. Furthermore, the hazards of genetic damage of stored sperm are uncertain.

Exercise. Therapeutic exercise programs are potentially beneficial in some chronic disease states. According to Hellerstein and Friedman (1970), general conditioning activities appear to result in increased frequency and satisfaction of sexual intercourse in males with coronary artery disease. This type of program may improve physical endurance so as to reduce fatigue during sexual activity in other cardiovascular, pulmonary, or neuromuscular states. Physical therapy designed to increase range of motion of contracted hip or knee joints may allow intercourse where it had previously been uncomfortable or impossible. Strengthening of weakened muscles and transfer and bed mobility training are other services which the physical therapist can provide. Prolonged stretch and local application of heat or cold tend to inhibit spasticity temporarily. If successful in the hands of a therapist, these methods can be applied by the patient or partner prior to sexual acts.

In the assessment of physical capacity of those with cardiovascular or pulmonary disease, several forms of monitored exercise may be undertaken. Continuous electrocardiographic recording with a Holter electromagnetic tape, blood pressure, pulse, and respiratory rates may be sensored during the Master's two-step test, rapid ascent of two flights of stairs, treadmill or free ambulation at 4 miles per hr, bicycle ergometry at 600 kilopon meters per min, or during sexual activity (Eliot and Miles, 1973; Hellerstein and Friedman, 1970; Zohman, 1973). These specific activities are all equivalent to or greater than 6.1 kilocalories per min of energy consumption, the estimated level of expenditure at orgasm according to Hellerstein and Friedman. Therefore, if these tests are accompanied by minimal or no signs and symptoms of distress, sexual intercourse can be safely recommended.

Patients with back disabilities can be subjected to lying, sitting, turning, twisting, hyperextension, and other positional changes to determine if pain will occur during sex acts.

As a form of exercise, coitus has several unique characteristics.

Its analgesic qualities have been pointed out by patients with pain associated with musculoskeletal disorders. Postcoital pain relief may last for hours in these people (Erlich, 1973). Spastic individuals have observed reduction or cessation of involuntary muscle activity for similar periods of time after intercourse (Griffith and associates, 1973).

Surgery. Surgical procedures may alter sexual performances in a variety of ways. Spasticity of lower limb muscles can be reduced by anterior rhizotomy, peripheral neurotomy, Bischoff myelotomy, or other neurosurgical techniques. Contracture releases, such as adductor tenotomies, may allow adequate hip abduction. Hip or knee prostheses, the Girdlestone procedure, or arthrodesis modify painful or contracted joints so as to allow intercourse with little or no discomfort in the arthritic patient (Erlich, 1973). Penile implant prostheses have already been described. Incontinence accompanying the neuropathic bladder may be a primary indication for a modified Bricker (ileal loop) procedure, particularly in the female patient. A very recent development has been the surgical implantation of a pneumatic artifical urethral sphincter (Scott, Bradley, and Timm, 1973). Impotence associated with arterial occlusive disease such as the Leriche syndrome may be improved by corrective vascular surgery (May, DeWeese, and Rob, 1969). Conversely, surgery may result in deterioration of erectile or ejaculatory function. These disparate possibilities must be carefully explained to candidates for such surgical procedures. Tubal ligation or vasectomy are reliable forms of permanent contraception. Hysterectomy has been performed in retarded or brain-damaged adolescents where menstrual hygiene and contraception are desired. Women with scoliosis, meningomyelocele, juvenile rheumatoid arthritis involving the hips, and other neuromusculoskeletal disorders which produce cephalopelivic disproportion should be considered early in pregnancy as potential candidates for eventual cesarian section (Erlich, 1973).

Contraceptives. Conventional contraceptive techniques deserve special consideration (Debrovner, 1971). Women having hypertension, gynecological malignant tumors, or vascular disorders with propensities to thromboembolic or constrictive disease should not be issued cyclic sex hormones. Intrauterine devices may silently perforate, light up pelvic infection, or be expelled in women with major sensory deficits such as incur in spinal cord lesions. The diaphragm is readily malpositioned by those with poor upper extremity sensation or strength, leading to the possibility of contraceptive failure. The condom may be difficult to apply for similar reasons. Placement of diaphragm or condom by the able-bodied partner is one possible solution to these problems.

INTERVENTION STRATEGIES APPROPRIATE TO PRIMARY DYSFUNCTIONS WITH SECONDARY COMPONENTS

Principles of treatment aimed at secondary dysfunctions have been outlined elsewhere in this book and, thus, have been broadly categorized as behavior modification and counseling techniques for the purpose of this chapter. Given the specifics of management relevant to the primary dysfunction, the professional should integrate this information with the treatment strategy appropriate to the individual case.

Behavior modification procedures can be applied to the learning of motor behaviors related to sexual performance. Even individuals with mental retardation or brain damage are capable of responding to programs where rewards for the designated behaviors can be controlled. Specific problems for which behavior modification may be indicated are: (1) learning the appropriate place and time for sexual activities; (2) learning behaviors of dating and courting; (3) learning mechanics of foreplay and lovemaking; (4) learning mechanics of preparatory activities; (5) learning mechanics of sex acts with special reference to balance, coordination, energy conservation, pain prevention; (6) learning to combat fear. In addition, counseling may be most useful in reassuring patients about fears concerning sexual activity and management of primary problems.

If treatment is begun while the patient is hospitalized, a specific room may be assigned for practice, but privacy must be assured. The attitudes of the staff will influence those of the patient and, therefore, all efforts should be directed at creating comfortable and accepting attitudes toward a sex education or reeducation program. Passes from the hospital into the home environment provide a natural and more comfortable milieu for practicing sexual activities. Patients may be instructed specifically or generally before the practice session, and time for feedback should be scheduled. The number of structured practice sessions depend on the needs of the individual case.

Treatment strategies may include individual counseling or team counseling with patient and partner. While there may be occasions for the former, we concur with Masters and Johnson (1970) that there is no uninvolved partner. Group sessions may assist individuals by hearing of others' difficulties and by learning from their successes and failures at coping with postdisablement problems. Groups may be structured around couples or individuals with a disability alone. These sessions are particularly useful for presentation of audiovisual materials and didactic presentations (Multi-Media Resource Center). We are convinced, however, that the mere presentation of information alone usually is not sufficient to lead to behavior change and the resolution of sexual dysfunctions.

Masters and Johnson (1970), in their second volume, discussed the issue of surrogate partners, and we agree with their stance. The disabled individual may not always have a partner but this should not be allowed to preclude a critical aspect of the rehabilitation program. Occasionally, patients or partners seek gratification with an alternate partner while maintaining the original marital unit. Whether or not this is a reasonable course of action depends on the individuals involved and their value systems.

The issues involved in the sex education of disabled children are not that different from those relating to ablebodied children. The question of who does the teaching leads to the same answers: family, school, professionals (Fischer and Krajicek, 1974). The disabled child should have maximal opportunity to develop social skills and self-confidence as a person in preparation for the acceptance of the adult role. As questions arise about sexual functioning, answers should be given matter-of-factly, and specific details may be gained from knowledgeable professionals. Concerns about "abnormal sex drives or behaviors" of brain-damaged or retarded children should be reinterpreted as lack of controls over the appropriate place and time (Freeman, 1970). There is little to no evidence that these individuals have drives which are *different* from those of able-bodied individuals. Rather, the issue can be more successfully treated by behavior modification directed at learning the appropriate expression of the sex drive, appropriate being defined by the parent and professional.

SUMMARY

This chapter has defined the problems of sexual dysfunction associated with physical disabilities by differentiating between primary (organically caused) and secondary (behavioral) dysfunctions. Both types of dysfunction usually are present where sexual difficulties occur in physical disability states. Treatment of these problems is often best done by a professional health care team knowledgeable in the medical-physical modalities and behavioral and counseling techniques.

Secondary factors discussed include premorbid psychosocial influences and attitudes plus mechanisms of personal devaluation and desexualization, fears, and anxieties about the primary disability. Some further distinctions in these factors were identified in cases where the disability occurs in early life or congenitally.

Methods of evaluation of these problems have been alluded to in terms of premorbid, present, and future expectations of physical, psychosocial, vocational, and educational function.

Principles of management have been considered from the viewpoint of when to initiate treatment, who is best qualified to treat, how to introduce the subject to the patient, the importance of treating the sexual partner, and the need to recognize and respect the value systems of the sexual unit.

Specifics of management of primary dysfunctions associated with disorders of the locomotor system and commonly associated medical conditions were reviewed. Preparational activities, positions of sexual acts, alternate sex behaviors, and special precautions were described. Other medical-physical modalities which received attention were prostheses, drugs, exercise, surgery, and contraceptives.

Intervention strategies discussed included: behavior modification programs, training and practice of sexual activities in a suitable environment, individual and cocounseling, group education and counseling, surrogate partner training, and sex education for disabled children.

REFERENCES

Bailey, J. A., Checkles, N. S., and Johnson, E. W. 1968. Sexual counseling of the spinal cord injured patient. Paper presented at the Fifth International Congress of Physical Medicine, Montreal.

Belt, B. G. 1973. Some organic causes of impotence. Med. Aspects Hum. Sexuality, 7: 152.

Bensman, A., and Kottke, F. J. 1966. Induced emission of sperm utilizing electrical stimulation of the seminal vesicles and the vas deferens. Arch. Phys. Med. Rehabil., 47: 436.

Bors, E., and Comarr, A. E. 1960. Neurological disturbances of sexual function with special reference to 529 patients with spinal cord injury. Urol. Survey, 9–10: 191.

Braddom, R., and Johnson, E. 1969. Mecamylamine in control of hyperreflexia. Arch. Phys. Med. Rehabil., 50: 448.

Brown, C. 1970. *Down All the Days*. Stein & Day, New York.

Cole, T. 1975. In: Griffith, E. R., and Trieschmann, R. B. eds. Management of Sexual Dysfunctions Associated with Physical Disabilities. Proceedings of the Plenary Session of the American Academy of Physical Medicine & Rehabilitation and American Congress of Rehabilitation Medicine, Washington, D. C., October, 1973. Arch. Phys. Med. Rehabil., 56: 8.

Comarr, A. E. 1970. Sexual function among patients with spinal cord injury. Urol. Int., 25: 134.

Cooper, I. S., and Hoen, T. I. 1952. Metabolic disorders in paraplegics. Neurology, 2: 332–340.

Cummings, V. 1975. In: Griffith, E. R., and Trieschmann, R. B. eds., Management of Sexual Dysfunctions Associated with Physical Disabilities. Proceedings of the Plenary Session of the American Academy of Physical Medicine & Rehabilitation and American Congress of Rehabilitation Medicine, Washington, D. C., October, 1973. Arch. Phys. Med. Rehabil., 56: 8.

Debrovner, C. H. 1971. Sexual and medical consideration of contraception. Med. Aspects Hum. Sexuality, 5: 118.

Eliot, R., and Miles, R. 1973. What to tell the cardiac patient about sexual intercourse. Resident-Intern Consultant, Oct., p. 14.

Erlich, G. 1973. Sexual problems of the arthritic patient. In: Erlich, G., ed., *Total Management of the Arthritic Patient*. J. B. Lippincott, Philadelphia-Toronto.

Fischer, H. L., and Krajicek, M. J. 1974. Sexual development of the moderately retarded child: how can the pediatrician be helpful? Clin. Pediatr. (Phila.), 13: 79.

Ford, A. B., and Orfirer, A. P. 1967. Sexual behavior and the chronically ill patient. Med. Aspects Hum. Sexuality, 1: 51.

Fotheringham, J. B. 1971. The concept of social competence as applied to marriage and child care in those classified as mentally retarded. Can. Med. Assoc. J., 104: 813.

Freeman, R. D., 1970. Psychiatric problems in adolescents with cerebral palsy. Dev. Med. Child Neurol., 12: 64.

Grabstald, H., and Goodwin, W. E. 1973. Devices and surgical procedures in the treatment of organic impotence. Med. Aspects Hum. Sexuality, 7: 113.

Griffith, E., Timms, R. J., and Tomko, M. A. 1973. Sexual problems of patients with spinal injuries: an annotated bibliography. Dept Phys. Med. Rehabil., Univ. of Cincinnati, Coll. of Med., Cincinnati.

Griffith, E. R., and Trieschmann, R. B. 1975. Sexual function of the spinal cord injured woman. Arch. Phys. Med. Rehabil., 56: 18.

Guttmann, L. and Walsh, J. J. 1971. Prostigmin assessment test of fertility in spinal man. Paraplegia, 9 (1): 39.

Hellerstein, H. K., and Friedman, E. H. 1970. Sexual activity and the post-coronary patient. Arch. Intern. Med. 125: 987.

Hierons, R., and Saunders, M. 1966. Impotence in patients with temporal lobe lesions. Lancet, 2: 761.

Hohmann, G. 1972. Considerations in management of psychosexual readjustment in the cord injured male. Rehabil. Psychol., 19 (2): 50.

Hohmann, G. W. 1975. In: Griffith, E. R., and Trieschmann, R. B. eds., Management of Sexual Dysfunctions Associated with Physical Disabilities. Proceedings of the Plenary Session of the American Academy of Physical Medicine and Rehabilitation and American Congress of Rehabilitation Medicine, Washington, D. C., October, 1973. Arch. Phys. Med. Rehabil., 56: 8.

Howard, E. J. 1973. Sexual expenditure in patients with hypertensive disease. Med. Aspects Hum. Sexuality, 7: 82.

Jackson, R. W. 1972. Sexual rehabilitation after cord injury. Paraplegia, 10: 50.

Kass, I., Updegraff, K., and Muffly, R. B. 1972. Sex in chronic obstructive pulmonary disease. Med. Aspects Hum. Sexuality, 6: 32.

Kurnick, N. 1956. Autonomic hyperreflexia and its control in patients with spinal cord lesions. Ann. Intern. Med., 44: 678.

Loeffler, R. A., Sayegh, E. S., and Lash, H. 1964. The artificial os penis. Plast. Reconstr. Surg., 34: 71.

Masters, W. H., and Johnson, V. E. 1970. *Human Sexual Inadequacy*. Little, Brown and Company, Boston.

May, A., DeWeese, J., and Rob, C. 1969. Changes in sexual function following operation on the abdominal aorta. Surgery, 65: 41.

McDowell, F. H. 1968. Sexual manifestations of neurologic disease. Med. Aspects Hum. Sexuality, 2: 13.

Morales, P. A., Suarez, J. B., Delgado, J., and Whitehead, E. D. 1973. Penile implant for erectile impotence. J. Urol., 109: 641.

Mourad, M., and Chiu, W. S. 1974. Marital-sexual adjustment of amputees. Med. Aspects Hum. Sexuality, 8: 47.

Multi-Media Resource Center (Films). 340 Jones Street, Box 439 E., San Francisco, Ca. 94102.

Oaks, W. W., and Moyer, J. H. 1972. Sex and hypertension. Med. Aspects Hum. Sexuality, 6: 128.

Pearman, R. 1972. Insertion of a silastic penile prosthesis for the treatment of organic sexual impotence. J. Urol., 107: 802.

Pfeiffer, E., and Davis, G. C. 1972. Determinants of sexual behavior in middle and old age. J. Am. Geriatr. Soc., 20: 151.

Rubin, D. 1972. Sex in patients with neck, back and radicular pain syndromes. Med. Aspects Hum. Sexuality, 6: 14.

Rubin, I. 1968. Sexual adjustments in relation to pregnancy. In: Vincent, C. E., ed., *Human Sexuality in Medical Education and Practice*. Charles C Thomas, Springfield, Ill.

Rusk, H. A. 1964. Principles in the management of psychiatric problems. In: Rusk, H. A., and Taylor, E. J., ed. assistant, *Rehabilitation Medicine* Ed. 2 C. V. Mosby Company, St. Louis.

Rusk, H. A., Covalt, D. A., Fisher, S. H., Marks, M., Sullivan, J. F., and Diller. L. 1967. Roundtable: sex problems in paraplegia. Symposium presented at the N. Y. Univ. School of Med. Medical Aspects Hum. Sexuality, 1: 46.

Schoffling, K., Federlin, K., Ditschuneit, H.,and Pfeiffer, E. F. 1963. Disorders of sexual function in male diabetics. Diabetes, 12: 519.

Scott, F., Bradley, W., and Timm, G. 1973. An implantable prosthetic urinary sphincter for treatment of urinary incontinence. Scientific Exhibit. American Congress of Rehabilitation Medicine, American Academy of Physical Medicine and Rehabilitation, Washington, D. C.

Shontz, F. C. 1971. Physical disability and personality. In: Neff, W. S., ed., *Rehabil. Psychology*. American Psychological Association, Inc., Washington, D. C. 33.

Tarabulcy, E. 1972. Sexual function in the normal and in paraplegia. Paraplegia, 10: 201.

Trieschmann, R. B. 1975. In: Griffith, E. R., and Trieschmann, R. B. eds. Management of Sexual Dysfunctions Associated with Physical Disabilities. Proceedings of the Plenary Session of the American Academy of Physical Medicine and Rehabilitation and American Congress of Rehabilitation Medicine, Washington, D. C., October, 1973. Arch. Phys. Med. Rehabil., 56: 8.

Trieschmann, R. B. 1974. Coping with a disability: a sliding scale of goals. Arch. Phys. Med. Rehabil., 55: 556.

Wright, B. A. 1960. *Physical Disability: A Psychological Approach*. Harper, New York.

Young, J. 1963. Use of guanethedine in control of sympathetic hyperreflexia in persons with cervical and thoracic cord lesions. Arch. Phys. Med. Rehabil., 44: 704.

Zohman, L. R. 1973. Cardiac rehabilitiation: its role in evaluation and management of the patient with coronary heart disease. Am. Heart J., 85 (5): 706.

Surgical Intervention in the Treatment of Sexual Disorders

JAMES J. RYAN, M.D.

The clinician caring for patients with problems involving sexual diability should be familiar with surgical procedures which could be of assistance. As these problems are of wide scope and are seen by clinicians of many different disciplines, and the surgery itself is performed by many surgical specialists, it is difficult for anyone to have an intimate familiarity with all relevant operative procedures. This discussion will center about problems of moderate frequency and surgical techniques of well established reliability. The operative details of the surgical techniques themselves will not be reviewed in depth. Rather the indications, timing, general length of hospital stay and disability, probability of "success," and possible complications will be discussed. In this area expanding breadth, increasing therapeutic efforts by those in many specialties, and the rapid evolution of "newer and better" techniques assures the transience of much herein mentioned.

A basic "problem" orientation will be used to introduce topics, and the bisexual male-female division of problems, while admittedly overly simple and uncontemporary, has been adopted. The limitations of this are apparent in the consideration of intersex problems and of surgical sexual reassignment as treatment of gender dysphoria syndromes.

THE SOURCES OF THE PROBLEMS

The sources of sexual disability are numerous. Some clearly arise in anatomic deformity or physiological dysfunction, *e.g.*, congenital anomalies. In problems based on anatomic-physiological abnormalities, the anatomic and physiological rearrangement attending surgical procedures recommend themselves most easily. If we somewhat narrowly and mechanistically restrict consideration of "sexual disabilities" to inabilities and deficiencies in penile-vaginal intercourse, then our concerns are confined to the external genitalia of both the male and female. Examples of such problems in the male would be abnormal urethral location in the penis, abnormal curvature of the penis sufficient to complicate vaginal penetration, and erectile disorders. In the female, it might be even more restricted to hypoplasia or congenital absence of the vagina. But such a narrow consideration of sexual disabilities, while obviously an inadequate representation of the commonly presenting spectrum, would be an equally inaccurate presentation of the benefits which can accrue from well established surgical procedures.

Many features which are from the anatomical and physiological standpoints entirely "normal" or "irrelevant" can be of sufficient concern to impair sexual interaction. The impairment lies in the patient's perception of this feature and subsequent dissonance arising from disagreement with his conception of himself—his body image. Properly considered as problems of "body image deformity," their surgical modification or elimination can in some cases diminish self-reproach or self-consciousness and increase self-esteem and facilitate ease of personal interaction—at times sexual interaction. As such results all emanate from the psychological impact of the surgery on the patient, the surgeon is clearly no longer directly in charge of the results. How the patient will react to the results of surgery is not entirely predictable. Nevertheless, surgery is very frequently and successfully performed for problems of body image deformity. While deformity of almost any part of the body can impair sexual interaction, for practical purposes we shall center our attention upon the more common areas: the breast, the genitalia, and the trunk and torso.

MALE OR FEMALE? —THE PROBLEM OF INTERSEX

The intersex problem arises in physical abnormality, sometimes conspicuous at birth, and sometimes subtle and not evident until magnified by growth. It may thus present in the neonate or later in childhood or adolescence. The age of presentation is of extreme relevance. The newborn child with ambiguous genitalia needs a gender assignment allowing maximal fulfillment of the gender role. Even with the more appropriate assignment, considerable surgical revision of the external genitalia and possibly internal sexual organs as well as lower urinary tract may be necessary to provide an anatomic basis for successful sexual activity. While the details of diagnosis are beyond the scope of this discussion, several practical points concerning the limitations of surgical intervention should be kept foremost in mind.

Firstly, it is virtually never indicated to assign the male gender to an infant whose phallus obviously is inadequate. Plans for later improvements and revisions seldom can be realized. Although there are plastic surgical procedures to simulate the penis or create a pseudopenis from pedicle flap tissues, these are of sufficient difficulty to make satisfactory incorporation of the lower urinary tract unpredictable. As regards sexual function, these tube flaps are not erectile. The scarring at sites from which this tissue is borrowed is usually considerable. To assign an infant to the male gender, hoping he will accept these disabilities in the future, would seem imprudent under most situations (Young, Crockett, Stoller, Ashley, and Goodwin, 1971). Thus, an assignment of female gender in the majority of infants with ambiguous genitalia offers greater likelihood of satisfactory sexual fulfillment as surgical efforts can create cosmetically and functionally satisfactory female external genitalia.

The importance of recognizing these problems in infancy cannot be overstressed. Decision regarding sexual assignment could be considered a "social emergency" in the neonate (Hendren and Crawford, 1972). In some disorders involving ambiguity of genitalia, additional therapeutic considerations necessitate accurate and expeditious diagnosis, for example life-threatening adrenal deficiency (adrenogenital syndrome), preservation of fertility (female pseudohermaphroditism resulting from adrenogenital syndrome), or elimination of gonads with increased malignant potential (testicular feminization). Most importantly, an initial appropriate gender assignment may later raise the socially and psychologically disastrous necessity of either a change of sex role, seldom accomplished successfully beyond the age of 1 or 2 years or a markedly compromised sexual identity (Money, Hampson, and Hampson, 1955).

Evaluation of these children requires a thorough knowledge of the embryology of the urogenital tract. Methods of investigation must include (1) a detailed history, (2) a careful physical examination, (3) nuclear chromatin studies, (4) cytogenetic characterization, (5) roentgenographic examination, (6) biochemical evaluation, (7) endoscopy, and (8) laparotomy and gonad biopsy. The history should detail possible androgenic drug ingestion by the mother during pregnancy, as well as any familial history, particularly among maternal aunts, of sterility, amenorrhea, or possible hernia repairs involving gonads. On physical examination, the external genitalia are most revealing. In a case of hypospadias, absence of one or both testes from the scrotum should be thoroughly investigated. Clitoral enlargement is strongly suggestive of other pathology. Rectal examination in the neonate with palpation of a uterus enlarged by maternal hormones can be a most helpful finding.

Nuclear chromatin studies for chromatin bodies as described by Barr are seen in 20% or more cells from genetic females and not more than 1 to 2% of cells in normal males. Cytogenetics, or the direct study of chromosomes, will allow increasingly specific classification of these syndromes, as it has with Klinefelter's syndrome designated 47-XXY and Turner's syndrome designated as 45-XO.

X-ray examinations, particularly cystourethrography with the injection of dye into the lower urogenital opening, can be helpful in delineating anatomy of the lower urinary tract and disclosing the presence or absence of a vagina. However, even such a negative study does not exclude the presence of a vagina, and careful endoscopic examination will be necessary.

Biochemical studies and urine test for 17-ketosteroids and 17-hydroxycorticosteroids are of value. In most cases, the final step of laparotomy and gonad biopsy is mostly for fact finding and not definitive removal of such structures. On purely social grounds, decision as to the sex of rearing must often be made long before one has the data at hand to be certain of the pathogenetic hormonal problem.

Readily evident anatomic facts should strongly influence the gender assignment. To permit assignment of the male gender to an infant whose ambiguous genitalia incorporate a phallus, the phallus must be of adequate size. It may, however, incorporate an abnormal location of the urethral opening, this being either short and below the penis, the problem of hypospadias, or on the dorsum of the penis, *i.e.*, epispadias. Both of these problems occur often enough in situations where there is no ambiguity about gender that they will be discussed in the subsequent section with more common problems of male genitalia. Where there is ambiguity or the absence of one testis from the scrotum, a scrotal prosthesis may be easily inserted in the scrotum at an appropriate age, and the newer soft Silastic simulates a testis in tactile quality. Where an insufficient phallus is present (microphallus), if part of a hormonal deficiency state, replacement therapy may produce enlargement adequate to allow functioning in the male gender role. There is no reliable surgical technique to significantly enlarge an inadequately small penis. Thus, with a grossly inadequate phallus, assignment of the female gender is most appropriate, and numerous surgical techniques can be called upon in the creation of cosmetically and functionally acceptable external genitalia.

If female gender assignment is made, there are numerous

operative procedures for creating esthetically and functionally adequate external genitalia. In the presence of microphallus or extreme clitoromegaly, amputation or clitoridectomy was pursued in the recent past. More recently, with the thought that later sexual activity might be enhanced by preservation of the glans or enlarged clitoris, clitoroplasty has been performed (Hendren and Crawford, 1972). This an operation to recess the shaft of the enlarged organ back under the pubis and leave the most sensitive glans or clitoral tissue appropriately located. The long term follow-up results of this in terms of enhanced or adequate sensual functioning must be awaited.

The creation of a vagina, or vaginoplasty, can vary from simply providing an adequate introitus or external opening to a vagina which is already in large measure present or, if there is total absence of the vagina, to total reconstruction. In the former instance, depending on the degree to which the vagina does approximate and open onto the perineum, a relatively simple procedure of cutback or flap vaginoplasty can be performed in the infant at the time of clitoral recession. In the cases incorporating the least deformity of the lower urogenital tract, no further surgery beyond infancy may be required and sexual function be entirely adequate. However, in the more marked cases with total agenesis of the vagina, reconstruction by creation of a vaginal pouch between the rectum and urinary structures to the level of the peritoneum is usually deferred until young adulthood. As such agenesis can occur as a principal problem in an otherwise normal adult female, the surgical procedure for total vaginal reconstruction will be discussed subsequently with problems of female genitalia. The facts that a stint must be worn in place and, preferably, frequent intercourse engaged in to maintain the vaginal capacity make the reasons for deferral to early adulthood quite obvious.

Thus, while a thorough evaluation and accurate diagnosis in the child with ambiguities of external genitalia are mandatory to anticipate ancillary problems and to direct accurate long term therapy, the practical limitations on the surgical construction of adequate functioning external genitalia must always be kept preeminently in mind if a gender assignment is to be made which will incorporate optimal adult sexual function.

In the most unfortunate instances in which older children or adults are seen with intersex problems and the gender assignment has been inappropriately made, the same limitations of surgical therapy remain. If a male gender assignment was made and has been fully accepted by the patient and his family psychologically and socially, then change of such assignment past the age of 1 or 2 is frequently too disruptive to be entertained (Money and associates, 1955). If the external genitalia are markedly deficient, unfortunately the same limitations as regard reconstruction or enlargement of the penis persist. Occasionally, with no alternative, extensive surgical procedures can be undertaken in the hopes of establishing an adequate simulation of a phallus. The limitations of this procedure have already been mentioned. An extremely small microphallus cannot be enlarged surgically with any predictable success (Young and associates, 1971). If a marginal but adequate penis is present, then scrotal prostheses may be of benefit. If breast enlargement to bothersome proportions is a part of the problem, then reduction can be performed through inconspicuous incisions about the areola if the enlargement is not massive. The marked improvement in chest contour can more than justify considering such surgery, and this will be detailed later under gynecomastia. In other instances where a female assignment has been made, the same procedures as might have been carried out in infancy can be performed; external genitalia and a vagina of acceptable functional and esthetic quality can be created. If breast development is seriously deficient, then enlargement by augmentation mammoplasty can be particularly successful. This procedure, more commonly performed for body image deformity, will likewise be discussed later. The limitations of surgical accomplishment in the case of inappropriate gender assignment cannot be stressed enough. The maladjustment and psychological problems seen in these patients can be of massive proportions, and the best of surgical results may fall far short of providing a functional level acceptable to the patients. The thorough psychological evaluation, counseling, and therapy, while essential in all cases, become the major hope for salvage and sustenance for these individuals. Gender reversal after age 2 or 3 may be too disruptive to patient and family to be entertained. Above all, however, they must be counseled and supported to realize the limitations their anatomic deficiency imposes but also be introduced to the innumerable ways compensatory outlets can be pursued. (For further information regarding the child with ambiguous genitalia, see Hendren and Crawford, 1972.)

PROBLEMS IN THE MALE

External Genitalia

Several congenital problems may affect the male external genitalia. The most common problem involving the penis is that of hypospadias, an abnormal location of the urethral opening on the undersurface of the penile shaft. More rarely epispadias, a similar condition with an abnormal opening of the urethra on top of the penis, and also rare problems of penile torsion and penile curvature can present. The scrotum is most commonly involved by absence of the testis.

Hypospadias

Hypospadias is an abnormal location of the urethral opening on the undersurface of the penis rather than at its tip. This has a wide spectrum from the opening being located between the scrotum at its base or anywhere along the shaft of the penis to a minimally troublesome and almost normal opening at the base of the glans rather than its tip. A frequency of 1 in every 300 to 400 male births makes this a most common congenital problem. While numerous operative procedures have been developed, all require meticulous execution to assure good results.

General principles of hypospadias care begin with a careful evaluation of the urethral opening. Occasionally this is stenotic and must be enlarged, and it is important that this be done by enlarging the superior, not inferior, aspect, as that would allow the urethral opening to recede farther proximally and increase the difficulty of definitive repair. No child with hypospadias should be circumcised, as this is often the tissue that will make a difference between a successful repair and a difficult or nearly impossible reconstructive task. Patients are followed at 6-month intervals from birth until the genitalia have enlarged enough to facilitate surgery. This is usually between 1½ and 2 years of age. Growth of the penis slows somewhat after age 2, but the fascial layers become increasingly fibrotic, making dissection somewhat more difficult.

Frequently associated with the abnormal urethral opening is a bend in the penis ventrally, referred to as chordee, resulting from a tough fibrous band extending from the urethral meatus to the edge of the hooded prepuce or foreskin. At present, correction of this as well as a reconstruction of the urethra, urethroplasty, to extend this from its abnormal location to the tip of the penis, can both be accomplished in one operation. There are numerous techniques using local tissues in the form of either flaps or free tubed skin grafts, but the operator performing this should be sufficiently familiar with the variety of techniques to adapt them as the difficulty of the circumstances demand. There are five characteristics of successful hypospadias repair: (1) complete straightening of the penis; (2) a urethral meatus brought to the tip of the penis; (3) a normal voiding pattern; (4) normal penile appearance; and (5) normal erectile function. Presently in knowledgeable, skilled surgical hands, this goal can be approached in 80% of hypospadias cases. Entirely normal adult sexual function is thus possible (Horton and Devine, 1973; Wood-Smith, 1964).

Epispadias

Uncomplicated epispadias is a rare condition occurring in both males and females in approximately 1 in 30,000 to 1 in 100,000 births. Here the urethral opening is on the dorsum of the penis, again proximal to the tip. Principles of surgery are not dissimilar to those reviewed for hypospadias except that epispadias is very often associated with a major ventral abdominal wall defect and includes extrophy of the bladder as well. While rare, this is a major deficit, and its reconstruction is dificult. A normal penis and normal sexual function can rarely be achieved with present surgical techniques in combined extrophy of the bladder and epispadias. In epispadias alone, the success should approach that with hypospadias (Horton and Devine, 1972).

Erectile Disorders

There are several erectile disorders of the penis which can frequently be improved by surgical intervention. These are penile torsion and curvature (most commonly Peyronie's disease), priapism, and impotence.

Penile Curvature. While curvatures of the penis may be congenital, most commonly associated with hypospadias, they may be associated with a shortening or contracture of any of the fibrous layers surrounding the inner corpora cavernosa or corpora spongiosum of the penis, the former being the vascular erectile bodies contributing principally to penile enlargement and erection. Trauma or injury inducing scarring in these fascial layers with associated inability to expand symmetrically can lead to curvature with erection. This can be a congenital disorder first seen in the neonate. In these cases, if extreme and of functional significance at that time, correction by surgery can result in marked improvement. It may then necessitate reoperative surgery in early adult life.

The most common disorder of penile curvature in adulthood is Peyronie's disease. The presenting symptom is usually deviation of the penis and pain with erection. The patient may detect a hard, tender knot within the penile shaft, and most commonly the pain slowly and spontaneously subsides. Following this, there is frequent curvature of the penis. The etiology is felt most likely to be a vasculitis inducing a fibrosis in the tunica albuginea or fibrous layer surrounding the corpora cavernosum. While various treatments have been used with success [vitamin E (Scardino and Scott, 1949), steroid injections (Desanctis and Furey, 1967)], a recently developed surgical procedure has met with good success (Horton and Devine, 1973). Surgical resection of the fibrous plaque from the tunica albuginea with its replacement by a dermal graft, thus preventing contracture and minimizing recurrent scar formation at the site, has produced an excellent initial correction of the problem which has remained over the period of follow-up of several years. The procedure does require hospitalization for 4 to 7 days and general anesthesia. Resumption of normal sexual activity several weeks later has been the usual case. Several limitations of surgery should be cited—that of occasional injury to one of the nerves in resecting a rather large plaque, a possible development of flail midportion of the penis should the resection have to extend deeply into the corpora cavernosum on one side, and recurrence and worsening of the condition with surgery in the initial phases of the disease prior to the formation of a well localized, discrete fibrous plaque (Horton and Devine, 1973; Nesbit, 1965).

Priapism. Priapism is the condition of prolonged erection of the penis, usually unaccompanied by sexual stimulation, with attendant pain. Broadly classified as primary and secondary priapism, the causes of the latter are innumerable, being either neurogenic, infectious, mechanical, or hematological. The basic pathology is venous stasis and persistence of erection with the arterioles to the corpora cavernosum fully opened, while the venules and arteriovenous shunts are partially closed. With prolongation, this can produce relative venous occlusion at the junction of the cavernous spaces with the collecting veins. In this situation edema of the corpora trabeculae occurs, and mechanical resistance to subsequent venous drainage develops. This can lead eventually to occlusion of the arterioles and subsequent gangrene of the corpora, ending in fibrosis and a permanent penile contracture and deformity. Thus, the importance of providing improved venous drainage is evident.

Priapism is a surgical emergency and time is crucial. Two objectives are to be sought: (1) restoration of the venous drainage from the corpora and (2) prevention of damage to the erectile mechanism. Forms of medical therapy have not been generally successful. Needle aspiration may be employed with a large gauge needle inserted in the base of the corpora on each side (Harrow, 1969). Removal of most of the dark venous sludge and evacuation of the corpora to the point of bright bleeding are necessary. Irrigation with saline has been recommended. A more recent operation has been the use of the saphenous vein anastomosed to the corpora spongiosum in an attempt to establish decompression (Grayhack, McCullough, O'Connor, and Trippel, 1964). While an emergent matter, the treatment is not without complications, and loss of sexual potency in patients is quite common (Grace and Winter, 1968).

Impotence. Impotence, for the purpose of this discussion, is defined as the inability to obtain or maintain a penile erection adequate to effect vaginal intercourse. The causes for impotence are numerous and can frequently be psychogenic as well as organic. While the indications for surgery have by many authors been confined to cases of established organic impotence, for example, secondary to nerve damage and pelvic surgery, others have reported its use in cases of psychic impotence. A successful surgical procedure used over the past 15 years is the insertion of a Silastic penile implant (Loeffler, 1973). The procedure is carried out in the hospital, most frequently under general anesthesia. Through a 1-inch incision on the dorsum of the shaft of the penis, a pocket is made between the two corpora cavernosum. The Silastic rod, approximately 1 cm in diameter, is then placed with a blunt end back at the origin of the corpora underneath the pubis and the distal tapered end placed at the distal limits of the corpora within the junction of the glans. Few complications have been reported, with extrusions occurring in only 5 of 200 reported cases. While the penis differs from the normal erectile state, the implant provides sufficient support to facilitate vaginal introduction and, in some cases, subsequent erection. Even without this, however, patients have reported being able to conduct intercourse in a fashion satisfying to both partners.

Brief mention might be made of a new penile implant attempting to simulate more closely the erect and detumescent states of the penis (Scott, 1973). This is a hydraulic cylinder with a scrotal fluid reservoir which is placed within the penis in a similar fashion to the rod. This, then, can allow inflation of the implant, providing increased penile rigidity, and when deflated, return of the more normal flaccidity. This is at present still in developmental stages though a number of successful clinical installations have been reported. Caution is advisable, however, in that past experience with similar inflatable prostheses has indicated an increased incidence of complications with time.

Scrotum

The only scrotal problem seen with any frequency is an absent testis. This may be congenital or secondary to trauma or possibly resection necessitated by testicular disease. The absence of one or both testes in the male of any age can cause psychological difficulty. While only one testicle is necessary for fertility, the absence of the other can have significant personal meaning and be a point of considerable sensitivity. Children may be subject to embarrassment if disrobed before others and thus may avoid activities requiring this. In the adult, the intimacies of sexual contact can unmask this sensitivity. Where a problem exists, the placement of an appropriate testicular prosthesis can be of great help. The most preferred prosthesis is silicone having a resilient texture similar to the normal testis (Prentiss, Boatwright, Pennington, Hohn, and Schwartz, 1963). These come in two sizes, small for children and larger for adults, but the difference in size is not sufficient to motivate many requests for revision of one inserted in childhood. The operative procedure is not complicated, can be performed under local anesthesia if necessary, requires a minimal hospital stay, and has a minimal attendant disability or limitation of activity.

The Male Breast

Gynecomastia. The male breast, while of no physiological consequence, can be the site of body image deformity. Excessive breast enlargement, coming to resemble the female breast, can be most disturbing to the adolescent male. Pubertal enlargement and tenderness of the male breast are common. They may be transient, and as the tenderness subsides the size of the breast returns to normal. However, the enlargement can continue almost to female proportions. At the point breast enlargement inhibits social activities and interaction, surgical extirpation of the breast tissue should be considered.

Surgery for gynecomastia can be performed through a small incision at the edge of the areola and the hormonally sensitive breast mass is removed (Webster, 1946) (Fig. 11.1). This must be done with great care to not produce a "dish deformity" of the chest, but when properly performed it can result in an excellent cosmetic result, eliminating embarrassment at appearing without a shirt. The operation requires admission to the hospital, can be performed under local or general anesthesia, and necessitates a hospital stay of 2 to 3 days. Activities are limited for a period of 4 weeks. It is strongly recommended that, when any breast enlargement in an adolescent male progresses to the point where he limits his activities or interactions because of embarrassment of appearing without a shirt, surgical extirpation of the breast mass be considered. While mild enlargement may subside, marked enlargement seldom totally regresses.

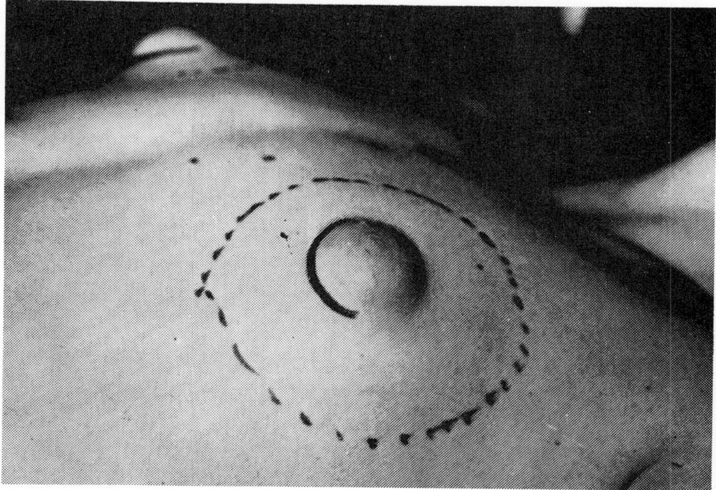

Fig. 11.1. Gynecomastia of 2½ years duration in 15-year-old boy. Infra-areolar incision and extent of enlarged breast tissue to be excised.

PROBLEMS IN THE FEMALE

Genitalia

Vaginal Agenesis. While the fundamental problem in the congenitally absent vagina is anatomic, the significance, both psychological and physiological, should not be underestimated. When at puberty menses are absent, a sense of deformity and incapacity may often ensue. And later, when normal coitus is not possible, frustration is natural.

The causes of vaginal absence are several. Some are genetic, as Turner's syndrome with resultant sexual immaturity, but vaginal agenesis on a genetic basis is infrequent. Hormones, endogenous or exogenous, influencing the fetus during the 5th week of intrauterine life can interfere with the normal female development. A part of this may be hypoplasia or absence of the vagina. And lastly a failure of end organ response can be cited as in the case of patients with "testicular feminization" where genetic maleness is combined with an external female body habitus except for the absence of a vagina.

Where the hypoplastic vagina fails to open through a normal introitus, this opening can often be provided in infancy as a part of surgical modification of other aspects of the external genitalia, as is necessary with ambiguous genitalia. Where there is total absence of the vagina and total reconstruction is necessitated, a different timing of surgical intervention is necessary.

The treatment of choice for total reconstruction of the congenitally absent vagina is development of a cavity between the rectum and urinary structures and insertion of a thick split thickness skin graft (McIndoe, 1949). This should be deferred until the pelvic structures are near adult size. The insertion and continuous use of a stint for some 6 months following surgery to prevent contracture and constriction of the skin graft is required. In addition, frequent intercourse helps maintain and prevent this contracture. The amount of "natural" physiological function that can be expected is exemplified by the case of a patient with this type of reconstruction having delivered three babies vaginally (Moore and Simonis, 1969).

Possible complications of injury to the adjacent urethra or rectum while forming the cavity should be mentioned as they constitute major complications occasionally requiring additional surgery in the form of urinary diversion or colostomy. Rarely, sepsis will cause loss of the skin graft and subsequent contracture of the cavity. necessitating a repeat operation after a period of delay and rest of the tissues. However, in the vast majority of cases, the operation can be performed successfully with creation and maintenance of a vaginal cavity of sufficient size and depth to allow intercourse.

Clitoromegaly

Cliteromegaly usually must be of significant proportions to be perceived as a problem. If this is the case, the procedure of clitoral recession with delivery of the clitoral crura back deeper along the pubis can be effective. This does require hospitalization and general anesthesia but a minimal hospital stay and a minimal period of disability. As clitoromegaly can result from androgenic excess at any age, ovarian tumor must be ruled out.

Clitoral Hooding

Occasionally either a marked diminution of size in the glans clitoris or marked hooding of a normal organ will minimize clitoral contact. A relatively minor procedure of clitoral circumcision can be performed to uncover the clitoris and make it more subject to direct stimulation. This has been reported to directly increase the sensitivity and pleasure of contact. Direct clitoral contact is not necessary for sexual response and the degree to which it is found pleasurable varies among individuals. It should be noted this is to be differentiated from the historic operation of female circumcision which is still performed in portions of the world: in essence an amputation of the clitoris and portions of the labia, thus to directly diminish the pleasure of sexual contact. The present operation can be performed under light general anesthesia with a minimal hospital stay and a short period of disability.

Vaginal Capaciousness

Penile-vaginal disparity most frequently arises from excessive capaciousness of the vagina, particularly the entrance or introitus to the vagina. This is most common following multiple vaginal deliveries. This increased capaciousness may contribute to a significant diminution of pleasure with intercourse. This condition of vaginal enlargement is frequently attended by anterior and posterior vaginal wall laxities with urological or rectal dysfunction. In this state, a generalized operation for improvement can be performed and is frequently described as an anterior-posterior vaginal repair.

The operative procedure itself in addition to reinforcing the tissues of the anterior and posterior walls can be designed to significantly reduce the volume of the vagina, and with care a reinforcement of the perineal body and the posterior aspect of the vaginal introitus and thus a tightening or narrowing of the vaginal entrance can be effected. This operative procedure requires general anesthesia and necessitates a hospital stay of several days. It is usually not accompanied by any serious complications. Abstinence from sexual activity of some 6 weeks is recommended. Considerable improvement in both urological and rectal function may ensue.

The Female Breast

Congenital Absence of Asymmetry. While commonly an object of body image deformity, one particularly significant congenital problem of the female breast is absence, or marked hypoplasia. Absence can be associated with deficiency of the underlying pectoral muscle and deformities of the hand on the associated side, Poland's syndrome. More common is unilateral hypoplasia leading to asymmetry of the breasts. Often, this not evident until puberty and becomes progressively prominent with development. Some difference in size and shape between the breasts is common and seldom of concern until approximately a 20% differential in weight or volume exists. Differences greater than this become readily noticeable, and their correction is desired. In the case of total absence, deformity becomes evident earlier, and the psychological impact to a developing girl can be great. Though surgical treatment might be deferred, the patient and family should be seen early and assured that when breast development has progressed sufficiently, corrective surgery can be performed.

Two techniques by which the breasts are brought into better symmetry is an augmentation of the small side and occasionally a modified reduction or alteration of shape of the larger side. Augmentation mammoplasty is widely used and will be discussed later in the context of body image deformity. Augmentation will correct the size disparity, but the disparity in shape may persist. The shape of the better developed breast must frequently be altered. This is done by the technique of nipple and areolar transposition to a new site and tailoring of the skin envelope as is done for a reduction mammoplasty breast or ptosis correction. These will also be discussed in more detail subsequently. While perfect symmetry is seldom attained, it can be very closely approached, usually well within the limits of normal variation in breast sizes. The operation is performed under general anesthesia in the hospital with a stay of 3 to 5 days and can be performed in one stage. With further development, should symmetry again decrease, the same procedures can be repeated or modified as the patient might desire.

Micromastia—the too Small Breast. The female breast is frequently the center of a sense of body image deformity. A sense of inadequacy or disproportionate smallness of the breast is a concern of these women and while not obviously impairing their sexual interaction, carries a sense of inadequacy and may interfere with activities and dress. The breasts can be enlarged from small states of micromastia, either congenital or post partum, by augmentation mammoplasty

Augmentation mammoplasty is almost exclusively performed presently by the insertion of Silastic prostheses behind the breast (Fig. 11.2). The degree of augmentation is determined by the size of the patient's chest as the pocket behind the breast has definite anatomic limitations. An appropriately sized prosthesis can be placed in the cavity developed behind the breast and anterior to the thoracic muscles. The operation usually is performed through a small incision along the edge of the areola. With the pocket appropriate formed, a matched size prosthesis is inserted. This operation is commonly performed in the hospital but can be performed in outpatient ambulatory surgical facilities. It may be performed under local or general anesthesia, seldom requires a hospital stay of more than 2 days if hospitalization is chosen, and requires limitation of activities for 4 to 6 weeks.

The results of augmentation mammoplasty are almost uniformy pleasing to the patients (Fig. 11.3a, b). The breasts are

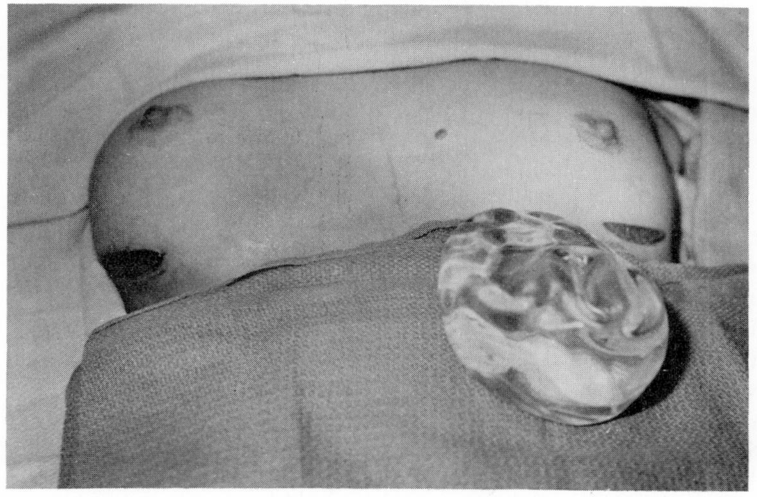

Fig. 11.2. Augmentation mammoplasty. The Silastic implant about to be inserted on the left side through an inframammary incision.

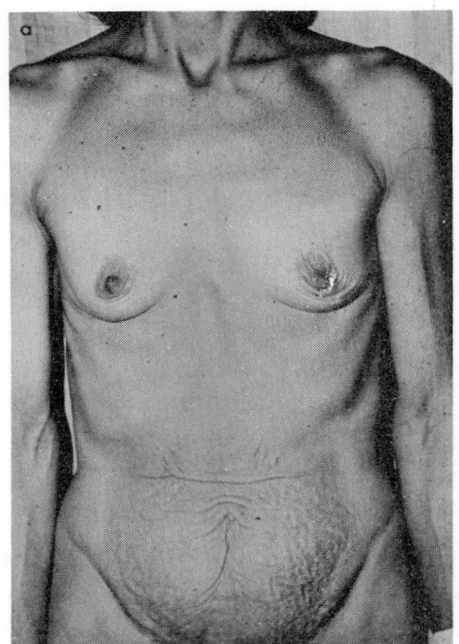

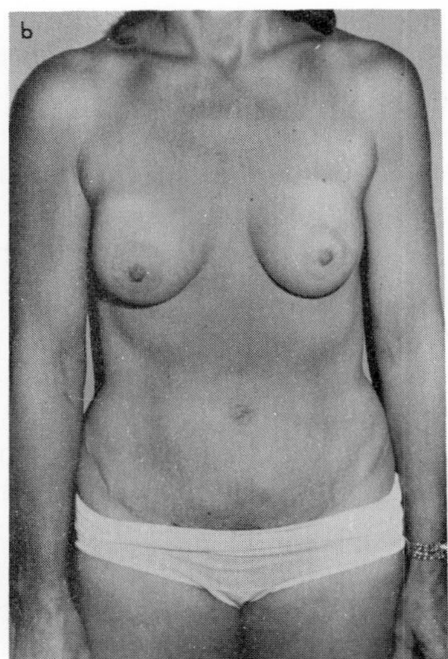

Fig. 11.3.a. Thirty-seven-year-old post partum woman with depressive weight loss referred by psychiatrist regarding intense displeasure with her breasts and abdomen. b. Same patient 1 year after augmentation mammoplasty, abdominal lipectomy, and 15-lb. weight gain.

clearly enlarged, and with the newer prostheses, tactile quality in the feel of the breast is near normal. Follow-up evaluation has almost uniformly revealed an improved sense of body image, a feeling of "things are as they always should have been." Initially following augmentation there is increased breast play in sexual activity which returns to near preoperative levels in 6 to 9 months in most cases. A persisting pleasure with the improved appearance in body image is evidenced by a long-term alteration of activities and dress styles.

Complications attending augmentation mammoplasty most commonly are seroma or hematoma about the implant. This occurs in less than 3% (DeCholnoky, 1970). Rarely infection can become a problem which may necessitate removal of the implant. This, however, can be replaced after the infection is brought under control, and an intervening period of 6 months is allowed for complete healing of tissues. Long-term surveys of over 10,000 cases of augmentation mammoplasty have not revealed any increased incidence of breast disease with the newer Silastic implant (Hoopes, Edgerton, and Shelley, 1967).

Macromastia—the too Large Breast. As extreme smallness or micromastia can be a problem, so can excessive breast size. In the adolescent female, a rapid enlargement to gigantic proportions can occur and is described as "virginal hypertrophy" of the breast (Fig. 11.4). This is apparently a marked end organ sensitivity to the normal hormonal stimulus of puberty. In addition to the emotional and psychic trauma of grotesquely large breasts, there can be extreme physical problems with both inter- and inframammary skin rashes, shoulder stress and pain, and a slumped and altered posturing in an attempt to mask the breast size. Under these conditions, surgical extirpation of the breast mass should be strongly considered.

More commonly the breast enlargement is more gradual and simply results in a breast of excessive size, out of proportion with the remaining body dimensions (Fig. 11.5). Disproportionate breast size can be a source of embarrassment by its conspicuousness. These patients will not uncommonly relate the desire to look "simply normal." In addition to problems with skin rash, shoulder stress, and posture previously mentioned, there is restriction of dress, difficulty of procuring clothing of the proper size, and not infrequent avoidance of activities which would reveal the extreme breast size. Under these conditions, the same operative technique can be readily recommended—that of reduction mammoplasty (McKissock, 1972; Strombeck, 1971).

Reduction mammoplasty consists principally of alteration of three elements of the breast; a reduction of the actual breast mass, a proportional reduction in the skin of the breast to produce a pleasing shape, and then a proper relocation of the nipple and areola on the breast. The operation does involve some evident scarring in that there is a circular scar about the nipple

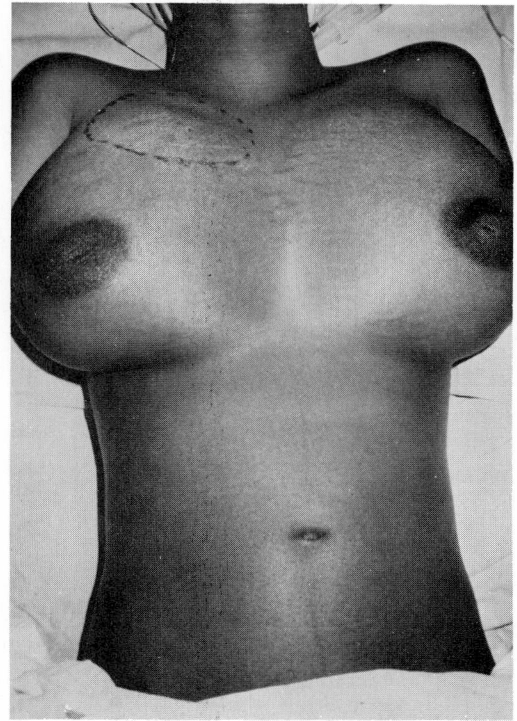

Fig. 11.4. Virginal hypertrophy in a 12-year-old girl. Marks outline discrete mass.

and areola, a vertical scar then running to the inframammary crease or fold below the breast, and a transverse scar just above the inframammary crease. None of these scars are at all conspicuous with a bra or halter. Newer techniques of transposing the nipple and areola to its new site preserve good nipple sensation, and indeed the technique can occasionally be modified to allow lactation and nursing following its performance. This is a major operative procedure requiring hospitalization, general anesthesia, and a stay of 5 to 7 days. Activities are limited for 6 weeks. Complications are those of bleeding with possible hematoma formation and bruising occurring in 5 to 8 percent of cases. Less frequent complications are those of infection (less than 1% and rarely, partial or complete loss of the nipple or areola owing to impaired blood supply. With the newer techniques and in the absence of infection, this last complication is very rare.

Ptosis—the Sagging Breast. An additional feature of the breast which the patients may find disturbing is alteration in breast

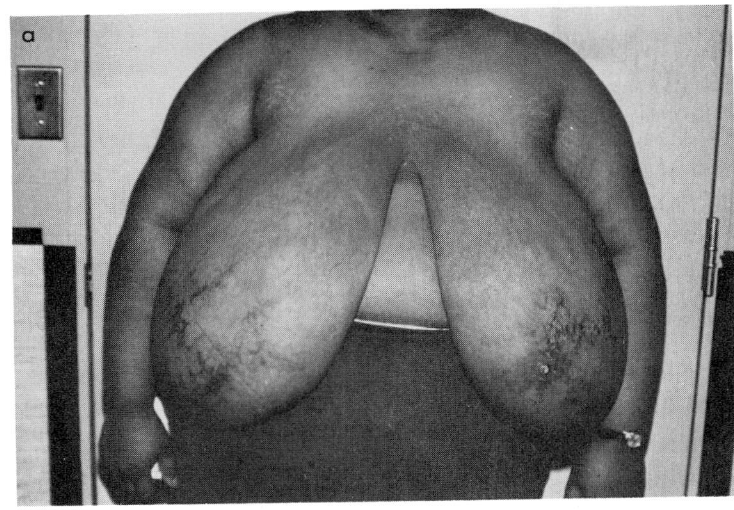

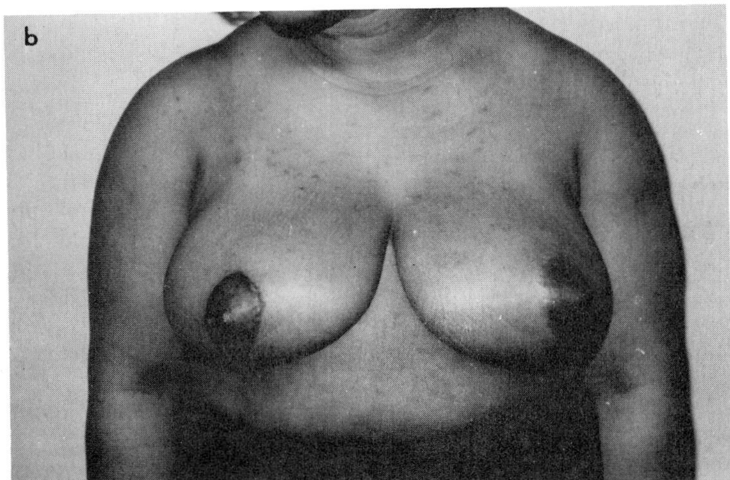

Fig. 11.5.a. Extreme macromastia in 42-year-old obese woman. b. Two years after reduction mammoplasty with removal of nearly 10,000 g of tissue and 125-lb. weight loss.

shape with aging. With normal aging, particularly following childbirth, as the breast becomes smaller, it may lose its youthful, conical shape and take on a ptotic, pendulous appearance (Fig. 11.6). Some women find this most distressing, and while pleased with the size of the breast, would desire a more pleasant, youthful appearance. Correction can be achieved by a modification of the reduction mammoplasty technique; no glandular mass is resected, but the nipple and areola are repositioned, elevated to a new site, and the skin tailored to the breast

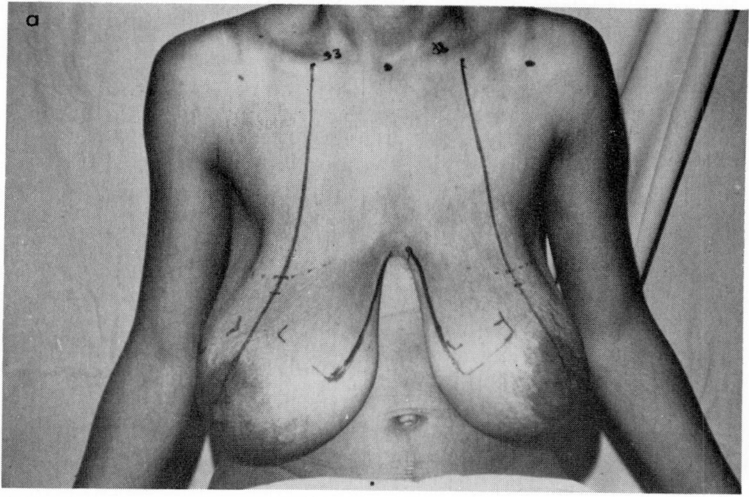

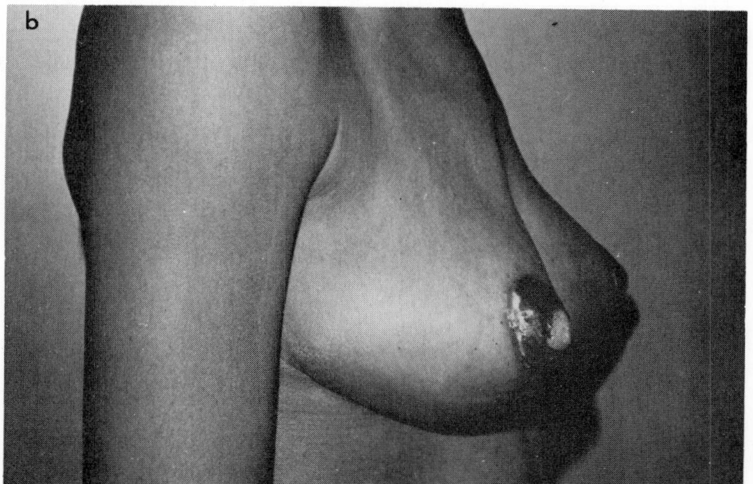

Fig. 11.6.a. Marked breast ptosis in 32-year-old woman. Measurements and markings for new nipple location and skin-breast excision. b. Same patient 3 months post operative. Nipple pigmentation slowly returned over 9-month period.

mass to give a more youthful, conical shape. This necessitates the same scarring previously described, but in most cases the patients feel that the improved appearance more than justifies the inconspicuous scarring. The details are similar to that of full reduction mammoplasty, though the operation is less complicated and incidence of complications is thus proprotionately less.

Thus, the numerous problems of the breast creating a sense of deformity can oftentimes be improved by one or a combination of the above procedures. The size can be altered by augmentation or reduction, and the shape can likewise be altered. While not to be anticipated and certainly not assured, it is no exaggeration to say that many patients have a dramatic alteration in life style following such surgery. The change in apparel, the change in activities previously avoided, and a general sense of improved pleasure with oneself is frequently seen.

Contour Deformities of the Abdomen and Thighs Attending Localized Obesity

Marked skin redundancy of the lower abdomen in an apron-like fashion can result following marked weight loss (Fig. 11.7). This skin excess can likewise occasionally be seen in the inner thigh areas as well as excessive apparent depositions of fat in areas of the buttocks and upper thighs. These may be so extreme as to virtually cover the genital areas and be attended by extreme problems with skin rash, personal hygiene, and physically impaired sexual interaction. More commonly they are of much more moderate degrees. A mild but very common contour deformity is seen in the lower abdominal protuberance which may result following several pregnancies. Here, despite vigorous exercise and a good restoration of muscle tone, persistent prominence of the abdominal skin below the umbilicus and above the pubis may persist. There are numbers of different

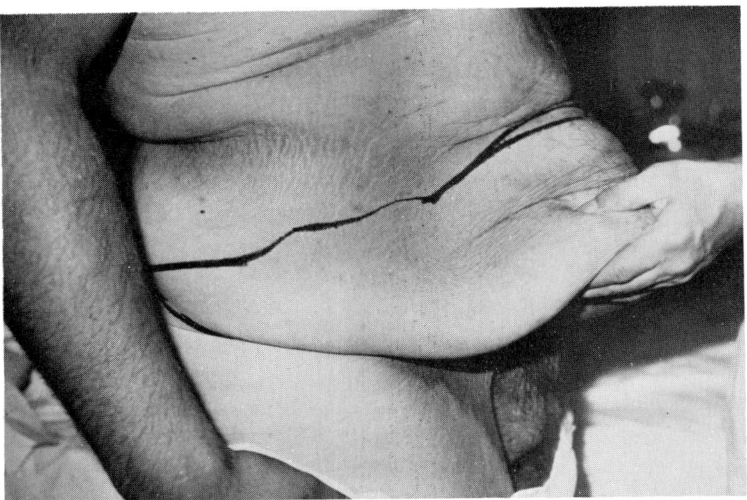

Fig. 11.7. Abdominal contour deformity (abdominal apron) following 175-lb. weight loss.

operative procedures, most commonly abdominal lipectomy and surgical reduction of the thighs which, by eliminating these unsightly excesses of skin and subcutaneous tissue, and thus restoring a more normal body contour, can improve self-image and thus foster ease of personal interaction.

Abdominal lipectomy consists of a transverse incision made just above the suprapubic lower abdominal crease usually confined within the prominent anterior bones of the iliac spines bilaterally (Grazer, 1973; Pitanguy, 1967). This is carried down to the plane just above the abdominal muscles and fascia, and the entire abdominal skin is then widely undermined up to the edges of the ribs superiorly. The umbilicus is then circumscribed, the abdominal skin is pulled inferiorly, the excess is removed, and the umbilicus is then brought out through a new incision in an appropriate location. This not infrequently results in total removal of all skin that previously was contained between the umbilicus and the suprapubic incision. The resultant scars are an inconspicuous circular scar about the new umbilicus usually contained within it rather than around it and a transverse scar running just above the pubis in the natural skin fold occurring in this area (Fig. 11.3b). The procedure necessitates hospitalization and general anesthesia and strict bedrest for 5 to 7 days thereafter. Activities are restricted for several more weeks. Complications are seen in less than 5% of cases and consist of bleeding and fluid collections beneath the abdominal flap which may on occasion necessitate reoperation. Infection, likewise, is infrequent and has not occurred in a personal series of 26 cases. The abdomen is once again smooth, and any stretch marks contained in that removed skin between the umbilicus and suprapubic areas are likewise eliminated.

A similar procedure can be done on the inner aspect of the thighs, the scars hidden in the perineal groin creases, the medial thighs undermined, and excess skin and subcutaneous tissue removed. Again, this necessitates hospitalization and general anesthesia, strict bedrest for a week to 10 days, and then limited ambulation for several more weeks. The only complication of any frequency is that of some bleeding beneath the flaps postoperatively but occurring in less than 4% of cases. Scars can usually be placed so as to be less offensive than the redundant skin and fat. Similarly, lipodystrophies of the outer thighs and buttocks occasionally occur, and these can be eliminated by carefully tailoring and placing the incision in the gluteal thigh creases. Here, however, the scars occasionally can become sensitive and tender and sitting can be uncomfortable for a period of time following such surgery.

A number of problems have been reviewed which, while in no way physiologically constituting sexual disability to the extent that they do impair body image, can in individual instances impair sexual interaction. A sense of body image deformity of almost any part can, to the degree it preempts one's attention, interfere with the necessary interaction for complete sexual gratification. Perhaps in a way anything that makes one more self-preoccupied perhaps makes one less capable of a meaningful exchange. Thus, deformities of almost any part of the body, even those of facial appearance, when improved and corrected can in some instances greatly facilitate personal interaction which may result in improved sexual interaction. This is, however, variable among patients and should not be the principal reason for cosmetic surgery. In the patient who is properly motivated and realistic about the limitations, a proper improvement in his sense of well-being can often be anticipated.

SEX REASSIGNMENT SURGERY IN GENDER DYSPHORIA SYNDROMES

A great deal has been written regarding the surgery of sexual reassignment. The description of transsexualism, often applied to such cases, might best be limited to the description of the postoperative patient upon whom sexual reassignment surgery has already been completed. The psychiatric disorder itself would seem most appropriately described by the more recent term, "gender dysphoria syndromes." The present status of surgery in this area was well stated recently, "It must be emphasized it is not yet established that surgical alteration will be the best method of treating the adult transexual, but it is established that such treatment may offer significant relief for many patients" (Edgerton, 1973). Certainly in childhood and adolescent presentations of these problems, the mode of therapy should be psychiatric. In adult cases, again this would seem the primary mode of therapy. Only when psychiatric therapy has been unsuccessful in the adult should sexual reassignment surgery be considered as palliation for a most unfortunate emotional state. It seemingly seldom constitutes a cure for the problem of gender reversal (Meyer and Hoopes, 1974).

Surgical procedures for reassignment from male to female involve castration, penectomy, and elimination of redundant scrotal skin. The reconstructive procedures then consist of fashioning esthetically and functionally acceptable external genitalia and, most importantly, a functioning vagina of adequate depth to permit intercourse. In addition, if breast size is inadequate after hormonal therapy, augmentation mammoplasty can be performed. Numerous techniques have been reported for performing the ablative procedures, and all or portions of the reconstructive procedures in one or, more commonly, two stages. If the anatomic situation is such that the penis is of adequate size and the penile skin sufficient, and the penis adequately retrodisplaced toward the perineum, then this skin can be used for fashioning the introitus and all or part of the vagina. This, however, carries a higher complication rate than a two-stage reconstruction and is difficult to achieve with the usual anatomic arrangement in that the penis is much further anterior than the ideal vagina would be. Thus, frequently penectomy, castration, and use of the penile and scrotal skin to form the external genitalia are accomplished as a first stage. When this has healed, the total vaginal reconstruction can be carried out as earlier described, making a vaginal cavity from the surface of the perineum between the rectum and urethra and prostatic tissues up to the level of the peritoneum. This is then lined with a split thickness skin graft from the thigh or buttock and put in place with a stint which is then worn for several months. This of course necessitates two hospitalizations, each of the operations performed under general anesthesia, and each requiring a hospital stay of 1 to 2 weeks. Sexual activity must await complete healing. The surgery can provide entirely acceptable external genitalia and vagina, from both a functional and esthetic view. There is no clitoral structure as such. In cases in which the glans of the penis has been preserved to simulate a clitoris, the usual results were a dysesthetic rather than pleasurable sensation, so this is seldom performed at the present time.

The female to male surgical reassignment consists of the ablative procedures of hysterectomy, vaginectomy, and reduction of the breasts to proper size. The reconstructive procedures then are creation of a scrotum, placement of testicular prostheses, and penile reconstruction (Edgerton and Bull, 1970; Noe, Birdsell, and Laub, 1973). The ablative procedures can be carried out with good and predictable success as a single stage; however, if the breasts are of normal female size, the reduction will almost always carry attending scars more than just circumareolar if reduction to a normal male contour is to be achieved. While scrotal simulation and testicular implants can be carried out with good and predictable results, penile reconstruction is the great deficiency in this reassignment surgery. Ideally the penis should be a proper urinary conduit as well as a functioning sexual organ. The numerous procedures described for "penis" construction are the creation of a tubed pedicle flap either from abdominal or less commonly thigh tissues transferred onto the mons pubis, then attempted incorporation of the urinary system by urethral lengthening and lastly, if it is to function in intercourse, provision usually for insertion of a Silastic rod. The stages needed are numerous, seldom less than four and often many more. The problems with urethral lengthening and incorporation of the urethra into the tubed pedicle are numerous. Scars on the abdomen are unavoidable and often conspicuous to the point of being esthetically objectionable. And at the completion of the most successful penile simulations, one has a fairly insensitive. nonerectile structure which only with great imagination can be conceived of as a penis. While some patients have been pleased with the results, the tremendous effort, the frequent complications, and the limited achievement must be carefully borne in mind before considering such operative endeavors.

SUMMARY

Clinical problems with attendant sexual disability, for which surgical procedures of established reliability offer improvement, have been reviewed. Those arising from congenital problems constituting an anatomical-physiological impairment as well as those arising from a sense of body image deformity have been discussed. A familiarity with such procedures may call to mind the possibility of surgical benefits when such patients present themselves.

REFERENCES

DeCholnoky, T. 1970. Augmentation mammoplasty. Survey of complications in 10,941 patients by 265 surgeons. Plast. Reconstr. Surg., 45: 573.

Desanctis, P. N., and Furey, C. A., Jr. 1967. Steroid injection therapy for Peyronies disease: a 10 year summary and review of 38 cases. J. Urol., 97: 114.

Edgerton, M. T. 1973. Transsexualism–a surgical problem? Plast. Reconstr. Surg., 52: 74.

Edgerton, M. T., and Bull, J. 1970. Surgical construction of the vagina and labia in transsexuals. Plast. Reconstr. Surg., 46: 529.

Edgerton, M. T., Knorr, N. J., and Callison, J. R. 1970. The surgical treatment of transsexual patients, limitations and indications. Plast. Reconstr. Surg., 45: 38.

Grace, D. A., and Winter, C. C. 1968. Priapism: an appraisal of management of 23 patients. J. Urol., 99: 301.

Grayhack, J. T., McCullough, W., O'Connor, V. J., and Trippel, O. 1964. Venous bypass to control priapism. Invest. Urol., 1: 509.

Grazer, F. M. 1973. Abdominoplasty. Plast. Reconstr. Surg., 51: 617.

Harrow, B. R. 1969. Simple technique for treating priapism. J. Urol., 101: 71.

Hendren, W. H., and Crawford, J. D. 1972. *The Child with Ambiguous Genitalia*. Year Book, Chicago.

Hoopes, J. E., Edgerton, M. T., and Shelley, W. 1967. Organic synthetics for augmentation mammoplasty: their relation to breast cancer. Plast. Reconstr. Surg., 39: 263.

Horton, C. E., and Devine, C. J., Jr. 1973. Hypospadias. In: Horton, C. E., ed., *Plastic and Reconstructive Surgery of the Genital Area*, Chap. 18, p. 273. Little Brown and Co., Boston.

Horton, C. E., and Devine, C. J., Jr. 1972. *Hypospadias and Epispadias*. CIBA Clinical Symposia, Vol. 24, No. 3.

Horton, C. E., and Devine, C. J., Jr. 1973. Peyronies disease. Plast. Reconstr. Surg., 53: 503.

Horton, C. E., and Devine, C. J., Jr. 1973. Plication of the tunica albuginea to straighten the curved penis. Plast. Reconstr. Surg., 52: 30.

Loeffler, R. A. 1973. Surgical treatment of impotence in the male. In: Horton, C. E., ed., ***Plastic and Reconstructive Surgery of the Genital Area.*** Chap. 51, p. 635. Little Brown and Co., Boston.

McIndoe, A. H. 1949. The treatment of congenital absence and obliterative conditions of the vagina. Br. J. Plas. Surg., 2: 254.

McKissock, P. K. 1972. Reduction mammoplasty: the vertical dermal flap. Plast. Reconstr. Surg., 49: 245.

Meyer, J. K., and Hoopes, J. E. 1974. The gender dysphoria syndromes. Plast. Reconstr. Surg., 54: 444.

Money, J., Hampson, J. G., and Hampson, J. H. 1955. Hermaphroditism: recommendations concerning assignment of sex, change of sex, and psychologic management. Bull. Johns Hopkins Hosp., 97: 284.

Moore, F. T., and Simonis, A. A. 1969. Per via naturalis following reconstruction of the vagina. Br. J. Plast. Surg., 22: 378.

Nesbit, R. M. 1965. Congenital curvature of the phallus. J. Urol., 93: 230.

Noe, J. M., Birdsell, D., and Laub, D. R. 1973. The surgical construction of male genitalia for the female-to-male transsexual. Plast. Reconstr. Surg., 53: 511.

Pitanguy, V. 1967. Abdominal lipectomy. Plas. Reconstr. Surg., 40: 384.

Prentiss, R. J., Boatwright, D. C., Pennington, R. D., Hohn, W. F., and Schwartz, M. H. 1963. Testicular prosthesis: materials, methods, and results. J. Urol., 90: 208.

Scardino, P. H., and Scott, W. W. 1949. The use of tocopherols in the treatment of Peyronies disease. Ann. N. Y. Acad. Sci., 52: 390.

Scott, F. B. 1973. Discussion of devices and surgical procedures in the treatment of organic impotence. Hum. Sexuality, 7: 119.

Strombeck, J. O. 1971. Reduction mammoplasty. Surg. Clin. North Am., 51: 453.

Webster, J. P. 1946. Mastectomy for gynecomastia through a semicircular intra-areolar incision. Ann. Surg., 124: 557.

Wood-Smith, D. 1964. Hypospadias. In: Converse, J. M., ed., *Reconstructive Plastic Surgery*, Saunders, Philadelphia.

Young, H. H., Crockett, A. T., Stoller, R., Ashley, F., and Goodwin, W. E. 1971. The management of agenesis of the phallus. Pediatrics, 47: 81.

TWELVE

The External Male Genitalia: The Interplay of Surgery and Mechanical Prostheses

JOEL M. NOE, M.D., DONALD R. LAUB, M.D. and WERNER SCHULZ

Traumatic loss of or damage to the external male genitalia has provided the major impetus toward the development of a satisfactory surgical technique to reconstruct the penis (Bogoras, 1948; Fleming, 1970; Frumkin, 1944; Gillies and Millard, 1958; Hoopes, 1969; and McIndoe, 1948). Penile construction has also been necessitated in cases of congenital anomalies and neoplastic, infectious, or metabolic destruction. Sex reassignment surgery from the female-to-male anatomic status represents yet another situation in which phallus construction has been employed.

In attempting to create a penis which is psychologically satisfying to the patient, both cosmetic and physiological criteria must be considered. The surgically formed phallus should be cosmetically acceptable and, ideally, should simultaneously serve as: (1) a urinary and seminal conduit; (2) an instrument for coitus; and (3) a source of erogenous stimulation. This unique combination of cosmetic and functional requirements has made penile reconstruction a challenging undertaking for the surgeon. Of the etiological categories of patients requesting phalloplasty, the female-to-male transsexuals are some of the more difficult cases in that: (1) total reconstruction (or more accurately construction) is required; (2) there are neither penile remnants nor scrotal tissue available as sensitive skin donor sites; and (3) a construction of the total male urethra is necessary. Because sex reassignment surgery does represent the extreme in terms of the numbers of problems that must be coped with to achieve a

psychologically satisfying result, it serves as an excellent model to illustrate techniques applicable to more general cases of penile defect.

SURGICAL METHODS

Traditionally there have been two methods for reconstructing the penis—the tubed flap (Ali, 1957; Bergman, Howard, and Barnes, 1948; Bogoras, 1936; Edgerton, Knorr, and Callison, 1970; Evans, 1963; Farina and Frier, 1954; Gelb, Malament, and LoVerme, 1959; Gillies and Millard, 1948; Noe, Birdsell and Laub, 1974), and the use of scrotal skin (Chappell, 1953; Goodwin and Scott, 1952; Goodwin and Thelen, 1950; and Millard, 1966). A third technique, specific to sex reassignment surgery, involves surgical alteration of the hormonally hypertrophied clitoris (Tank, Pauly, McCraw, Petty, Rowland, and Durfee, in press).

Tubed Pedicle Flap

The most popular technique of penile reconstruction has been the tubed pedicle flap. In 1936, Borgoras, utilizing an abdominal tubed pedicle flap, succeeded in reconstructing a penis, the major portion of which had been lost to trauma. Rigidity was provided by implanting an autogenous rib graft in the tube.

This basic technique was used by Frumkin (1944) in achieving one of the first total phallus reconstructions. Besides an abdominal tube flap to recreate the shaft of the penis and a rib cartilage graft for rigidity, Frumkin developed a second tubed flap for reconstructin of the urethral canal. In his series he used both the scrotum and forearm as donor areas for this second flap.

Gillies and Millard (1948) advanced the concepts of Frumkin by extrapolating on a suggestion of Maltz. Gillies formed two abdominal tubed flaps, one of which was inserted inside the other as a future site for the urethra. At a later stage a rib cartilage graft was incorporated into the tube to provide rigidity.

Since the forties, surgeons have modified Frumkin's and Gillies' procedures in a variety of ways: (1) the source of tissue used to create the flap; (2) the manner in which the flap was migrated to the genital area; (3) the method of constructing the urethra; and (4) the type of implant inserted into the tube to attain rigidity and the stage at which this was carried out.

Even with these improvements, there are still several disadvantages to the tubed flap method: (1) a number of stages are required to develop a tube, migrate it to the genital area, construct a urethra, and add an os penis; (2) the abdominal wall is scarred in the process of forming the tube; and (3) the neophallus lacks sensation. [One of Gillies' cases reappeared in the literature 9 years later, after sustaining a hotwater bottle burn of the penis, most likely secondary to the relatively anesthetic tube (Evans, 1963).]

Use of Scrotal Skin

A second method devised for reconstruction of the penis has involved the use of local tissue and local flaps. Chappell (1953), Goodwin, and Scott (1952) and Kaplan and Wesser (1971) have advocated this method, citing several advantages: (1) few stages (often only two) are necessary to achieve a satisfactory result; (2) the simplicity of construction; (3) the use of sensitive skin to create the phallus produces a relatively sensitive organ; and (4) there is no abdominal scarring. However, this technique is not without problems. Generally the cosmetic result has been less than acceptable—a hairy, corrugated penis.

Surgical Alteration of the Clitoris

A third technique, specific to sex reassignment surgery, involves the use of techniques developed for the correction of hypospadias. Tank and his associates (in press), after determining that the transsexual patients who presented at their clinic were most interested in the creation of an organ which would permit them to stand to urinate, surgically altered the hormonally hypertrophied clitoris. They lengthened the clitoris by dissecting it free of its suspensory ligament and mobilizing as much as possible the clitoris, corpora, and labia minora. A new urethral canal was fashioned out of mucosal flaps taken from the labia minora. Tank and his associates have reported patient satisfaction with the results of this procedure.

Summary of Current Techniques

In reviewing these categories of surgical techniques, it can be noted that dramatic surgical results in the formation of the penis have not been attained as yet. In many instances, surgeons have elected not to attempt either insertion of a permanent baculum for rigidity or creation of a urinary conduit. Attendant complications of extrusion or reabsorption in the case of implantation of a permanent baculum or fistulae or stricture in urethral construction have been observed frequently.

An alternative to surgical formation of the penis is the use of a prosthesis. A synthetic penis, ideally fabricated, would have the advantage of not requiring surgical intervention with its attendant risks of complication, scarring, time lost from work, and expense.

The most readily available prosthesis, which can be easily obtained commercially, is constructed of pink vinyl. This apparatus is held in place by a belt. Its primary function for the patient is use as an instrument of penetration in coitus, but it is less than satisfactory in several respects: (1) it cannot be used as a urinary conduit; (2) it cannot be worn under street clothing because of its permanently erected appearance; (3) it does not have sensibility (although it may conduct some sensation back to the pubis where it is positioned on a plastic base); and (4) it is less than an anatomic duplicate. However, this prosthesis does serve an important psychological purpose by improving the confidence of the patient in his ability to function sexually.

A more anatomically accurate prosthesis can also be purchased. Since this penile replica lacks rigidity, it serves only a cosmetic and not a functional purpose unless the individual wearing the device is particularly creative. To provide function for a prosthesis of this type, an interlocking metal mechanical skeleton has been developed. Simulated erection can be achieved by inserting this baculum into the artificial penis and locking it into place. Besides its more satisfactory cosmetic appearance and its ability to function in coitus (with the use of an additional apparatus), this artificial phallus also meets another important psychological need of the patient—it can be worn on a continuing basis because of its flaccid state. The development of a new ileostomy cement and Dow Corning's Medical Adhesive B have provided a further advantage to this prosthesis; they permit the patient to wear the artificial phallus for the two- to five-day life of the adhesive without the discomfort and psychological encumbrance of a belt. Patients have reported variable success with this combination of devices.

Since 1964 investigation on a design for a more physiologically accurate baculum has proceeded at Stanford University Medical Center. Rather than the steel skeleton which is locked into place manually, a single action hydraulically operated implant is used. The basic unit consists of an erection tube, a one way valve with a controlled leak time and a bulb for activation. Ten minutes after activation, the pressure in the phallus is reduced to about 50%. In the case of extended intercourse, rigidity can be restored by renewed pressure on the master cylinder.

These prostheses and the mechanical inserts discussed circumvent the need for surgical intervention. They are less costly than surgery. They do not require time away from work. They do not produce scarring. There is no attendant morbidity. However, they are obviously less than satisfactory, particularly in that they do not meet the psychological need for providing an auto-organ.

Prosthetists agree that surgical constructions, even those that are rough cosmetic approximations with limited function and sensation, are preferable to artificial devices. The patient needs to feel that the restored organ is a part of him rather than a removable object that is taken off and placed on the bed stand at night. A surgically constructed lobster claw hand with pinch and sensibility is still considered superior to any prosthetic hand. No external breast augmentation, regardless of how perfect in consistency and shape, provides as much patient satisfaction as a less perfect prosthesis which is implanted *beneath* the skin. A final example of the same body image phenomenon is seen in patients with a missing ear. Even a perfectly fabricated artificial ear inevitably ends up in a drawer. A much cruder, surgically created ear which is composed of the patient's tissues alone or the patient's tissues in combination with a synthetic implant is more readily accepted by patients. Experience has indicated that even when surgical restoration is fraught with complications and the end result of surgical reconstruction is less than ideal, patients select surgery rather than prosthetic replacements.

SEX REASSIGNMENT SURGERY

The Stanford University Medical Center experience with phallus construction has been focused on the gender dysphoric patient (Fisk, 1974) who requested sex reassignment surgery from the female-to-male anatomic status. The use of surgical therapy to treat problems of personal dissatisfaction with the sex of anatomy has gradually evolved over the last 2 decades. The first public recognition that such problems existed and that surgical treatment was possible occurred overnight with the Christine Jorgensen case in 1953 (Hamburger, Stürup, and Dahl-Iverson, 1953). This was in a sense the "public birth" of modern transsexual surgery. Since the initial shock, resistance in the medical community toward acceptance and treatment of this problem has gradually abated.

While over-all advances in caring for gender dysphorics have been made, development of satisfactory surgical techniques for the female transsexual have lagged significantly behind procedures created to meet the needs of their male counterparts. Because dramatic surgical results in the formation of the penis were not available, the female-to-male patients who initially presented to the Stanford program had to be self-sufficient, relying more on their own ingenuity than the miracle of surgery to make a successful adjustment to the male role. As a consequence, they exhibited a more complete though still somewhat stereotyped maleness assisted by various hormonal and sociocultural adjuncts: (1) Physical appearance. Hormones have been used and result in the growth of facial hair, increased libido, and a deeper voice. Muscle development has been achieved through weight lifting. (2) Dress. A greater variety of attire has been noted lately although the accoutrements of the universally present cigar or cigarette, cowboy hat, and tattoo are prevalent. (3) Mannerisms. A swaggering style of walk and an aggressive handshake are common. (4) Personality. The female gender dysphorics consistently present as hardworking, stoic, and independent "good" citizens.

Stanford Experience

The literature was reviewed, the needs of these patients assessed, and various alternatives weighed:

1) Could a device be designed that would be capable of complete erection and relaxation?
   a) Were suitable materials available?
   b) Could such a device be surgically implanted?
2) Would an external male genitalia constructed solely from human tissues be preferable? Would it be feasible?
3) Would a combination of human tissues and synthetic material devices be better? If so, what combination would be best?
4) What was the relative "price" to the patient in terms of risks, complications, and probable results of each of the above approaches?

After considering these questions, it was decided to use the abdominal tube technique complemented by prosthetics in the hope of providing the patients with a penis which was both cosmetically and functionally satisfactory. It was thought that the interplay of surgery and prosthetics would produce the psychological advantages of an auto-organ but simultaneously reduce the "price" in terms of the number of required surgical procedures and their consequent morbidity.

The surgical procedures, however, were only one phase of a pilot project which was designed to offer a multidisciplinary treatment for the gender dysphoric individual. Genital surgery was viewed as the final phase, intervening only to make anatomy conform to an already successful life style in the male role, as judged by psychological, social, and economic criteria.

Because the presence of large breasts may interfere with living as a male during the trial period, mastectomy has been selectively performed to assist the transition to the male role.

Phalloplasty

The technique used at Stanford for the construction of a penis requires two stages: (1) formation of a bipedicle, midline, lower abdominal flap (see Figs. 12.1, 12.2, 12.3, and 12.4); and (2) releasing the upper end of the tube and constructing the glans penis at the same time (see Fig. 12.5). An optional third stage can be performed at the same time as the second stage or performed at a later date; it involves fusion of the labia and insertion of testicular prostheses.

During the first stage, an abdominal tubed pedicle flap is formed in such a way that the abdominal skin is brought inside the tube. A split thickness skin graft provides covering for the outside of the tube. The second stage involves release of the tube and fashioning of the tip to approximate the glans and corona. The tube is left open at both its proximal and distal ends to facilitate hygiene within the tunnel. The tunnel also permits the use of a temporary baculum. No attempt is made to amputate the clitoris or to interfere in any way with its sensibility.

Hysterectomy and salpingo-oophorectomy are performed during the second stage through the midline scar which was created when the donor site of the flap was closed. It is imperative that hysterectomy not be accomplished prior to the first stage as either a midline or Pfannenstiel incisional scar compromises the blood supply of the pedicle flap. Many of our complications have occurred in patients who underwent hysterectomy prior to entering our program.

The final cosmetic appearance can be enhanced by fusing the labia to create a scrotum and inserting testicular prostheses into the labia majora. These testicular devices are available commercially from Dow Corning Company and Heyer-Schulte. Generally they are formed by silicone, either premolded, smooth-solid silicone, bags filled with gel consistency silicone, or gel or solid silicone covered with a velour material.

Attempts have been made to achieve a more accurate mimick-

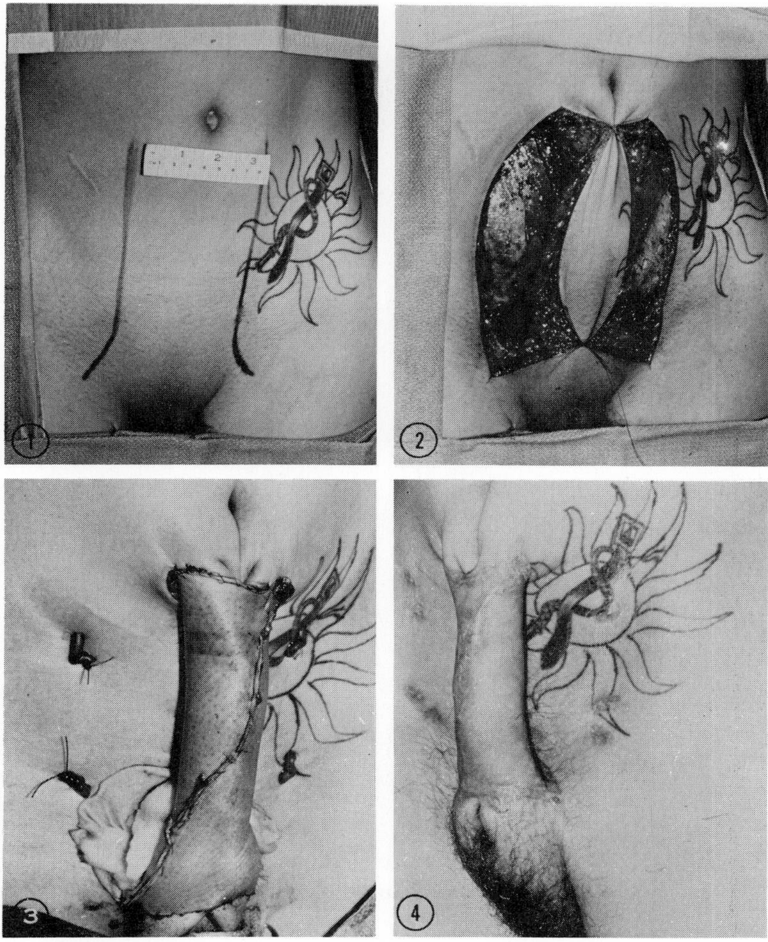

Figs. 12.1 to 12.4. The two-stage method used for constructing the penis. Essentially the creation of a tube within a tube. The inner tube facilitates hygiene and acts to hold the baculum for intercourse and the silicone tube for urination. (Reprinted with permission from Noe, J., Birdsell, D., and Lamb, D. The surgical construction of male genitalia for the female-to-male transsexual. Plast. Reconstr. Surg. 53: 511, 1974.)

ing of the male genitalia by using testicular prostheses which are fabricated from stainless steel covered with room temperature vulcanized silicone to provide greater density and weight. It was hypothesized that the skin of the labia would assume a more scrotal appearance as it stretched and sagged under the gravitational force of the overweighted testicular prostheses. This has not occurred to date, however (Noe, Birdsell and Laub, 1974).

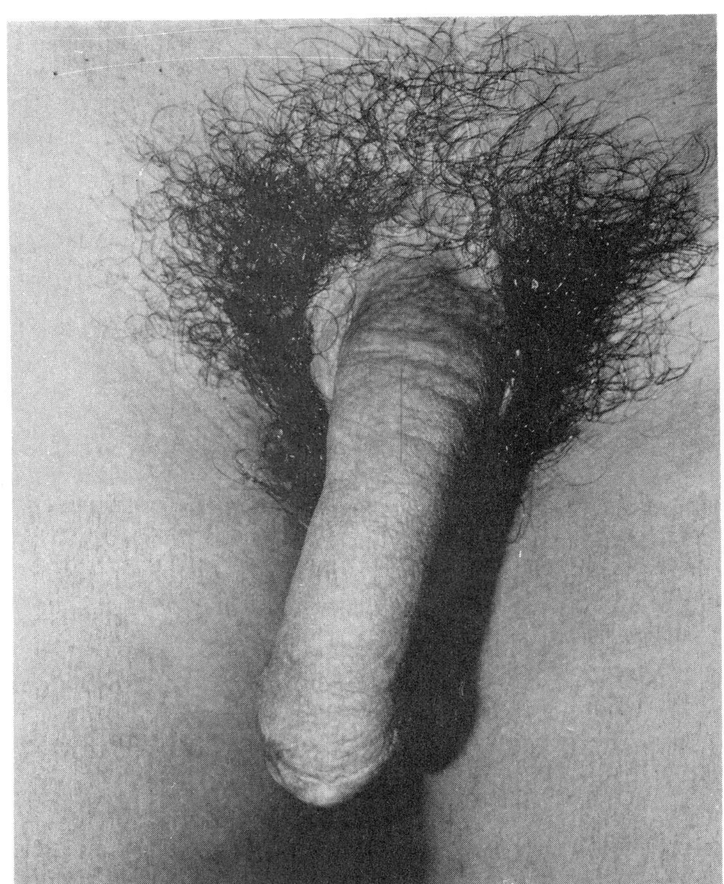

Fig. 12.5. An example of a penis constructed by the method described in this chapter.

Rigidity

When phalloplasty was first performed at Stanford, only rudimentary forms of stiffeners were available. These nylon prostheses were inserted into the proximal aspect of the neophallus. The nylon composition of the baculum resulted in chronic inflammation and the permanently erected status that was produced by its insertion caused difficulty during urination. Since then, refinements have been made in the baculum (see Figs. 12.6 and 12.7). Experience has indicated that the use of a temporary baculum which is inserted prior to intercourse is the best method of providing rigidity for coitus and

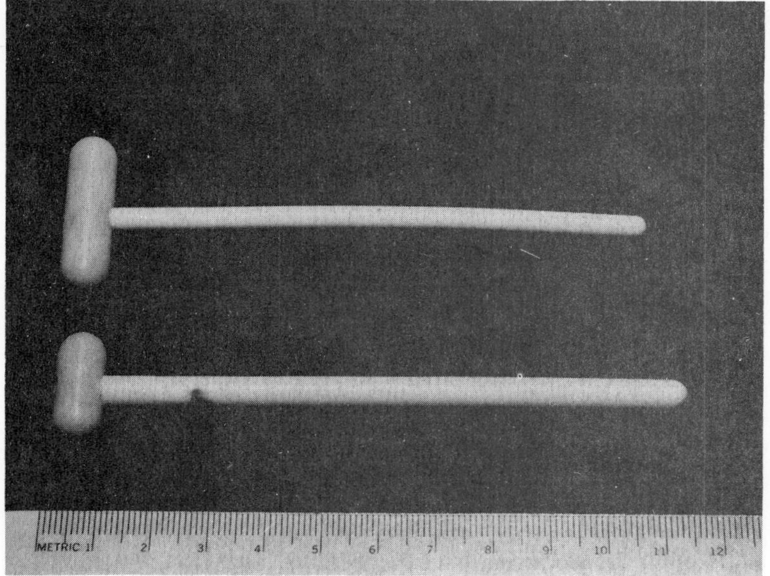

Fig. 12.6. Two baculums. These are used at the time of intercourse to attain erection of the penis and self (clitoral) stimulation.

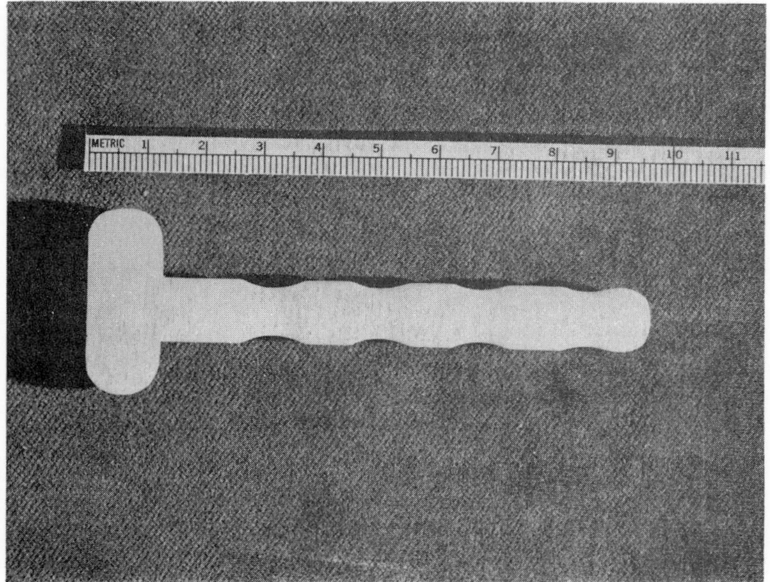

Fig. 12.7. A baculum.

minimizing the dangers of extrusion inherent in a permanent implant which has been placed in an organ lacking sensibility.

The T-shaped silicone baculum is inserted through the proximal opening of the tube, the base of the neophallus. The silicone rod rests on the pubic symphysis so that erection is transmitted out from the bony area through the penis. Conversely, external pressure on the tip of the neophallus is transmitted back to the clitoral area, affording some stimulation (Fig. 12.8).

Brantly Scott, (Scott, Bradley, and Timm, 1973) has developed a device which could be a major breakthrough in providing rigidity for phalloplasties. He has devised an apparatus which is surgically inserted to correct impotence in males. This baculum consists of a cylindrical penile prosthesis which is placed in the shaft of the penis. The penile prosthesis is connected by tubing to a reservoir buried in the prevesical space and pumps which are set in the scrotum. The prosthesis remains in a relaxed state until erection is required for coitus. At that time, rigidity is achieved by applying pressure on the pumps.

If this technique could be employed in transsexual surgery, it would offer several psychological advantages to the patient: (1) it would be a permanent prosthesis embedded in the patient's tissues; (2) the function provided would be more physiological in nature, eliminating the need for manual insertion of a baculum;

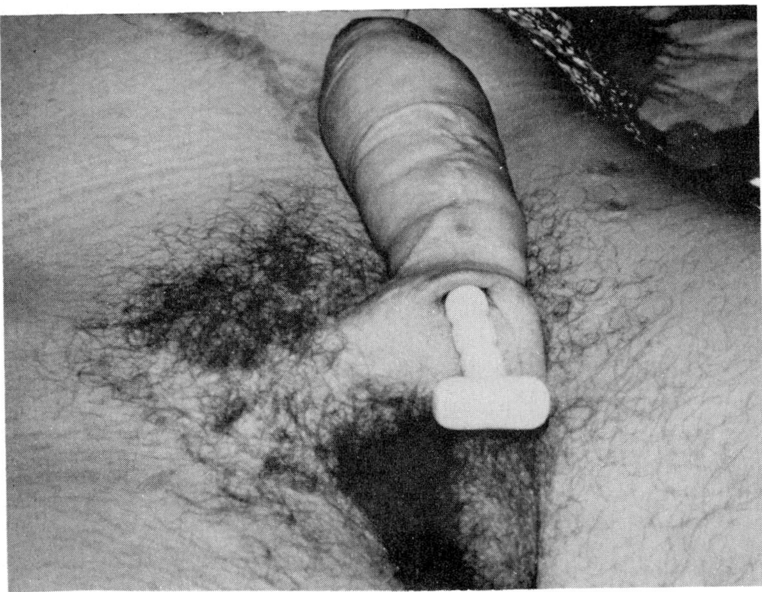

Fig. 12.8. Baculum in place inside inner tube of penis. Penis is now erect. The T-bar rests on the clitoris, leading to stimulation during intercourse.

and (3) the probability of extruding the prosthesis would be reduced in that the implant would only be rigid during coitus.

Urinary Conduit

No attempt has been made to construct a urethra in the phalloplasties performed at Stanford. It is felt that the difficulties and complications outweigh the psychological benefits of being able to stand to urinate. Instead, some of our patients have recently employed a device designed by Werner Schulz. A catheter-like apparatus is placed at the urethral meatus so that urine passes through silicone tubing into the central tunnel of the phallus (Fig. 12.9). With this device and a brief practice session, patients have been able to stand to urinate, avoiding the attendant complications of surgery. The apparatus is inserted each morning and removed at night. The five patients currently using the device have reported satisfaction with the results.

SUMMARY

In penile construction much remains to be achieved to produce a penis that meets the psychological, cosmetic, and physiological

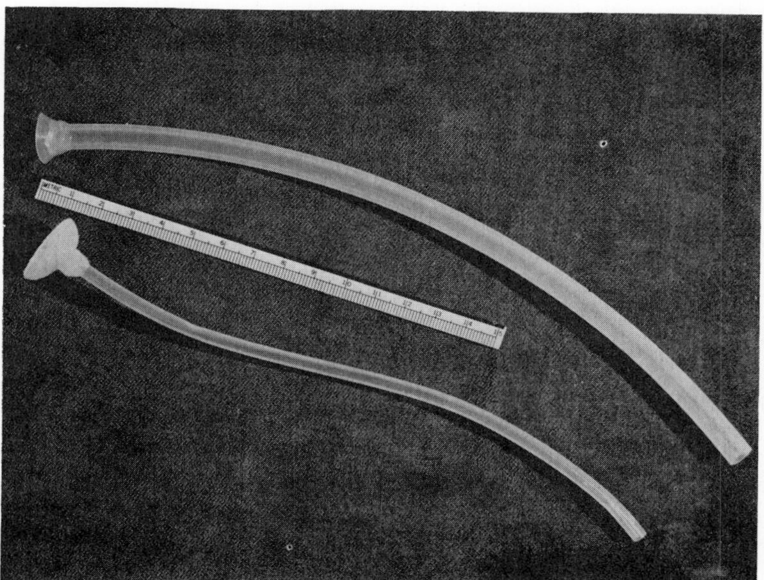

Fig. 12.9. The silicone tube is inserted into the bladder and then exits through the inner tube of the penis. It allows the patient to urinate in a standing position.

needs of patients requesting such surgery. The ongoing support—medical, surgical, psychiatric, hormonal legal, and social—in the patient's rehabilitation must be synchronous with their unique needs, not only with their medical and psychological requirements but also with these devices. As can be seen, at present an interplay of surgical techniques and mechanical devices appears to work best.

REFERENCES

Ali, M. 1957. Surgical treatment of the male genitalia. J. Internat. Coll Surg. 27: 352.

Bergman, R. T., Howard, A. H., and Barnes, R. W. 1948. Plastic reconstruction of the penis. J. Urol. 59: 1,174.

Blum, V. 1938. A case of plastic restoration of the penis. J. Mt. Sinai Hosp. 4: 506.

Bogoras, N. 1936: Über die volle plastische Wiederherstellung eines zum Koitus fähigen Penis. Zentralbl. Chir. 63: 1,271.

Chappell, B. S. 1953. Utilization of scrotum in reconstruction of penis. J. Urol. 69: 703.

Edgerton, M. T., Knorr, N. J., and Callison, J. R. 1970. The surgical treatment of transsexual patients. Plast. Reconstr. Surg. 45: 38.

Evans, A. J. 1963. Buried-skin-strip urethra in tube pedicle phalloplasty. Br. J. Plast. Surg. 16: 380.

Farina, R., and Frier, E. G. 1954. Total reconstruction of the penis. Plast. & Reconstr. Surg. 14: 351.

Fisk, N. 1974. Gender dysphoria syndrome—the conceptualization that liberalizes indications for total gender reorientation and implies a broadly based multi-dimensional rehabilitative regimen. West. J. Med. 120: 386.

Fleming, J. P. 1970. Reconstruction of the penis. J. Urol. 104: 213.

Fogh-Andersen, P. 1964. Transsexualism: an attempt at surgical management. Scand. J. Plast. Reconstr. Surg. 3: 61.

Fogh-Andersen, P. 1956. Transvestism and transsexualism. Surgical treatment in a case of autocastration. Acta Med. Leg. Soc. 9: 33.

Frumkin, A. P. 1944. Reconstruction of the male genitalia. Ann. Rev. Soviet Med. 2: 214.

Gelb, J., Malament, M., and LoVerme, S. 1959. Total reconstruction of the penis. Plast. Reconstr. Surg. 24: 62.

Gillies, H. D., and Millard, D. R. 1948. Congenital absence of the penis. Br. J. Plast. Surg. 1: 8.

Goodwin, W. F., and Scott, W. W. 1952. Phalloplasty. J. Urol. 68: 903.

Goodwin, W. E., and Thelen, H. M. 1950. Plastic reconstruction of penile skin: implantation of the penis into the scrotum. J.A.M.A. 144: 384.

Hamburger, C., Stürup, G., and Dahl-Iverson. E. 1953. Transvestism. J.A.M.A. 152: 391.

Hoopes, J. 1969. Operative treatment of the female transsexual. In: Green, R., and Money, J. eds. *Transsexualism and Sex Reassignment*. p. 335. The Johns Hopkins Press, Baltimore.

Kaplan, I., and Wesser, D. 1971. A rapid method for constructing a functional sensitive penis. Br. J. Plast. Surg. 24: 342.

Kluzak, R. 1968. Sex conversion operation in female transsexualism. Acta Chir. Plast. 10: 188.

Laub, D., and Fisk, N. 1974. A rehabilitation program for gender dysphoria syndrome by surgical sex change. Plast. Reconstr. Surg. 53: 388.

McIndoe, A. 1948. Deformities of the male urethra. Br. J. Plast. Surg. 1: 29.

Millard, D. R. 1966. Scrotal construction and reconstruction. Plast. Reconstr. Surg. 38: 10.

Morales, P. A., O'Connor, J. J., and Hotchkiss, R. S. 1956. Plastic reconstructive surgery after total loss of the penis. Am. J. Surg. 92: 403.

Mukhin, M. V. 1968. Total phalloplasty. Acta chir. plast. 10: 130.

Noe, J., Coleman, C., Laub, D. and Sato, R. In press. Construction of the external male genitalia: the Stanford experience. In: Proceedings of the Harry Benjamin Fourth International Conference on Gender Identity. Edwards Brothers, Ann Arbor.

Noe, J., Birdsell, D., and Laub, D. 1974. The surgical construction of male genitalia for the female-to-male transsexual. Plast. Reconstr. Surg. 53: 511.

Scott, J. B., Bradley, W. E., and Timm, G. W. 1973. Management of erectile impotence: use of implantable inflatable prosthesis. Urol. 2: 80.

Tank, E. S., Pauly, I. B., McCraw, L. H., Petty, W. M., Roland, W. D., and Durfee, R. B. In press. Genitoplasty in female-to-male transsexuals. In: Proceedings of the Harry Benjamin Fourth International Conference on Gender Identity. Edwards Brothers, Ann Arbor.

THIRTEEN

Psychodynamic Treatment of the Individual with a Sexual Disorder

JON K. MEYER, M.D.

This chapter outlines the uses of individual psychotherapy in the treatment of sexual disorders. By individual psychotherapy is meant treatment of the individual patient, focusing on his associations and utilizing a nondidactic approach in the context of an open-ended time frame. On the therapist's part, a skill in the use of transference and a familiarity with psychodynamic and psychogenic constructs are essential. Included within the category of individual psychotherapy is dynamically oriented, open-ended psychotherapy ranging in frequency from one time per week to four or five times per week. There are differences within this spectrum in the depth of fantasy material elicited, the strength and accessibility of transference, and the degree of therapist activity, but these techniques are separable in concept from behavioral, counseling, and group approaches.

The purpose of this chapter is as follows: (1) to consider the role of neurosis and character disorder in sexual dysfunction; (2) to indicate the dynamic formulations of sexual disability; (3) to outline the precepts and assumptions of dynamic psychotherapy with special relation to sexual disabilities; and (4) to indicate the results of treatment in such problems.

THE ROLE OF NEUROSIS, CONFLICT AND CHARACTER MODIFICATIONS IN SEXUAL DISORDERS

Much has been written about the newer approaches to sex therapy indicating that it is unnecessary to be concerned about associated psychopathology in a patient with a sexual problem. A statement frequently made is that the sexual disorder is due to social factors (job loss, failure to be promoted), intercurrent events (an episode of impotence leading to anxiety and further impotence), interpersonal difficulties (chronic or acute disagreements with one's spouse), and educational failures (society's disparaging attitude toward sexuality). All these factors, indeed, may be involved.

In my experience, however, the sexual disability and some apparently minor symptom (a phobia for heights, an obsessive thought of minor inconvenience, or derealization in certain circumstances) frequently stand as the twin peaks of a massive underlying neurotic and/or character disorder constellation. The ramifications and interrelations of these symptoms are manifest only after treatment of the major sexual symptom is instituted. This is the opposite of the situation in which the primary complaints are of anxiety, disturbing obsessions, compulsions, phobias, or character problems; sexual difficulty is initially only mentioned in passing, or may be denied altogether. Nonetheless, 6 months later the patient will present an extensive list of sexual grievances.

Freud (1910) pointed out that lack of sexual satisfaction can occur where there is no lack of normal intercourse and that sexual trends may find only poor outlets in frank coitus. In the same writings, he captured what has become the basis of the dynamic approach to sexual disorder:

> . . . [N]ervous symptoms arise from a conflict between two forces—. . .libido (which has as a rule become excessive) and . . . repression . . . A good number of [neurotics] are . . . incapable of satisfaction . . . [I]f they were without their inner resistances, the strength of the instinct itself would point the way to satisfaction for them . . . (pp. 222–223).

"Symptoms arise from a conflict between two forces": the drive toward sexual satisfaction, which may be of high intensity, and correspondingly strong or stronger repressive forces. This conflict, with its substructure in fantasy and childhood history, is actively extruded from awareness and is, therefore, inaccessible to rational thought, conscious memory, immediate experience, the influence of suggestion, and educational or behavioral approaches.

TREATMENT

The psychotherapies based upon dynamic principles recognize the motive force of fantasy and conflict, particularly those fantasies and conflicts which are unconscious. Sexual difficulties are considered to develop out of the same matrix as other personality and neurotic problems. An important treatment assumption is that there is a sufficiently strong propensity for the expression and enjoyment of sexuality that satisfaction would be obtainable, except for the conflictual impediments.

BASIC CONSIDERATIONS

Fromm-Reichmann (1950) has outlined the purpose and the technique of dynamic psychotherapy somewhat as follows. Through the intervention of psychotherapy there is to be a "clarification" of difficulties with others (and oneself), including sexual difficulties. This is accomplished through the recall of forgotten memories and affects in the special context of the relationship with the psychiatrist. This relationship itself is the subject of intensive scrutiny. There is resistance to this process because of the painful nature of the associations and affects. In the light of the memories and the therapeutic relationship, communications and behavioral operations will be interpreted to provide essential clarification. Certain basic assumptions in this process require further elaboration.

First of all, there is the assumption that the sexual problem will most often be simply one manifestation, although an extremely important one, of a neurotic and/or personality disorder. Sexual gratification is held to be a single aspect of a more manifold capacity to feel positively toward persons and to secure bodily satisfaction from them (Fisher and Osofsky, 1967). Despite a monosymptomatic presentation, as treatment goes on increasing respect will develop for the pervasiveness, strength, and attachments of the neurosis and its character ramifications. For the patient this respect will come at the point where healthy components of the personality assert themselves and he sees that things indeed could have been, and can be, different.

Second, there needs to be the assumption on the part of both patient and psychiatrist that treatment is open-ended. It will take as long as necessary, until the patient is satisfied. The institution of artificial time parameters, as in the "Masters and Johnson" methods, focuses the work but allows resistance to cover embarrassing or conflictual material.

Third, the patient's responsibility is to report history, thoughts, fantasies, bodily feelings, and affects as they come to mind. He may be assured that agreement with this principle is easy, but that implementation is hard. Much important material will seem embarrassing, trivial, offensive, in violation of some external confidence, etc. The stance of the therapist is that the patient is to be as nonjudgemental in reporting thoughts and feelings as he will be in hearing them.

Fourth, it is the therapist's responsibility to aid the patient as much as possible in self-exploration. The therapist does *not* pat the patient on the back, approve, disapprove, or attempt to manipulate external reality. Open-ended questions about the material at hand will be helpful in furthering the work of exploration. The psychiatrist's responsibility is not to exhort toward success, but to remove the roadblocks to it—*i.e.*, the resistances. This is done most effectively by noting and commenting upon apparent roadblocks to free association and communication as they occur. If sufficient material is available to relate the presenting resistance to other patterns of behavior, this may also be useful.

Fifth, one can make no promise of "cure," but in general as history is reviewed, thoughts noted, affects expressed, and fantasies examined, certain capabilities will come to the fore. As resistances are overcome and conflict comes into the forum of conscious consideration, the patient will begin to report improvement in troublesome areas almost as an aside. The "as a matter of course" quality of the improvement will often come as a surprise to the patient. Improvement in the patient's life will usually be noted most dramatically just when the relationship with the psychiatrist has become the most difficult. This is an indication of the development of a full-blown transference neurosis.

Sixth, the treating physician has special responsibility for maintaining the structure of the situation in which treatment occurs. A time is selected when he can reliably be present and punctual. Freedom from other concerns—telephones and administrative matters—during this time is essential. The fee, of whatever magnitude, is worked out in advance and acceptable to both.

Fromm-Reichmann (1950) spoke of the "respect" due the patient. Such respect extends from the fact that the patient's problems in living are not too different in kind, although perhaps in degree, from those others have faced. Additionally, the patient's sexual difficulties are often a source of embarrassment, they are of moment to him, the onset of treatment is a frightening experience, and a high degree of hope is riding on the outcome.

Special mention is required for the therapist with sexual problems. While such problems may make him empathic, unless the therapist has been treated himself, his anxiety may become so alarming that treatment will be interrupted or defensively utilized for self-aggrandizement or self-treatment. The physician in reality should be nothing less than interested, compassionate, dependable, and concerned with his patient. Genuine concern for the patient does not extend to acting upon the temptation to share one's own experiences, intimacies, fallacies, and problems with the patient on an assumption of *quid pro quo* (Freud, 1912b).

TRANSFERENCE

The factor which brings conflicts and fantasies into awareness with convincing immediacy is the transference. Most of the truly effective therapeutic work will be in the context of the transference. Mack and Semrad (1967) have defined transference as follows:

> ... [T]o an increasing extent the patient's feelings toward the analyst replicate his feelings toward the specific people he is talking about ... The special type of object displacement ... is called transference (p. 315).

Expression of reaction patterns, affects, and fantasies in a current time frame, with immediacy, in a personalized context, is the living experience of the transference. The transference brings vividly alive, in a controlled and observed setting, both unsatisfied claims for love and sexual release and prohibited aggressive feelings. This phenomenon offers opportunity for real work. One cannot dismantle a neurotic construction purely in retrospect; or as Freud (1912a) put it, "*in absentia*." Free association, interpretation of resistance, and abstinence from immediate gratification in the treatment setting are the precursors of transference development.

Novey (1969) has commented upon the importance of transference in treatment, as follows:

> In the transference situation it is necessary ... to ... re-experience the old emotional states ... repeated in attenuated form and re-examined by means of a current replica of a historically significant person ... [T]he old emotionally laden experiences are lived out ... in a diluted form ... in which they can be detoxified ... (p. 90).

Transference operates in a dual way, both as the most powerful determinant of effective treatment and as the most powerful resistance to successful outcome. Prototypic patterns are given up only slowly and grudgingly, after considerable effort to justify rather than relinquish them. Care must be taken to emphasize that transference is essential in human interchange, being neither good nor bad in and of itself. The end point is not a patient free of transference, but one in whom its unrealistic, insatiable, and detrimental aspects have been examined and incorporated in a more mature frame of reference.

Over the course of treatment, the transference coalesces into a transference neurosis. As Freud (1914) stated:

> [W]e regularly succeed in giving all the symptoms of the illness a new transference meaning and in replacing his ordinary neurosis with a transference neurosis ... The transference thus creates an intermediate region between illness and real life through which the transition from one to the other is made (p. 145).

This transference neurosis represents an artificial illness, being occasioned by special circumstances. It is, nonetheless, real in its effects and has the advantage of accessibility.

The tool used in resolving the transference neurosis is the interpretation. As Strachey (1934) has pointed out in an old, but useful paper, the interpretation to be "mutative" must be given in repeated small doses timed to coincide with the emergence in the patient of emotionally laden material, tinged with archaic fantasy, and directed toward the therapist as a transference object.

In his early works, Freud (1912a, b, 1914, 1915) outlined characteristics of the transference particularly important for patients with a sexual problem.

> . . . each individual . . . has acquired a specific method of his own in his conduct of his erotic life . . . This produces what might be described as a stereotype plate . . . which is constantly repeated . . . in the course of the person's life (Freud, 1912a, pp. 99–100).

Portions of this template have passed through the process of maturation and development. Others have been detoured or deferred. These latter libidinal strivings are unlikely to be satisfied by events and persons within the sphere of reality. They are "held ready in anticipation," responding to existing prototypes as well as actively structuring elements in everyday life to fit that prototype. Erotic transference to the doctor, despite its semblance of reality, will exceed, both in amount and in nature, anything justifiable on rational grounds.

Transference manifestations are not to be expected simply in terms of verbal communications of affection, hate, etc. They will also be manifest in repetitive behavior both within the treatment hour and outside. When this behavior is explored, its relationships to history, fantasy, and affect will be revealed. Freud (1914) observed that the greater the resistance to remembering and reporting the more such cognitive activities will be replaced by repetitive behavior. This is particularly true of individuals whose pathology is reflected in character malformations.

A common occurrence in psychodynamic psychotherapy is that the patient "falls in love" with the physician. This love, however, distorts the purposes of treatment, causing treatment to be regarded as inconsequential, and temporarily prevents further progress. "Love" seems to come at precisely that point where the most difficult and painful material seemed likely to emerge.

It is necessary both to allow the development of transference love, and to resolutely withhold gratification of it. Dahlberg (1970) has indicated the untoward consequences of sexual intimacy, heterosexual or homosexual, with patients: treatment terminated unhappily, the patient at first feeling elated at the attention and triumphant at removing the psychiatrist from his pedestal but, in the final analysis, feeling betrayed. The more plain it is that the treating physician is neither tempted nor offended by transference blandishments, the more readily he will be able to extract benefit from the situation. Once the patient feels safe enough to express the preconditions for loving, the fantasies springing from erotic desires, and the detailed characteristics of his being in love, the infantile and conflicted roots will come to light (Freud, 1915).

SPECIAL PROBLEMS IN THE TREATMENT OF SEXUAL DISABILITIES

A multiplicity of difficulties may be reflected in a sexual dysfunction since sexuality is plastic, multifaceted, and involves other people or their representation in fantasy. In some instances greatest progress is made by direct pursuit of history and fantasies related to the sexual disability, while in others consideration of more "peripheral" material is highly therapeutic.

Issues of physical disability related to sexual malfunctions are more frequently seen by other medical specialties. Nonetheless, one should not overlook the psychic consequences of, for example, anomalous internal or external genitalia, the untoward masculinization of the adrenogenital syndrome, or the loss of self-esteem in microphallus or penile agenesis. Inherent variations in drive level seem to account for some disharmony among partners, requiring help in adjustment.

The capacity to trust sufficiently for mature intimacy is frequently limited by unresolved grief related to early separations, loss, or psychological distancing. Until this is dealt with, there is constant fear of repeated loss, and human relationships are approached with detachment, isolation, and a facade of independence. In treatment, the sense of deprivation and ultimately the anger must be lived through. In this situation the reliability and punctuality of the therapist are essential.

Gender identity problems are seen as part of a request for sex reassignment procedures. General pessimism exists in the literature regarding psychiatric interventions in the gender dysphoria syndromes. Nonetheless, some patients will readily respond to the suggestion for exploratory work. Since such work is in the patient's own best interest, it may reasonably be requested as part of any evaluation for sex reassignment procedures (Meyer, 1974a, b).

In the perversions the sexual aspect of the condition is frequently exciting, gratifying, and to some extent ego-syntonic. Frequently, external parameters are part of the initial treatment contact, for example: court referral, pressure from the spouse, or insistence on the part of employers. Once the anxiety or depressive precursors of the perverse action are dissected out, the activity may lose some of its seductiveness. There are always issues of heterosexual fear. The individual's capacity to maintain any relationship, including the therapeutic one, may be a limiting factor in some cases.

For most patients the overtly sexual material in the treatment will take on oedipal shadings. Desires for physical and emotional possession of the therapist are not pursued simply for personal satisfaction alone, but also in the context of a presumed competition with other patients or other figures in the therapist's life.

For the psychiatrist who, by virtue of serendipity or hard work, has achieved a reputation as a "sex doctor" the erotic transference may take on a special coloration. There is a tendency on the part of some patients to attribute to the therapist personal love-making skills and physical capacities which are, unfortunately, not often possessed. The assumption is that if things are not progressing well, this could be corrected by accepting the patient as a pupil or partner rather than as a patient. If this opportunity is declined, such unwillingness may be interpreted as willful withholding, or as demonstrating that the therapist is, in fact, a "paper tiger."

Masturbation serves to some extent as a stand-in for inadequate interpersonal relationships and in many respects serves to insulate the individual from feared wounds to his self-esteem. Time, place, occasion, frequency, and fantasies of masturbation provide information about the strength of drives toward sexual gratification and aggressive outlet, the prohibitions of conscience, and the attempts to mediate conflicting demands intrapsychically, culturally, and interpersonally. Hammerman (1961) has referred to masturbatory practices as the embodiment of character traits and fantasied constructs which are helpful in understanding the patient's problems. Uncovering the full depth of masturbatory practices "will yield a more rapid and fruitful understanding of the character structure, along with the emotional abreaction necessary to insure conviction in the patient" (Hammerman, 1961, p. 308).

A number of patients present with problems of multiple pseudo-intimacies which seem adolescent in many respects, but which are based on earlier conflict. A special comment might be made on the treatment of "swinging" couples or individuals. "Swinging" provides the addicting element of risk-taking, offers far easier gratification and discharge than is possible through a therapeutic process, operates in the service of denial, and provides narcissistic rewards. Similar secondary gain is apparent also in the less well rationalized and institutionalized "affairs" or "liaisons."

Not infrequently in the authors' experience, after treating a couple using the Masters and Johnson techniques, one partner, or both, has realized for the first time the presence of internal intrapsychic resistances to working through sexual problems. Such occurrences will become more frequent as the Masters and Johnson techniques and other behvioral measures are more widely employed. The very limitations of the short term, dual sex therapy format in dealing with conflict, fantasy, and unconscious motivation often throws these factors into bold relief for the patient. Individual psychotherapy may be very profitably employed after "Masters and Johnson" type work.

TREATMENT RESULTS

Results from individual therapy of any substantial series of general sexual disabilities have been in short supply in the literature. Recently, however, O'Connor and Stern (1972) published a retrospective survey of the effects of psychotherapy and psychoanalysis upon sexual symptomatology in 96 cases, 61 females and 35 males, treated in the Psychoanalytic Clinic of Columbia University.

Without considering the specific sexual disability, 25% of females and 57% of males were "cured." "Improvement" rates were 36% and 17% for females and males, respectively. Improvement for the female included more pleasure in the sexual act, positive attitudinal changes, and orgasm during foreplay but no orgasm during intercourse itself. As the authors point out, it is easier for the female to improve without cure than for the male, since male difficulty is primarily failure of performance rather than satisfaction. The more serious the psychopathology and the longer standing the symptom, the less likelihood there was for successful outcome. Patients treated analytically showed an improvement rate of 77% versus 46% for those in standard psychotherapy.

Clearly, further effort, largely prospective, is required to document the therapeutic effectiveness, mechanisms of effect, limitations, parameters of patient selection, and other aspects of the dynamic therapies in relation to other treatment modalities. Cooper (1969) has made relevant suggestions as to the necessary components of such research:

> Specific needs include: (1) greater empiricism; (2) more stringent criteria for inclusion in any study which should be explicit,

> prospective, controlled, modest. . ., and replicable by others; (3) the use of objectively validated measuring instruments. . .to supplement clinical data; and (4) the application of appropriate statistical methods (p. 354).

CONCLUSION

One of the striking findings from any comprehensive review of the literature surrounding sexual practice and treatment is the manifold disagreement. At this point in time, however, the formulations of dynamic psychiatry provide a comprehensive and clinically substantiated approach to the understanding and treatment of emotional disorders, including sexual ones.

The precise point or significance of the dynamic observations is that much of what is operative in human life is inaccessible to conscious recollection without special effort. This material is accessible only under circumstances of long contact with the patient, the use of free association, and observation of transference manifestations.

It appears that in *initial evaluation* individuals may be seen in whom the sexual difficulty seems to be an isolated phenomenon. Whether such conclusions can be maintained through a course of treatment is problematical. It is more common at initial evaluation, however, to find sexual and other psychiatric difficulties in association. The accumulated clinical experience in dynamic therapy indicates that sexual disabilities rarely occur free of character and neurotic problems and that the sexual disability cannot be dissected entirely free from contributory, intrapsychic conflict. These conflicts, without being dealt with, impose limitations upon the degree of sexual rehabilitation over the short term, upon the capacity for intimacy, and upon the maintenance of improvement.

In terms of the breadth and depth of what may be accomplished, individual, dynamically based psychotherapy is the ultimate treatment of choice for sexual problems with neurotic and characterological bases. In and of itself such treatment will often lead to restoration of adequate sexual functioning along with relief from other symptoms or life problems. The special role of individual psychotherapy, however, is as a releaser from intrapsychic conflict. This release then allows the patient to be teachable by life and by peers or if necessary, by didactic, hierarchial forms of therapy. Kestenberg (1968) stated the point of educability very well:

> In psychoanalytic treatment the patient becomes teachable, but the treatment situation does not allow for training, which only performance of function can give. That must be relegated to the

> physical sphere of learning ... if need be, taught by those practitioners who devise pedagogical methods to inculcate skills" (pp. 513–514).

To develop adequate sexual function requires a capacity to learn, which may be disabled by the conflicts investing sexual life. These conflicts are best removed through dynamically oriented, individual psychotherapy. It is at this point that short term, didactic treatment, which also involves the partner of the now educable patient is, perhaps, most efficacious.

REFERENCES

Cooper, A. 1969. Factors in male sexual inadequacy: a review. J. Nerv. Ment. Dis. 149: 337.

Dahlberg, C. 1970. Sexual contact between patient and therapist. Contemp. Psychoanal. 6: 107.

Fisher, S., and Osofsky, H. 1967. Sexual responsiveness in women: psychological correlates. Arch. Gen. Psychiat. 17: 214.

Freud, S. 1910. "Wild" psychoanalysis. In: Strachey, J., ed., *Standard Edition of the Complete Psychological Works of Sigmund Freud*, Vol. 11. London: Hogarth, 1953, pp. 221–227.

Freud, S. 1912a. The dynamics of the transference. In: *Standard Edition*, Vol. 12, pp. 99–108.

Freud, S. 1912b. Recommendation to physicians practicing psychoanalysis. In: *Standard Edition*, Vol. 12, pp. 111–120.

Freud, S. 1914. Remembering, repeating, and working-through. In: *Standard Edition*, Vol. 12, pp. 147–156.

Freud, S. 1915. Observations on transference love. In: *Standard Edition*, Vol. 12, pp. 159–171.

Fromm-Reichmann, F. 1950. *Principles of Intensive Psychotherapy*. Chicago: University of Chicago Press.

Hammerman, S. 1961. Masturbation and character. J. Amer. Psychoanal. Ass. 9: 287.

Kestenberg, J. 1968. Outside and inside: male and female. J. Amer. Psychoanal. Ass. 16: 457.

Mack, J., and Semrad, E. 1967. Classical psychoanalysis. In: Freedman, A., and Kaplan, H., eds., *Comprehensive Textbook of Psychiatry*. Baltimore: Williams and Wilkins, pp. 269–319.

Meyer. J. 1974a. Clinical variants among applicants for sex reassignment. Arch. Sex. Behav. 3: 527.

Meyer, J. 1974b. Psychiatric considerations in the sexual reassignment of nonintersex individuals. In: Meyer, J., guest ed., *Sex Assignment and Reassignment: Intersex and Gender Identity Disorders*. Special issue of Clinics in Plastic Surgery, 1(2): 275–283.

Novey, S. 1969. *The Second Look: The Reconstruction of Personal History in Psychiatry and Psychoanalysis*. Baltimore: Johns Hopkins.

O'Connor, J., and Stern, L. 1972. Results of treatment in functional sexual disorders. N. Y. State J. Med. 72: 1927.

Strachey, J. 1934. The nature of the therapeutic action of psycho-analysis. Int. J. Psychoanal. 15: 127.

Index